A Passion for Mountains

THE LIVES OF DON AND PHYLLIS MUNDAY

A Passion *for* Mountains

Phyllis Munday with infant Edith and friends
camped below Mount Sifton in the Hermit Range, 1921.

Kathryn Bridge

Rocky
Mountain Books
Calgary–Victoria–Vancouver

Copyright © 2006 Kathryn Bridge
First edition

All rights reserved. No part of this publication may be reproduced, stored in a retrieval system or transmitted in any form or by any means—electronic, mechanical, audio recording, or otherwise—without the written permission of the publisher or a photocopying licence from Access Copyright, Toronto, Canada.

Rocky Mountain Books
#108 – 17665 66A Avenue
Surrey, BC V3S 2A7
www.rmbooks.com

Library and Archives Canada Cataloguing in Publication
Bridge, Kathryn Anne, 1955–
    A passion for mountains: the lives of Don and Phyllis Munday / Kathryn Bridge.

Includes bibliographical references and index.
ISBN-13: 978-1-894765-69-5
ISBN-10: 1-894765-69-9

1. Munday, Don, 1888–1950. 2. Munday, Phyllis, 1894–1990. 3. Mountaineers—Canada—Biography. I. Title.

GV199.92.M86B75 2006   796.522092   C2006-903363-3

Edited by Elaine Jones
Cover and book design by Frances Hunter
Front-cover photo of Munday climbing party approaching rock pinnacle near Mount Waddington, 1934: BC Archives I-61647
Back-cover photo of Don and Phyllis Munday on summit of Mount Victoria, 1925: Smith collection

Printed in Canada

Rocky Mountain Books acknowledges the financial support for its publishing program from the Government of Canada through the Book Publishing Industry Development Program (BPIDP), Canada Council for the Arts and the British Columbia Arts Council.

Contents

Map of B.C. 6

Introduction 7

Chapter One — Early Years and the B.C. Mountaineering Club | 14

Chapter Two — Wartime | 48

Chapter Three — Recovery and Discovery | 58

Chapter Four — Climbing on the Coast | 90

Chapter Five — The Alpine Club of Canada | 122

Chapter Six — Mystery Mountain Years | 158

Chapter Seven — Icefields and Mountains | 196

Chapter Eight — Later Years | 212

List of Ascents 224

Endnotes 228

Selected References 235

Acknowledgments 236

Photo credits 236

Index 237

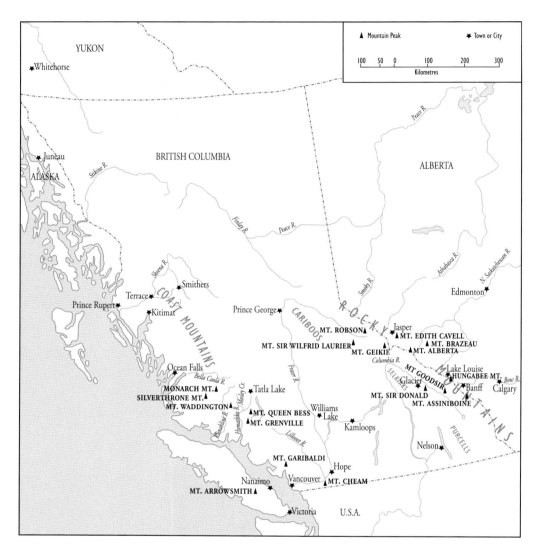

Selected Mountains, Towns and Cities in British Columbia

Introduction

FOR SHEER PHYSICAL PROWESS, grit and single-mindedness, the achievements of Canada's Don Munday and Phyllis (née James) Munday are extraordinary and remain impressive even by today's standards of extreme pursuits. In the world of mountaineering, they were known as "the Dean of Mountaineering" and "the Grande Dame of the Mountains." The Mundays were prodigious in their pursuits, climbing mountains and exploring the British Columbia wilderness for 40 years. Their legacy includes an impressive 150-plus mountains climbed and some 40 first ascents—that is, they were the first people known to have reached the very top of a particular mountain. Between 1925 and 1936, they penetrated an unsurveyed mountainous area of the B.C. coast. Their ongoing exploration ultimately led to the accurate mapping and delineation of the most important glacial system on the Canadian Pacific coast and included identifying Mount Waddington, the highest mountain completely within B.C.

They climbed in the period before and after the First World War, an era before the present system of highways existed, before the use of airplane or helicopter drops, before the introduction of plastics, nylon or Gore-Tex, before Global Positioning Systems or cellular telephones, and before sponsorship. They climbed in an era of steamship or railway travel, specialized in bushwhacking from the sea up to the alpine, carried tinned foods in canvas frame packs, wore wool clothing, used homemade wooden skis and oriented themselves with a compass and hand-drawn maps. They funded the trips themselves, taking time off from work and relying on the support of friends.

In many ways they were an odd couple. Physically they were opposites. Don was small in stature, thin and wiry. His experiences in the First World War had aged him, giving him a graver view of life and a seriousness of purpose. Phyllis (or Phyl, as she was known to almost all) was six years younger than Don, long-limbed and several inches taller. She was robust, exuding health and vitality. She was gregarious and sociable. Both were passionate about the outdoors, about climbing and about active involvement in their mountaineering clubs.

Phyl was a committed Guider who volunteered her time for more than 60 years in the Girl Guide movement, holding increasingly responsible and influential roles, both locally and provincially. She received numerous honours and decorations in her lifetime, not only for her mountain climbing, but also for her service to others. For her mountain rescue and nursing of an injured hiker she was given the first Girl Guide award for valour, the Bronze Cross, in 1925. In 1938 the Alpine Club of Canada membership voted her an honorary member and in 1971 named her honorary president. She held honorary memberships in the American Alpine Club (1967), the Appalachian Mountain Club and the Ladies' Alpine Club in England (1936). The Canadian Council of Girl Guides awarded her the Beaver in 1947—the highest honour a Guider can achieve. In 1967 she was named Dame of Grace for her voluntary work in the St. John Ambulance Brigade. The University of Victoria conferred on her the title and degree of Doctor of Laws (1973). In 1972 she was presented with the Order of Canada.[1]

Don was a prolific journalist and writer. During the First World War, he wrote records and accounts for Army headquarters, and he later became assistant editor of the *B.C. Veterans' Weekly,* the *Scarlet and Gold* and the *Shoulder Strap,* periodicals of the Royal Canadian Mounted Police. He was always extremely active in mountaineering organizations, serving as vice-president of the B.C. Mountaineering Club and editor of its publication for several years running in the 1920s. He was awarded the Silver Rope by the Alpine Club of Canada (ACC) in 1934 and elected as the western vice-president, a position he held from 1946 until his death in 1950. Don was appointed to the Editorial Board, the Glaciological Committee and the Ski Committee of the ACC. He served two terms as president of the Vancouver branch of the Canadian Authors Association (1949–50). He was a Fellow of the Royal Geographical Society (1928) and held membership in the Canadian Geographical Society, the American Geographical Society and the Arctic Institute of Canada. Don was also a member of the British Glaciology Society and the International Committee on Snow and Ice.[2] He was awarded honorary membership in the Appalachian Mountaineering Club in 1949.

Don's stories recounting Phyl's and his climbing adventures appeared in the Vancouver *Sun* and *Province* over several decades, and he wrote for a wide variety of journals and magazines. His authoritative articles on climbing, exploring, glaciology, snowcraft, birds, animals and flowers appeared in the Alpine Club of Canada's *Journal* with great regularity for 30 years. In 1948 his book *The Unknown Mountain* was published to great acclaim. It has been continuously in print and remains a classic of mountaineering. He was an ardent and skilful photographer, and a poet.

No one book can do justice to the extraordinary breadth of achievements and contributions that these two individuals—singly and together—packed into their full lives. Instead, this book focuses on their love of mountains and their climbing, which spanned from about 1910—a decade before their marriage—through the 30 years after their marriage until Don's untimely death in 1950. During these 40 years, the Mundays climbed on the west coast of Canada in and around Vancouver and north of the city, in what was then the largely unknown and little-surveyed territory of the Coast Mountains. They climbed in the Rocky Mountains of British Columbia and Alberta, and in the Selkirks and the Columbia Ranges. They did so at a time when such outdoor recreational pursuits were odd, not the norm. As a climbing team they were unique, especially when they defied convention and took their infant daughter with them.

"Dogged persistence" was the descriptor applied to them in regard to their eight-year quest to successfully ascend the highest peak of Mount Waddington, the mountain they identified and pursued. They followed their instincts (and Don's compass bearings) on extraordinary expeditions into what would soon be revealed (through the Mundays' own mapping and photography) as one of Canada's largest icefields, contained within an unparalleled geography of alpine mountains, tortuous river valleys and changeable weather.

After twice attaining the secondary peak of Mount Waddington (in 1928 and again in 1934), Don and Phyl ultimately abandoned hope of ever successfully ascending its uppermost summit. "Why, there isn't *any* one mountain worth throwing your life away on," remarked Phyl to a young climber decades later. "Even though we started out on a quest for our Mystery Mountain, we ended up with a lifetime of options, and a lifetime of adventures."[3] Instead they set their sights on the surrounding mountains and glaciers—all fresh and invitingly unclimbed or traversed.

The lure of mountains—of exploring and mapping untrodden places—was not a usual preoccupation for men or women in the 1920s and '30s, but neither was it unknown. National and local mountaineering clubs enjoyed steady membership and organized regular camps and climbs. The Mundays, as climbers and club members, had much in common with their companions, including an appreciation of natural spaces. They understood the importance of transcending the urban experience of their daily lives, of getting to the rural spaces and beyond that into "the wilds" or what was then viewed as wilderness. In an age marked by an emphasis on urbanization, the desire to get away from city life was not shared by many, but it was precisely this desire that bonded club members and made them distinct. These club members generally were English-speaking, British-descended members of the middle classes who had leisure time. Almost half (40 percent) of the Alpine Club of Canada members were female.[4] These women climbed mountains and actively participated in club responsibilities and excursions, yet among them Phyl was an exception. Not only was she remarkably strong and fit, but she also had an enormous drive to do more than just participate alongside her male counterparts. She wanted to challenge herself and push her limits at a time when such female seriousness was deemed unwise by many contemporaries.

Gender distinctions both within climbing clubs and in the broader social context shaped the Mundays' perceptions of themselves and also shaped other climbers' ideas of the gendered separateness of skills and abilities. If Phyl had not married Don and climbed with him, would she have been able to achieve distinction on her own? She certainly had the physical conditioning and talent to climb, even outperforming many of the male climbers in her circles. But would she have been disadvantaged by these male climbers' perception of her gender as inferior? "Manless" climbing—that is, women-only parties—gained real ascendancy only during the 1970s (although some British women climbers of the Pinnacle Club in the 1920s prided themselves on "manless" and "guideless" achievements). For a young woman in 1918, the insistence on gender differences might have been too difficult to overcome. For, after all, "A man hates a 'mannish' woman; but when a slight girl equals him at his favourite sport and yet retains her womanliness, he readily admits her claim to a place 'on the rope' and admires her greatly in consequence."[5]

From before the First World War and through to the 1940s, biological differences between men and women dictated one's destiny. A woman's role was to reproduce and raise children. It was thought that the physical and mental energy this function required could be threatened or eroded if a woman indulged in strenuous activities not directly related to her biological purpose. Physicians often argued that women's childbearing functions would be impaired if they focused too much on higher education or pursued "manly" sporting activities.[6] Recent studies of the Alpine Club of Canada and of Canadian mountaineering affirm the male gender bias, despite outward encouragement of women's participation on climbs.[7]

So in this milieu, Don and Phyl climbed—together as much as their personal lives would allow. Shortly after they met in 1918, they began to plan joint climbs. Early experiences on some of these initial excursions foreshadowed a reliance upon each other that would only be broken with Don's death in 1950.

In this book, the voices of Don and Phyllis Munday are used as much as possible to tell their life stories and to document, first-hand, the ascents and explorations they undertook. Don was a prolific writer, and his published and unpublished accounts, along with Phyl's, form the core of this book. This was possible because the diaries, manuscripts, photos and other documents that Don and Phyl kept were later donated to several archives by their daughter, Edith. In addition, some material is still in family hands.

Don was a matter-of-fact writer. His published articles—in newspapers, newsletters and journals—and his classic, *The Unknown Mountain,* are thorough, detailed accounts of climbing expeditions and club outings. His writing style is formal and reserved, generally understating the excitement and adrenalin-filled moments or the long and wearisome slogs to the mountain base. His intent was to document accurately the encumbrances overcome or avoided, the exact hour of awakening, of breakfast, of ascending and descending, of catching return transport home, and myriad other such facts and legitimizations of the ascents. He often writes in the third person, disassociating his personal viewpoints from that of the party as a whole. While we may wish for a more lively account, we lack for nothing in its completeness.

His unpublished manuscripts—those about geography and his activities in exploration in particular[8]—are somewhat different, though, often written in the first person or filled with commentary and opinion. This is the wilful, strong personality. This is the man of firm beliefs, confident and a little arrogant in his surety. Don's adventure fiction (often thinly disguised autobiography mixed with stereotypical damsels in distress) is overly sentimental. His poetry has its moments—especially the published verses—but is uneven. In contrast, his climbing diaries, like those of his wife, are terse and minimalist. Recording in pencil in a tiny crabbed hand on a small notebook, he puts down only the basics, as an *aide-mémoire.*

Only a few years' worth of Don and Phyl's climbing diaries have survived through time. We know they created more—Don also wrote a diary during the First World War—and family members have referred to them, so perhaps one day they will surface. In Phyl's small portable diaries she records her frustration on the climbs, the mistakes made or obstacles overcome. She makes light of her physical discomfort, rarely mentioning the arthritic pain that was always present, instead recording her mental turmoil, especially about her separation from Edith. Edith's image—a photograph showing her as a Brownie, a fairy dancer, or a young woman—was carefully pasted to the inside cover of each diary. Phyl clearly was torn during the necessary separations that enabled her and Don to climb.

Phyl also wrote publicly. A number of newspaper articles focus on her perspective as a mother living an unusual lifestyle, and of her beliefs in nature and the responsibilities we all have as its custodians. For many years she undertook an important volunteer position as editor of the Alpine Club of Canada's *Journal*, yet contributed surprisingly very few articles. She was very definitely a behind-the-scenes worker. Manuscript drafts for her unpublished *Mountain Memories* show that she had a much more engaging writing style than her husband. It is a pity she did not write of her own activities more often.

She did, however, speak publicly on many occasions, giving lectures and talks about climbing and nature, often illustrated with her own photography. Phyl lived for 40 years after Don, and during this time gave several radio, television and private interviews. These recorded interviews are invaluable and provide details of her childhood and of her climbing remembrances that only Phyl herself could give.

It is never easy to stop researching and to start writing. With sources as rich and voluminous as the Mundays' writings and photographs, the temptation to want to know everything in great detail has to give way to practicality. I have deliberately decided to give Don and Phyl the authoritative voice in this book by quoting extensively in an attempt to bring an intimacy to the text. The aim here is to pass on their passion for climbing rather than to talk about their records and analyze what they recorded and what they did not, to deconstruct their textual records, or pose theoretical perspectives. Such interpretation would suit another study, another time.

This book is intended for a general audience. It traces the remarkable achievements of two people who enjoyed a climbing partnership that was unparalleled in their time and serves as an example and inspiration for all of us today. Although Phyllis Munday was the subject of an earlier book, and her life story has been featured in several books about pioneering women, Don's life has not received the same attention. I hope that *A Passion for Mountains* will do justice to his achievements, as he undertook difficult and important climbs over several years prior to the First World War and before meeting Phyl.

A note about the photographs: Don and Phyl carried cameras and took photographs to document their climbs and the territories in which they explored. Neatly tucked away in repurposed letter envelopes lie many thousands of the negatives they created. Sometimes the envelopes contain terse notations such as "Waddington" or "Klinaklini" or "Grouse Mountain." Sometimes there are no words, just a date. Sometimes the negatives match the notations, sometimes they don't. At some point, I am sure, there was a system.

It is a challenge to identify images, to second-guess when the negatives have been misfiled. It is important that anyone with a photograph collection identify people, places and dates. Doing so will benefit not only archivists and historians, but also family members who may later inherit or research such collections. If people aren't identified, the place and date not given, later generations looking for clues may be at a loss to know their significance. In this digital age, this task is especially important, as images fly from computer to computer.

Lastly, a word about measurements. The Mundays lived in the age of imperial measurements. They hiked miles not kilometres, calculated feet and inches, not metres, weighed pounds instead of kilograms. I have retained the imperial measurements in the Mundays' quotes, but in my narrative I use metric, as it is today's standard. Mountain heights are also given in metric measurements.[9]

BCMC camp in Garibaldi. Black Tusk in distance, July 1914.

Chapter One EARLY YEARS AND THE B.C. MOUNTAINEERING CLUB

THE MUNDAY AND JAMES FAMILIES moved to Vancouver within a year or so of each other. In the years prior to the First World War, the city boomed with industries and commerce, spreading out into rich delta land. Set on the shores of the great Fraser River and the Pacific Ocean, Vancouver sits in a spectacular setting with mountain ranges to the north, east and south. It is small wonder that then as now, Vancouverites could feel the lure of mountains, the possibility of adventure and breathtaking vistas.

Walter Alfred Don Munday

Don Munday was born in Portage La Prairie, Manitoba, on March 16, 1888.[1] His parents were William Thomas Munday, a Quebec-born carpenter by trade, who became sheriff of the young town of Portage La Prairie, and Jessie (née Arkell), who emigrated from England to Canada at the age of five.[2] Don was the eldest child, with a brother, Albert Rupert, born 1889 in Birtle, Manitoba, and a sister, Caroline Pansy, born 1894 in Medicine Hat, Alberta.[3] Don's father died when he was quite young and the widowed Mrs. Munday and three children moved to Medicine Hat for a few years and then, by 1906, back to Manitoba. Within a few short years, Don and his siblings, along with their widowed mother, moved once more, this time to Vancouver.[4] The family lived in a substantial frame house on East 29th Avenue, in what was then known as South Vancouver.

Don was a wiry 5 feet 6 inches in height and weighed only 140 pounds. His blue eyes were piercing in his tanned face; his brown hair had a tendency to flop forward over his brow. Like his father, Munday worked as a carpenter, but he also had aspirations as a writer. He was influenced by the nature poets of the nineteenth century, especially Americans Ralph Waldo Emerson and Henry David Thoreau, but also Canadian poet Archibald Lampman, about whom Don wrote: "this distinctly Canadian poet has endeavored to rear standards of conduct ... that any aspiring heart may embrace safely."[5]

Top: Don Munday in fancy dress at age two (left) and as a youngster, ca. 1900 (right). Bottom: Don at age 20, crafting his poetry.

Don's poetry was an expression of a romanticism that influenced his world view. He succeeded in having individual poems accepted for publication in journals such as the *Westminster Hall Magazine, The Christian Guardian, B.C. Magazine* and other western publications. He also wrote articles and stories, a few of which were published before the war, before he focused his career on journalism. Don kept diaries and also documented some of the early climbing adventures of his coterie, contributing articles to the Vancouver *Province*.[6]

Moving from the prairie flatlands, Don thrived in the coastal environment of ocean, forest and mountains, which more closely resembled the natural world as described by the Romantic poets. By the time he was in his early twenties he was a confirmed climber. In October 1910, at the age of 22, he joined the British Columbia Mountaineering Club (BCMC), and by November the following year he had achieved status as an active member.[7] Active membership required mountaineering competency as proven through witnessed climbs of designated peaks.

The BCMC began as the Vancouver Mountaineering Club in 1907, formed by a nucleus of keen hikers, some of whom climbed. Within months the Club organized excursions to explore new territory, and by so doing trained the members, as they participated, in mountaineering skills. By the second annual meeting the name was changed to the B.C. Mountaineering Club. Early in 1910 the club secured a site of five acres on Grouse Mountain, north of Burrard Inlet, and the work of building a clubhouse began.[8] That same year, one climber claimed there was "hardly a peak that greets the northward view of the Vancouver range from the city that has not been reached by the active members,"[9] a testament to the thoroughness of this group.

Climbers first had to travel by small ferry to the "wild" north shore of Burrard Inlet (to what would later become North Vancouver) where Grouse Mountain and other snowy peaks beckoned. They worked their way up the Lynn Creek, Seymour and Capilano River valleys, climbing everything in sight. So by the time Don appeared on the scene, most of the mountains visible from the city had already been climbed and climbed again, often in endless variation. Many club members focused instead on reducing the ascent times or attempting new routes.

It is impossible to know for certain when Don began venturing out of the city and onto the mountain slopes, but the summer before he took out membership in the BCMC he climbed with several members who were to

Launch carrying climbers bound for The Lions, ca. 1917–18.

become among his closest companions. It was after a one-and-a-half-day trip to White Mountain (now known as Burwell) that Don expressed the following thoughts: "though not my first introduction to the mountains, [this trip] was the means of ushering me into a circle of mountaineers among whom I was destined to win friends, few, but true friendships, that have stood the tests of all vicissitudes of trail and camp and climb, severer tests than those to which more conventional friendships are subjected. Are not such friendships sufficient reasons alone for a feeling not far removed from Mountain-Worship?"[10]

The first records of Don's climbing adventures appear in the press in 1911. In May of that year, a party of eight BCMC members that included Don Munday climbed the saddle and western side of the Eastern Lion. Their route was designed to push the limits of what might be accomplished within a 24-hour period. They left from the BCMC club cabin on Grouse Mountain in the wee hours of the morning, and returned in time to catch the last ferry across Burrard Inlet that night.

> The party consisted of Miss L.A. DeBeck, Miss E. Fowler and Messrs. W. Gray, F. Smith, W.A.D. Munday, H. Korten, T. Park and J. Park. Leaving the cabin at 3 a.m., a descent was made by candle light by way of Trythall's to Capilano Road, just below the Canyon View Hotel. Five o'clock saw the party at the Capilano Hotel, and after crossing

EARLY YEARS AND THE B.C. MOUNTAINEERING CLUB | 19

Picnicking climbers on The Lions, May 24, 1911.

the intake bridge the trail was followed to Sisters Creek. The summer route lies up the creek bed, but the snow made this impossible so a four-mile tramp through the woods was necessary to the base of the couloir, which runs to the snowfield on the southeastern exposure of the peaks. The condition of the snow was very good, and at 11:25 a.m., the highest point on the saddle was attained.

After a short rest the party roped up and commenced to traverse the base of the western face of the Eastern Lion. It was found, however, that the snow was not in sufficiently good condition to enable a large party to ascend the very steep slope to the rock above as it avalanched under pressure, and after several attempts the ascent of the remaining three hundred feet was abandoned. The return trip was commenced at 3:30, and the Capilano Hotel again reached at 8:45. After a well-earned dinner the remaining four and a half miles to the car were tramped, and the 10:30 ferry caught, bringing to a close a long and enjoyable day, during which some thirty-two miles were covered, and an altitude of close on 6,000 feet attained. The ladies of the party had the added distinction of being the first to reach the saddle at such an early season of the year.[11]

Looking for "virgin peaks," adventurous climbers and their rivals travelled deeper inland and northwards, exploring beyond the mountains already climbed, moving into unmapped and little-surveyed territories. A month after the May 1911 Lions trip, Don returned to the area, by an alternate route, with Fred Smith and William (Billy) Gray. They climbed the East Lion and Brunswick Mountain (1,785 metres) and the local newspaper covered the story.[12] In those days Brunswick was generally unknown ground, having been climbed only twice before. Writing about the trip years later, Don noted: "I was flattered to be asked to go with them ... Having made ... one or two other fairly strenuous trips in their company, evidently I qualified myself to be invited to go to Brunswick."[13]

They left Vancouver late on Friday evening, June 23, and crossed Burrard Inlet on the ferry, then caught the Capilano streetcar to its terminus. From there they walked to just beyond the Capilano intake (the city's water supply from the dam on Capilano River creating Capilano Lake) and settled down for a three-hour sleep. Rising in the dark, they hiked up Sisters Creek, which was then unlogged and without trails. Don takes up the account.

> "There's lots of bushwhacking in B.C., the coast in particular. The rest of B.C. is not too bad. So there was nothing in the way of transport at all, nobody had cars that I can recall. To climb The Lions we used to take a boat from English Bay usually, or Horseshoe Bay, to go up to the beach at the foot of The Lions. Of course, it's all houses now, you see—quite a difference."
>
> PHYLLIS MUNDAY TAPED INTERVIEW, 1973, BC ARCHIVES

After a bit of trouble with the waterfalls below the Eastern Lion, we arrived in the afternoon in dense fog on one of the ridges north of the East Lion ... We prowled along the ridge in fog to the saddle between the Lions, descended to find the gully from which the usual route starts, and in due course reached the top still in the fog ... Just as we turned to descend, the fog dropped a few feet below the peak, revealing evening light glowing on the higher peaks which pierced the billowing clouds. Reluctantly we climbed down into damp mist and got back to camp at dark.[14]

Camp was sleeping bags rolled out on the heather. On this trip, apparently, Billy Gray was a slave-driver and they hardly stopped to eat or sleep. But that night he "let us squander four hours in sleep!" before they were off—in perfect weather—the following day.

> We now had to cross two ridges and valleys, each a climb and descent of 1,000 feet, the northerly slopes quite rocky. The second ridge ran westerly to connect with Mount Harvey and revealed to our view the imposing pinnacle which stands under the northerly face. 2,000 feet up the rugged south east face of the prominent overhanging east end of Brunswick landed us on the summit ridge 3¼ hours from camp. Returning to camp in the same time we thus ascended and descended 7,000 feet in 6½ hours and still had 5,000 feet down ... We tramped down Capilano Road in rain.[15]

Forty-nine hours had elapsed since they started and during that time they had climbed and then descended and climbed again, several thousand metres in altitude and had slept barely eight hours. Assuming time off for meals, they had hiked or climbed practically all the rest of the time. The intent was to make the most of their weekend time off, and at this they were successful. Don summed it up: "We had accomplished all we had set out to do, and, having immeasurably enriched ourselves with memories of two eventful days of climbing, was not the temporary weariness a small price to pay?"[16]

The trip was also a reconnaissance. By climbing Brunswick, the climbers hoped to learn more about the landscape to prepare them for an unclimbed mountain that lay to the east. They thought that the vantage from Brunswick would enable them to work out how to approach Mount Hanover, some miles away in uncharted territory. But no route was visible. Don wrote: "The trip had not given us a clear idea of how to get at Mt. Hanover from Capilano. Existing maps were seriously at fault."[17] It would be two years before Don followed up on the quest.

Don packed a lot of climbing into 1911. He was part of a BCMC group climbing Golden Ears for a first recorded ascent, and on the Labour Day weekend, with 17 other climbers, he ventured once again to The Lions. In October, with Fred Smith and Billy Gray, he made a first ascent of Crown crater. This unaided rock scramble was daring in its time.

> The name "Crater" is misleading for it does not owe its formation to volcanic action at all—Crown is wholly granite. Imagine a huge hopper or funnel a thousand feet deep with a crooked spout, and with a split up one side. That is the Crater. Along its west and south rim is a thin and mostly overhanging wall of rock ... The general slope was fully

45 degrees. The surface was often rather smooth. Crevices were scarce and we often advanced on all fours ... About five hundred feet directly under the peak, we turned more to the right towards the Camel. Here the slope though steeper was a little more broken, a pleasant change after the long, smooth stretches below. So far we had had no chance to use the ropes. Smith and I were ascending a short, shallow chimney. He weighs considerably less than I do, and when I came to rely on the projections he had used, handhold and foothold, [the] other failed at the same instant. Some say that only by promptly wedging my knees against the sides of the chimney saved my friends from having something tragic to inscribe ... But that was soon forgotten, for every minute brought its own little problem ... Footholds are mostly in awkward positions. Surmounting the first bulging edge, one reaches a platform in the corner formed by two upright slabs. Then to the south is a big projection with a vertical crack about ten inches wide splitting it. One must ascend partly in and partly out of this crack. Descending it sometimes proves even more difficult. On one occasion I found getting jammed in it a peculiarly painful experience. A little higher a point which troubles some climbers is a slanting slab just under the first pine [tree] and very close to the brink of the cliff ... From the ledge below the split overhang, Smith and three of the party went round to the north a few yards and discovered a way up. I do not know exactly what they encountered, but understand that the heaviest of the three dragged himself up a difficult place by literally pulling Smith's leg. For several days afterwards Smith entertained grave doubts as to whether both his legs

Tom Fyles atop Crown crater, ca. 1916-1918.

were of the same length, but, I believe, was afraid to measure them for fear of verifying his suspicions.[18]

Don attended the 1911 BCMC Summer Camp, held in the Garibaldi area, its name taken "from the lone, imposing peak which dominates the view up Howe Sound and Squamish Valley." For Don, the magnificent scenery offered variety beyond his previous experiences. The area of Garibaldi was a study in contrasts: magnificent alpine meadows, glacial lakes, glaciers, snowfields, lava beds, volcanic cones and snow-covered crags. In his first book, Don later wrote: "Its scenic beauties are by no means limited to glaciers, snowfields, and gaunt upthrusts of rock only to be admired from afar by all except those strenuous mortals, mountain-climbers—its lakes and flowery table-lands and upland valleys invite excursions in every direction or offer the solace of rest amid their loveliness."[19]

For Don and most of his contemporaries, this area was a wilderness, devoid of human activities, pristine and pure. The acknowledgment and understanding that its beauties were well known to the indigenous people and included in their traditional territories did not occur to them. The club members recognized that this area was special. The wonder was that all this existed within easy access from Vancouver, yet was almost completely unknown to the populace. The impact of logging and mining had not yet been felt, although it seemed inevitable that industrial concerns would someday turn their sights on this area. Don and his BCMC companions would soon become articulate and exuberant advocates for the necessity of protecting this unique area from exploitation or development by mining or logging interests. Eventually after much debate, it would become a park.

In the pre-war years there was no railway to Squamish, nor road access. Getting to the Garibaldi area depended upon the Union Steamship Company's regularly scheduled trips from Vancouver. On August 6, 1911, eleven members of the club left Vancouver by steamer heading up Howe Sound. They arrived at Squamish Landing at 3:00 p.m. and then travelled overland north of the Mamquam River to the foot of Columnar Peak where they met Billy Gray, who had gone ahead to make ready the campsite. On August 9 all 12 climbers left camp en route to Mamquam Mountain (2,595 metres), which had been formerly named Santa Rosa. The mountain had been investigated the previous year and ascended for the first time only the month before. By 10:15 a.m. on August 11, both parties had climbed to its uppermost pinnacle.

Two days later, Don and the others also climbed Garibaldi (2,678 metres), and on August 16 Don and a slightly smaller party undertook a three-day climb over Garibaldi Glacier, ascending three new peaks: Rust Mountain, Copper Peak (later renamed Mount Carr) and Castle Towers.[20] During the course of the camp "a large party of camp members," presumably including Munday, also climbed Glacier Pikes and The Sphinx.[21] Don climbed Columnar Peak several times to hunt goats. Wild goats were a popular means of adding solid food to the climber's often sparse provisions.[22]

An extra dash of excitement prevailed that year, as recent forest fires had ravaged the trails (and the site of the previous year's camp) and smoke from the fires obscured the views from the peaks. A change in wind or weather might have required a rapid retreat.

In 1912, Don continued climbing. He had a close circle of friends within the BCMC, but also climbing friends who were not members. He preferred climbing with a small group, but occasionally with larger groups of mixed company. At the end of May, he and three others "including one lady" passed through the Seymour Valley and across to Squamish (or Newport as it was then known) by way of the Stawamus Valley. They made an attempt on the two peaks called The Sisters (now called Sky Pilot and Ledge)[23] from Summit Lake (now Loch Lomond), the source of Seymour Creek, but were overtaken by a snowstorm and had to retreat, vowing to return.

And they did, bringing with them two others. From June 29 to July 1, Don, Fred Smith, Ben Hanafin, Edward LePage and two women spent three fun-filled but challenging days climbing these two outstanding peaks in the Sawtooth Range, "a mass of jagged pinnacles which rise both east and west."[24] To reach the area they did not hike overland as before, but travelled by launch up Howe Sound to the beach at the copper-mining town of Britannia. From the beach, they climbed straight up through the bush, following the creek past the upper townsite to the base of Mount Sheer and then onwards to "Bowman's cabin" at the foot of a high waterfall, then onto an unnamed lake (possibly Utopia Lake). The Sisters towered above its farthest shore.

Their first target was the higher western spire (Sky Pilot). They made the ascent, took photos and added their own records to the cairn,[25] and then made an attempt on the eastern Sister (Ledge). The next day, just for fun, Don and Fred Smith scaled Mount Sheer (1,680 metres) before breakfast, leaving from camp at 4:30 a.m. and making the summit just an hour and 10 minutes later.

That same summer in late July, Munday and Smith, accompanied by C. Field, returned to the area via Britannia and had a busy eight or nine days during which they again climbed the western Sister (Sky Pilot). It was hot and relentlessly sunny, so one day they set out shortly after 4:00 p.m., knowing that the sun would be gone from the mountain's eastern face and the climbing consequently cooler. They ascended via a pass between the two peaks, then up an icy snow slope, zigzagging up the face to the top. There they uncovered the 1910 record and added theirs. But while on top, they got sidetracked. Don's friend Fred Smith provided the following account.

Our work was not over, however, as a small peculiarly shaped needle,[26] which rises beside the peak, to almost the same height, awakened our curiosity. From the peak it looks almost impossible as the top appears to be formed of delicately poised rocks. We were not satisfied with this view, however, and climbing down to its base, looked round at its opposite face. A little ledge ran across it to within a few feet of the top and it looked more solid than the other side. Roping up we commenced the attempt. To get to the ledge one had to swing themselves out and edge along a crack with their hands but it was easily accomplished as the rear man had good anchorage. Moving one at a time we slowly moved up the ledge, till we reached the upper end. Above, the rock rose some ten feet but there was a small crack and by working one's hand up it and swinging out, I was able to pull myself up and then F & M followed. It was an insecure perch, to say the least as we could scarcely move but it was the top and so we deposited another record and defied the man who said mules could go anywhere a man could.

The sun was now setting and so we could not linger long on the needle tip although the sensation of isolation that it gave was very pleasant. The descent was accomplished without any particular difficulty although one needed unlimited faith in the bearing powers of the rope. Regaining the main peak we paused for a minute to watch the sunset colors before starting the downward scramble into the rapidly deepening dusk.[27]

They then made a first ascent of the eastern Sister (Ledge) (1,920 metres), a craggy peak in that same compact ridge of peaks. Ledge was a challenge.

It is by far the more interesting from a climbing standpoint, as it rises a sheer tower and the route we followed appears to be the only one up it. Even that may perish before long as a rock from above could easily demolish enough of the ledge to make it useless. The summit is a flat platform of rock broken by deep crevices. At the Northern end one can stand on the edge and look straight down a thousand feet on to the glacier beneath, as this side is higher than the Southern.

We did not spend long on top as the sun was high in the heavens and the heat intense. Leaving a record in a cairn we returned to the ledge and started down. It was worse than the ascent as we dare not rope on account of the lack of holds and so we carefully crept along till the shoulder was reached and the worst part over. Back to camp we hurried and as it was past noon, we had our third meal, after which we rested for a few hours and I found a nice warm pool in which to take a paddle.[28]

Two days later the threesome had crossed over to the east side of the Stawamus River. Here they dried themselves out in a trapper's cabin, then transferred their packs to an old camping ground not far away "and set forth with light rucksacks, expecting to return by dark."[29] Their goal was to ascend a peak to the north they had named Eagle Head, which rises from the ridge forming the west boundary of the Stawamus Valley. The name was chosen for its profile as viewed from Ledge and Sky Pilot.

At seven in the morning they recrossed the Stawamus and began the ascent: "Above we could see nothing but towering slabs, so we followed whatever direction looked most promising ... The only method of ascent was by way of small cracks and ledges and we frequently had to traverse several hundred feet either to the right or left to find some means of ascent." As the lightweight, Fred Smith was often used as an extension ladder, being elevated on the hands of Munday and Field "to some projection above and then left to get up or fall off."[30]

Finally they struck the top of the ridge and were very pleased to note that, despite the continual traverses, they were close to the base of the peak. They looked up at the northeast face, which did not look very reassuring. "Between it and us lay a deep draw, which descended to the Stawamus and I imagine would afford a much better route than the one we had followed. It was now past noon and we had [had] a six hour climb without rest, so dinner was quite in order." The face looked impossible so they decided "to traverse its base ... and look at the north-west face." But it would be the north face

EARLY YEARS AND THE B.C. MOUNTAINEERING CLUB | 27

they finally selected. Up they scrambled. "By employing extension ladder tactics, we made good progress and at last, between three and four o'clock, gained the summit." [31] This was the first ascent of Eagle Head, later known as Mount Habrich (1,700 metres).

Back on the ridge they held "a council of war." It was Friday afternoon and they had to leave Newport on the steamer for Vancouver that Sunday. But they still wanted to explore the glaciers extending north from The Sisters. Could they do this, and still get to Newport? In the end, after assessing their food they decided to stay out all night, visit the glaciers in the morning, then return to their camp on the Stawamus where they had stashed their packs. From there they would hike into Newport. The food supplies were low: "enough tea for two brews, two soup tablets, a small piece of bannock, and three little pieces of chocolate. We also had three very healthy appetites. We tossed a coin, and the all night session won." [32]

From the Eagle Head ridge they climbed down to the divide to pitch camp, where they portioned the night into three watches of two hours each. Sometime after 3:00 a.m. they left in the misty dawn. To ascend the snout of the most easterly glacier, they roped up and cut steps until they reached a more level portion. They threaded their way through the crevasses, crossing ice bridges and moving ever southward. The semicircular form of the glacier inspired them to name it Stadium. They then crossed over to the west, travelling on the edge of another glacier, and then down a stream, which eventually led into the Stawamus. They crossed the river and reached the trail and then their packs. They had been gone 30 hours, with little sustenance for the most part, so it was into their packs and out with the tinned beans and canned apricots. One of them went fishing, and fresh trout added to the feast. The account concludes: "next morning we completed the rest of our journey to Newport which we reached in time to catch the boat for Vancouver. We were unshaved, ragged, and tanned; and some of those on

The essentials prior to the First World War *"One blanket carried in light canvas waterproofed packsack with leather shoulder straps and without a packboard. Total weight nearly over 30 lbs for a 2 day trip, 50–55 lbs for a weeks hike. One small hatchet with one person. Carbine rifle with a subchamber for small game. This rifle, with a Free Miner's Licence, which was carried by the rifle owner, allowed us to shoot game at any season for our own use. The cost was $5.00. Wild goats were prized for food on the trail—Indian River area."*

R.M. MILLS REMINISCENCES, TAPE 4-38, BCMC FONDS

the boat looked at us with pity but we needed it not, our only sorrow was that we could not have stayed out indefinitely and wandered into fresh fields."[33]

To cap off a busy summer, in August Don again attended the BCMC camp held in what would become Garibaldi Park. It was a different location from the previous year, for this camp was in the Black Tusk Meadows.

The BCMC camp was tremendously enjoyable; it was time well spent with like-minded people. Don was not the most gregarious individual, but somehow in the company of other climbers, he felt more at home than he did at any other time. Many club members contributed to the task of mapping the terrain. During this summer camp Billy Gray, then club president, "carried out plane-table and photographic work to complete the first topographic map of the Black Tusk area of the Garibaldi District." The map was published initially in the club's *Northern Cordilleran* in 1913

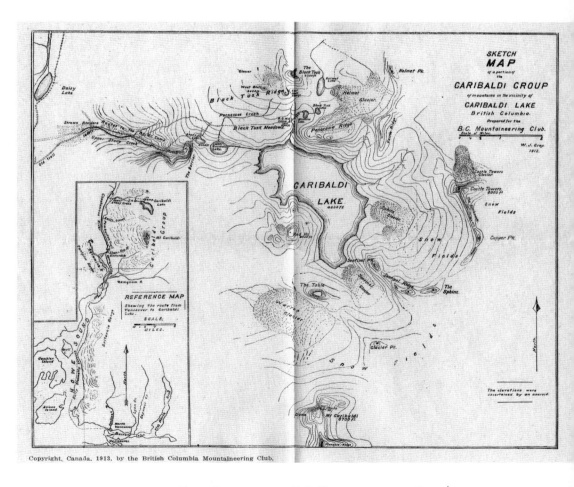

EARLY YEARS AND THE B.C. MOUNTAINEERING CLUB | 29

Top: Mount Hanover from Brunswick Mountain, ca. 1916–1918. Bottom: Garibaldi view, 1916. Left to right: The Sentinel, Garibaldi, The Table.

and was the only map available for 14 years.[34] To the compass orientations were added aneroid barometric readings and triangulation to determine elevations, which in turn facilitated accurate topographic delineation, removing guesswork. Establishing elevations of the mountains, glaciers and passes was extraordinarily important in opening up this area for further climbs. Other members documented the area through photographs and panoramic images taken from sufficient elevations (often mountain tops) to enable understandings of the glaciers and watershed systems. As interest in this area grew, climbers took it upon themselves to accurately record distance, direction and height, to sketch or photograph, and to add to the knowledge base.

On May 22, 1913, Don, Ben Hanafin and Edward LePage left Vancouver for Mount Hanover (1,747 metres). "Being engaged in mapping the mountains as well as climbing them, my friends and myself had a double incentive to attract us towards this mountain which seemed to rank second in height among those summits lying within a fifteen mile radius of Vancouver. It was with the idea of penetrating at the same time the veil of mystery hanging over the upper Capilano Valley that we decided to attempt to reach Mt. Hanover by way of Capilano Creek. A preliminary scouting trip served chiefly to impress upon us what a long, hard tramp was before us."[35]

The readiest means of approach was probably from Howe Sound, but as their earlier reconnaissance two years ago had failed to confirm a route from this direction, the Capilano Valley was selected in all awareness that this route still involved guesswork. At what point would they turn west away from the valley and towards the mountain? Would the mountain be seen from the upper Capilano, or would it be obscured?

Following the Capilano River was not considered particularly prudent by most climbers. No trails or roads existed, so the route would entail bushwhacking through the coast rain forest, not an easy proposition. Don wrote, "Its miles of heavy timber repelled climbers who one and all hate bush work."[36] But they gambled that they would find a way. Pushing them on was the rumour that rival climbers, notably the club vice-president and renowned peak-bagger Basil S. Darling, were attempting the very same mountain via Howe Sound. The race was on!

Don and Ben left on the evening of May 22. LePage was 24 hours ahead of them, on an advance scout. He met up with them at the first campsite, and after consuming canned beans and bacon, he unfolded a discouraging report of the region.

He had climbed a 4,000 foot mountain south of camp, naming it Enchantment Peak. From the summit he had obtained a clear view of the valley of Enchantment Creek by way of which it appeared necessary for us to approach Hanover. In addition he made some sketches of the district; these served to make his descriptions very clear, except in one very important feature, and that was some sort of a mountain mass lying southeast of Mt. Hanover. What was between that ridge and the peak was a matter for speculation.[37]

They gathered a good supply of dry wood and went to bed by daylight, hoping to get a few hours rest before striking off.

A deep layer of fragrant balsam boughs made an incomparable mattress...for a few hours we forgot the labour and the heat of trail and climb. That unclimbed mountain soon reasserted itself however; waking before 11 p.m. we lay in our sleeping bags and talked until midnight ... At 2 a.m. we lit our candles and set out upstream through the black shadows. It was nearly 3 a.m. when we came to the mouth of Enchantment Creek. By this time the stars were paling, and the blue-black mountain crests of which we caught glimpses were growing sharper against the whitening sky. The nature of the ground made candle light necessary for another twenty minutes; numerous little streams intersected the flat, boggy ground around the mouth of Enchantment Creek and these were treacherously bridged with snow. Keeping about one hundred feet above the stream we tramped for an hour and a half along the steep hillside on the south of the creek. At 5 a.m. we reached Roaring Creek, the branch of Enchantment Creek that drains the east face of Mt. Brunswick and also the sloped barrier ridge which hid Hanover from sight. We crossed the main stream by means of an exceptionally slippery log; then picked our way through the numerous channels into which Roaring Creek divides below a great accumulation of logs at the foot [of] its distinguishing feature, a hundred feet of cascades. We climbed to the top of the falls through very dense brush strangely free from snow. The barrier ridge behind which lay Hanover, was now directly in front, while further to the left

Looking southwest from White (Burwell) Mountain, showing (left to right) Dam, Goat and Crown mountains, ca. 1916–18.

was a broad slope leading up to the east face of Brunswick. On our right a narrow valley ran up steeply between Peak A and the barrier ridge. Whether this valley led to it was wholly problematical but the volume of water in its creek was a fair assurance that it extended high among the summits, and it might possibly carry us around to the prominent eastern ridge of Hanover. Firm snow was plentiful again and we mounted rapidly along the eastern slope until the bottom of the valley widened greatly and revealed what appeared to be some sort of a pass in front of us. We hurried up to the crest, and suddenly came out of the timber into the open. The valley, walled in by mountains and still in shadow, extended northward for half a mile, and held a frozen lake six hundred yards long. We bestowed the name of Lake Surprise upon it. The ice looked rotten in places; we kept along the east shore in hopes that the summit of Hanover would come into view over the ridge on the west side of the lake. At the head of the lake the valley turned sharply westward into a large semicircular expanse of snow, from which basin it swept steeply upward for 2,500 feet between the barrier ridge and a long wall of bare and imposing cliffs on the north. Somewhere above and behind those cliffs we expected to find the summit.

We had traveled without interruption for five and a half hours to reach an elevation of three thousand feet. Gathering a few boughs that had been scattered on the snow by slides from the cliffs above, we sat down for fifteen minutes and breakfasted in the pleasant sunshine into which we had emerged for the first time that morning. But when we got started up that long slope of soft snow the heat became intense; in spite of it we climbed 1,200 feet in the first three quarters of an hour. White [Burwell], Mt. Seymour, Cathedral and Crown came into view one after the other as we gradually rose above the ridges that had shut us in for so long. To the northward Mamquam, Garibaldi and the Sawteeth were soon added to the scene.

All about us were evidences of snow-slides, some of them recent. The sloping ledges of the long line of cliffs, coupled with the chances of avalanches from the snow-slopes above, did not tend to make rockwork attractive. However, at one point a steep ribbon of icy snow cut the wall of rock and offered a good route. Just when we turned up it we obtained a fine view of a snow-slide pouring like a cataract over the cliffs to the left. Upon mounting above the cliffs we found ourselves near the crest of a ridge that rose westward. Away up it, about 800 feet above us, we caught a glimpse of a sheer rock face crowned with a heavy cornice of snow. It was our first glimpse of our goal. The arête on which we stood was quite narrow, sloping sharply to the brow of the southern cliffs, while on our right the whole line of northern cliffs was capped with a long graceful cornice near the edge of which we had to travel. Knowing a rival party was attempting the mountains that day from Howe Sound, it was with mingled feelings that we pressed forward toward the crest. The gleaming expanse of snowy summits momentarily widening around us no longer called forth expressions of interest or delight—we were wholly intent upon gaining the peak. We finally surmounted a little snowy dome; there, just beyond, lay the summit's untrodden snow, and at 10:10 a.m. we stood upon it.[38]

The three men returned to their camp on the banks of the Capilano River before 6:30 that evening. "The meal that ensued was a brave repast, washed down with much jam, for the latter, through some mistake, we had an excessive quantity; and it was very funny to see my companions

Pansy Munday and Loretto Hanafin at camp, Garibaldi, ca. 1912–1913.

trying to eat slices of bread overloaded with jam, in such a manner that the semi-viscous mixture would not overflow on all sides at once. In the meantime the chances were good that my own share was dripping into my tea or beginning to ooze through my fingers."[39] They slept, and left the next morning at 8:30, just as cold rains began to fall. Five hours later they reached the streetcar line. Later they learned that their rivals had reached a ridge north of Hanover and camped there that same night. The following day with its rain and snow prevented them from pressing onwards and they had returned by way of Deek's Creek to Porteau where their launch waited and took them back to Vancouver.

In July 1913, Don and Ben Hanafin had company. Their sisters joined them for a climbing trip into Garibaldi. Caroline Pansy Munday was just

19 and a student at McGill University College (later the University of British Columbia). Loretto Clotilda Hanafin, aged 23, was a skilled mountaineer, and an active BCMC member. Three years later she would marry Fred Smith.[40] On this trip they entered Garibaldi from the southwest, along Mamquam Creek, and climbed Round Mountain, Lava Mountain (The Gargoyles) and then Garibaldi itself, climbing the west face. They added their names to the cairn, noting that they were the eighth recorded party to ascend (and the women the first), then went on to the Dome. They also attempted the pinnacle on Garibaldi but were forced to abandon the climb because of the snow conditions and the smoke from a recent forest fire, which obscured their vision and irritated breathing. They headed inland, tackling Mamquam by way of Tyee Glacier. Their ascent was the fourth, but Pansy and Loretto were the first women up. On July 22 they climbed Spire Peak (2040 metres), the highest of the northern Mamquam group, in an 8½-hour ascent. Don composed his poem *Spire Peak* just days later.[41]

Spire Peak—First Ascent

I

"I wish my mother could see me now!"
Somehow is not the thought that is mine
As I cling to this mountain's shattered spine,
With those scarred tremendous walls below
At the bases of which, on the gleaming snow
Are bounding no larger than specks of sand
Those rocks I dislodged with a touch of my hand.

II

Just another short scramble—the peak must be near
For dwarfed down below us near summits appear.
Up over this crag—Oh, hello what is this?
Brother Ben, take a look at this ghastly abyss,
This gap in the ridge—Just a scant forty feet
Lies the summit above us, yet we must retreat!
First, let us sit down, let us eat, let us think:
While we dangle our feet o'er eternity's brink,
"Oh for the drip of that snow-cave!" we cry,
As we cram some food down throats dusty and dry

36

III

Have you noticed the rocks are as hot as a stove?
Oh this is the kind of a scramble I love!
We came up that corner, and round tha[t] queer spike,
Just straddle that edge as you like—or don't like.
Down there are our axes—ah, there is the snow!
Now down to the cave in the gully we go.
Could music be ever more welcome to man
Than snow water dripping in this dusty can?
How that goat scampered off o'er the snow-slope like mad.
When we pass that black hole we will try a glissade.
We are still fairly fresh, and the sun is still high;
For a nearsighted look at the peak let us try.

IV

These spires are piled with a grave lack of care,
They are giddy, unsafe, and I'm dazed I declare
With circling their bases on these slopes of snow.
Whether that is the summit I don't fully know.

V

From my perch on this cliff 'tis a sheer drop below
To that glacier—transit is rapid you know—
Not sufficient inducement to take any chance,
So, look to your rope, while I try to advance.
To scale this last stretch of this tumble down spire
A steeple jack tired of life we require—
Grab hold of shadow, hang on to thin air,
And hoist yourself up with the tenderest care—

VI

Ah, now I have hold of the top of the wall
With both hands—hurrah, here's the end of it all!
What matter though rocks are not hot as a stove?
The snout of the Tyee I see down that clove—
The peak at my elbow juts six feet above—
Oh, this is the kind of a climb that I love!

The outbreak of the First World War in 1914 changed the lives of many in Don and Phyl's generation. It was considered "the war to end all wars." For men both young and old, volunteering for military service was expected and treated as a serious responsibility, although for many youth, the romanticism associated with the abstract idea of war was a heady cachet. The killing fields of Europe were not yet an acknowledged horror. Don volunteered for the 11th Irish Fusiliers, a local militia. For him, voluntary training in the militia was one thing, but enlistment in the army proper was another. Although some of his friends and climbing partners signed up, it was not until the end of June 1915 that he followed suit, and this after considerable internal moral struggle and probably a certain social pressure from those around him.

Don did not view war as an exciting opportunity and was not caught up in the patriotic fervor that made many young men enlist eagerly early on. Some of his fellow climbers such as Frank Carr (who was killed in action in 1915) would lose their lives. In fact, it may have been Carr's death in June that convinced Don to enlist.

After months of soul searching, Don hiked solo from the North Shore and climbed Cathedral Mountain (1,730 metres). He described it best in a diary he kept while overseas. "Yesterday was the second anniversary of my last mountain climb, 'Cathedral.' As I stood on the snowy summit of Cathedral my love for all my mountains cried out to me not to involve myself in the horrible business of war, not to leave all that was dear to me to fling my puny contribution into the scale of right. It was very hard to renew my resolve to enlist until a strange coldness crept down over the mountains as though their aspect declare[d] 'Unless you are worthy to make this sacrifice you are unworthy to frequent our shrines.'" [42] He enlisted two days later on June 29, 1915, at Vernon. Almost the same day as Don put his climbing career on hold, his future wife was just beginning hers.

Phyllis Beatrice James

Phyllis Beatrice James was born September 24, 1894, high in the hills at Kotagala in the district of Nuwara Eliya, in the British colony of Ceylon (now the country of Sri Lanka), only 180 kilometres from Colombo but almost 2,000 metres above sea level. She was the eldest daughter of Beatrice (née Swann) and Arthur Frank James, expatriate British citizens. Frank James

Young Phyllis James in a dramatic pose, ca. 1899.

was a manager for Lipton and then Ridgways Tea. The family lived on a tea plantation and led a pampered, colonial existence. Phyllis had a younger sister, Esmée Mary, nicknamed "Betty" (b. 1896), also born in Ceylon, and a brother, Frank Richard Ingram, nicknamed "Dick," born near Sydney, Manitoba, in 1902, after the family emigrated.

About 1901 the family pulled up stakes and moved back to England, en route to Canada. At the age of 50 Frank James was looking for a different life. Canada opened up from east to west coast with the completion of the Canadian Pacific Railway in 1885, and was promoted as an exciting immigration opportunity. To encourage travel, the railway offered special fares for immigrants intending to settle in the prairies or farther west. The James family moved first to Manitoba, but the next summer they continued west on the CPR into British Columbia, then south by sternwheeler along Kootenay Lake to Nelson, a booming mining town set amid the Selkirk Mountains and on the shores of Kootenay Lake's West Arm.

Left to right: Esmée (Betty), Phyllis and Richard (Dick) James, Nelson, ca. 1907.

What a cultural, geographical and climatic shock it must have been for this family to leave a colonial life in the tropics for the cold prairie winter and then the isolation of southeastern B.C. Beatrice James, for instance, now no longer enjoyed the luxury of servants. She had to learn how to cook, to bake bread, to clothe and care for her children on her own, without the benefit of others. Beatrice's competence was an influence on Phyllis, who later marvelled at her mother's ability to handle this transition.

Frank James now worked as a bookkeeper and secured employment in connection with the various mining concerns active on the western shores of Kootenay Lake. At first, the family lived in Nelson (whose population was about 9,000), where Phyl began school. But by 1903 or 1904, the family had moved about 20 kilometres away from Nelson, across the West Arm of the lake. They lived in a small wooden cabin, which, based upon Phyl's description of her childhood there, was probably partway up the hillside above the steamboat stopping point known as Kokanee Landing.[43] Access to Kokanee Landing—which is just east of today's Kokanee Creek Provincial Park—was by water. All supplies, passengers and mail came via SS *Moyie* and SS *City of Ainsworth*, the wood-fuelled sternwheelers that made regular stops at the landing. When winter set in, the lake froze over and became nearly impassable, making it difficult or impossible to obtain food and supplies. In later years Phyl recalled one particular winter. "And then the lake pool froze over all the way from Nelson right up to 13 Mile Point and we used to go out and skate and when the boats finally broke through we skated out to the boats and got fresh meat from them."[44]

The cabin, high enough to allow a nice vantage point over the lake, was on a bend in the road leading up to the Molly Gibson mine. This mine, like many in the southeastern part of the province, was a hardrock mine, producing galena ore, a lead crystal. The impurities in the galena were silver, zinc and sometimes gold; it was the silver that made it profitable. Mule skinners negotiated the steep turns in the road to Kokanee Landing from the mine, their wagons loaded down with bags of ore. From there, the ore would be transported by sternwheeler to the smelter.

Isolated from Nelson and its comforts, the James family was forced into self-sufficiency. The colonial life in Ceylon became a distant memory. Phyl and sister Betty were home-schooled by their mother. The years at Kokanee represented unprecedented freedom, for they were outside in fair weather, scrambling up the hill, exploring and learning about the forest and its animals. They took special delight in balancing on windfallen trees high above gullies and Kokanee Creek with its cascading waterfalls.

> I was always out on the hillsides and my chief joy then, to my mother's horror—she didn't always know quite what I was doing, actually, because there used to be a lot of windfalls of trees across the ravines. They were more like deep gullies but sometimes ravines, and I used to love walking across them. My poor mother, she'd have had a thousand fits if she'd known some of the logs that I'd crossed over. But they were fun to me and, of course, there wasn't anybody else there, just my sister and I. We were the only two children on that hillside ... So we had to make our own fun and that's the way we did it.[45]

Phyl recalled her childhood as a happy time. "I had a horse of my own, he didn't have a saddle, he was a boney old thing, slow, but, oh, I dearly loved that old nag. I used to ride around bareback all the time, riding all over the place. He did dump me one day, poor thing. He shied at a squirrel, why on earth he did goodness only knows, but I landed on the ground and then of course had to lead him around until I could find a log or something so that I could get back aboard again."[46] On her twelfth birthday, Phyl was given a .22 rifle, which she took out on her rambles, always on the lookout for grouse and other game suitable for the dinner table.[47]

In the summer, berry-picking was a chore that also involved adventure. Armed with several buckets each, the girls hitched a ride from the mule wagon heading up to the Molly Gibson mine. Partway up the dirt track the wagon stopped and let them off. The sisters headed into the bush in search of the lush blueberry bushes. As they filled their buckets the girls kept their eyes and ears attuned to movements and noises in the underbrush that might signal the arrival of a bear. This was just part of the way things were, a quite natural aspect of being in the woods. Knowledge of the forest animals and respect for the beauties of outdoor life—and also the dangers—was part of Phyl's childhood learning. As the buckets filled, the girls left them along the side of the track and then had the freedom to explore and play until the wagon came down the hill, filled with sacks of ore. When the driver spotted the blueberry-filled buckets, he reined in the team and gave a shout to the girls, who soon came running and climbed aboard. Tucked up in some comfort amid the ore sacks and blueberry buckets, they rode down to their house in time for dinner.

No record exists of the James family taking part in organized activities while living in the Kootenays, although it is interesting to speculate that some of the recreational pursuits undertaken by others in the community might have underscored Phyl's own young yearnings for the hills. In May 1903, the *Nelson Daily News* reported: "A party of two ladies and two gentlemen climbed to the summit of Granite Mountain on Sunday and held a picnic on top. A flag was hoisted on a tall dead tree and was clearly visible from the city yesterday. The party took three hours to make the ascent, and state that the trail is in good condition."[48]

Although the James family moved again in 1908, Phyl's remembrances of her time in the Kootenays illustrate its influence on her later life. The ability to explore and to be independent, such an essential part of these childhood days, were priorities in her adult life.

Exactly why the family left the Kootenays is unclear, but it might have been precipitated by the state of the mining industry that year, which included a fluctuating demand for ore and a major miners' strike. The harsh winter weather might also have been a factor. The idea was to immigrate to New Zealand, so they packed their belongings and returned to Nelson, where they boarded a train to Robson, then journeyed by sternwheeler up the Arrow Lakes to Arrowhead, the head of navigation. From there it was by branch line to Revelstoke, where they boarded a CPR passenger train travelling to the Pacific coast. The railway terminated in Vancouver and that was as far as they got; they never boarded the steamer for New Zealand.

In Vancouver they re-evaluated their plans. The economic climate was positive and the city was beautiful, balmy and full of potential. So they stopped, moving to a modest cottage on Keefer Street. Urban living (Vancouver was a growing city of 27,000 people in 1901 and 100,400 by 1911)[49] was another huge change for the family. Beatrice James was only too glad to be in Vancouver and liked city life. Frank James was athletic—for several years running he had been the Ceylon tennis champion—and once settled in Vancouver, he soon became a respected veteran player at the Brockton Point tennis club. Although he enjoyed physical exercise he had difficulties understanding his daughter's need to escape to the wilds. He hoped that her natural athleticism would be channelled into tennis, but Phyl would not be deterred. She loved "the wilds," as they called the forests and hills. In Vancouver, access to the forests was not as immediate as it had been at Kokanee. On Sundays the family often boarded a streetcar that took them close to Stanley Park, the large wild preserve of old-growth cedar and Douglas fir not far from the city centre. Here they picnicked and walked along the forested trails. Phyl had a habit of turning one ankle inwards as she walked, and her mother, following behind, would gently tap the ankle with her walking stick when this occurred, gradually curing Phyl of this problem. But walking on nicely maintained trails was not "the wilds" she longed for.

Sometimes Phyl's father took the children in the ferry across Burrard Inlet to the North Shore, then only lightly populated and mostly wooded. Beyond the slopes of Grouse Mountain in winter lay icy, snow-capped peaks. Grouse

Left to right: Dick, Phyl and Betty James, Vancouver, ca. 1910.

EARLY YEARS AND THE B.C. MOUNTAINEERING CLUB | 43

Mountain was a gateway to this wild land, which reminded young Phyl of the Kootenay landscape. From the ferry quay they walked up the streetcar line to grassy meadows at the foot of Grouse Mountain and were nearer the mountains and away from the busy city life. But it was an all-day trip to get there.

Luckily, Phyl soon found a mechanism for outdoor activity. It came by way of an announcement at St. James Church one Sunday in 1910. A Boy Scout troop was to be organized, so any interested boys should stay behind after the service to learn more. Phyl's brother Dick attended the meeting, and from him she learned about this brand-new movement initiated by Baden-Powell in England in 1909. Scouting involved camping, hiking, woodlore, pathfinding and other pursuits. The fact that it was targeted at boys, not girls, did not deter her in the least. In fact, Phyl was downright angry. It seemed so unfair. Her resolve was so strong that Phyl persuaded her mother—who disliked the outdoors—to agree to be Scout mistress if Phyl found the requisite six girls to form a troop. Soon the official forms were submitted, each girl listed on the form with her surname and first initials only. Thus P.B. James, E. James and four female friends soon formed a sanctioned Boy Scout troop.

Baden-Powell's sister established Girl Guides just a year after Scouts, but Phyl and her friends discovered that only later at a May parade when they met up with a Girl Guide company. Phyl and Betty and the other Scouts disbanded the troop and registered instead as the "2nd Vancouver Girl Guide Company." Guiding offered many of the same opportunities as Scouts and involved no deception.

Soon Phyl started going on rambles on her own or with the Girl Guides. "I used to go up Grouse on my own with a few Guides ... which used to worry my dad quite a lot because he didn't know mountains and didn't like them, I don't think. He'd say: 'You'd been up there last week only, what do you want to go again for?'"[50] Phyl countered her father's question with one of her own. "Why do you play tennis on the same court you played in last week? You have just played a game on that court, why play again?" It was an argument Frank James knew he could not win.

But still, in the years prior to the First World War, it wasn't considered normal for girls or women to thrive on outdoor activities; indeed, the clothing styles—long, cumbersome skirts, shoes lacking tread or outdoor hardiness—made it difficult. Horseback riding was sidesaddle; to ride astride in the city was scandalous. Bicycles were just gaining acceptance,

Phyl James as Girl Guide patrol leader, ca. 1910, and with her canoe, *Terra Nova*, at Burrard Inlet, ca. 1913–14.

but required sitting astride the wheels and pedalling vigorously. Not easy in skirts and petticoats. Even sweating was discouraged because of the laundry involved!

The Girl Guide movement was to become a cornerstone of Phyl's life. She remained active for over 60 years, beginning as a patrol leader, then becoming a lieutenant, a captain and later a commissioner. She contributed greatly on a provincial level, notably developing the Lone Guiding movement, which linked girls in isolated areas together by mail, and acting as Provincial Woodlore Commissioner.

Phyl's first mountain ascent was probably Grouse Mountain in 1912, when she led her Guide company in full dress uniform up Mosquito Creek and along the rough trail to the summit. There the Guides planted the Union Jack on its standard, claiming the mountain for Guides.

But Phyl was almost too old for Guides, aimed for ages 11 to 15. She managed to stay involved by taking on more formal leadership roles. At 16 she became a lieutenant, and then a full captain, assuming responsibility for organizing their camping and hiking expeditions. These early camping expeditions were the real test, for none of the girls had ever camped or stayed outdoors overnight. The Guides constructed tents by making templates, then cutting canvas and sewing the pieces together. One of these expeditions was to Bowen Island in Howe Sound, accessible from the city by steamer. At the Bowen Island camp, the Guides climbed Mount Gardner (767 metres), and Phyl earned her swimming badge by swimming in a full-length (and heavy) serge skirt in the ocean.

Much of Phyl's outdoors knowledge had its beginnings in her experiences organizing the girls, setting up campsites, cooking and working on proficiency badges. She also took first-aid courses, and had a certificate from St. John Ambulance. In 1916 Phyl organized wartime projects for her Girl Guide company. Fundraisers such as amateur theatricals brought in money for the Red Cross, and at Christmastime the girls sponsored a soldier's family and contributed to a food hamper and presents. Phyl's

Guides also collected books and magazines for the Vancouver troops involved in summer training at Vernon. Little did she realize that even at this stage, she had made a connection with Don.

An important mentor was Elsie Carr, who acted for a time as lieutenant in Phyl's Guide company. Elsie Carr came from a family of hikers and climbers,[51] and, most importantly, she belonged to an organization whose sole purpose was to unite people who loved the outdoors and had a passion for climbing—the British Columbia Mountaineering Club. Carr invited her protege on several climbs as her guest.

Another friend, Margaret (Marg) Worsley, brought Phyl and Dick James up to the BCMC cabin on Grouse Mountain in August 1915. Visiting the cabin and seeing how it was used, and meeting members, convinced Phyl that her love of the wilds could be legitimized through accepted social activities. The BCMC was an entree into a world Phyl had only dreamed about, a group of like-minded people who shared her passion for the wilds, who supported each other, teaching and encouraging skill development. Access to the outdoors through Guide camps and pursuit of badges was fine, but the BCMC offered her the next step.

Unfortunately, she had to wait. She was not yet 21 years old, the age of eligibility for club membership. According to BCMC records, Phyl James applied for membership on October 15, 1915, just days after her 21st birthday. Her application was accepted, and two months later—showing proof of two ascents—she graduated to active membership with full status.[52] From then on there was no stopping her.

Phyl James (far right), with Betty beside her, salute the flag on the summit of Grouse Mountain, 1912. Elsie Carr holds the flag.

Phyl James in the lead position, ascending Mount Bishop, June 1916.

Chapter Two   WARTIME

O<small>N JUNE 29, 1915, DON ENLISTED</small> and was assigned to the 47th Infantry Battalion as a private. In November of that year, after several months of training in Vernon, Munday and his fellow soldiers travelled across Canada on the Canadian Pacific Railway to Montreal, where they embarked for England on RMS *Missanabie*. In August 1916 Don and the 47th Battalion left Branshott Camp for Southampton, where they boarded the *Inventor*, bound for Le Havre, and then marched on to the battlefields.

Don Munday in uniform, 1915.

The 47th Battalion would serve under Major General D. Watson, as the 10th Brigade, 4th Canadian Division. Don served as a scout. A scout's principal responsibilities were to note the position of the enemy's strung wires and other obstacles, movements, sentry positions and trenching activities and then to take compass points that would enable guiding the men safely through these threats. Don's equipment included field glasses, periscopes used in the dugouts and trenches in daylight, and telescopes for night work. Scouts, like all soldiers, were armed with Ross rifles and then later Lee Enfield rifles. They carried 120 rounds of ammunition and were considered among the more accurate shooters. In reconnaissance expeditions they travelled mainly at night, taking shelter in farmhouses and other abandoned structures. They were the first to go forward, finding the the safe routes, snipping through the enemy wires, leaving entrypoints for their comrades who followed.

As Phyl later described it: "A scout's business is to see that the men get to the places they were supposed to when they were at the front and get them back again."[1] As a mountain climber who was familiar with the outdoors, Don's skills in the bush and in rough terrain and his abilities to navigate with a compass, take bearings and read a map qualified him for this most important and risky responsibility.

While overseas Don wrote a "Weekly Chronicle of the 47th Battalion," which appeared in New Westminster newspapers, providing a wonderful link for families and the community at large who waited back home. Establishing himself as a journalist would serve him well upon his return.

Don distinguished himself, fighting in the battle of the Salient in the summer of 1916, and in the autumn at the Somme. In April 1917 he was at Vimy Ridge (where he earned the military medal for valour at the Battle of the Triangle), then at Hill 70, and then in October at Passchendaele.[2] His wartime account notes that at the Somme he and his comrades were gassed with tear gas and at Vimy Ridge with chlorine gas.[3] Although he carried his regulation gas mask, his lungs caught the sting of chlorine in the aftermath of the attacks. Several times he was up for promotion, but turned promotions down, preferring to remain uncommissioned.[4]

It was at Passchendaele, on October 24, 1917, while returning from a scouting foray, that he was hit with a mortar shell and wounded. A piece of shrapnel tore through his left arm, entering at his wrist and exiting at the elbow.

> Now and then a "woolly bear" crashed overhead ... and it was one of these that got me near Dochy Farm. The shrapnel went through my left arm, shattering the ulna.
>
> Sometimes men do not know at once that they are hit, but I believe this is only the case with flesh wounds. When a bone is hit there is not an instant of doubt about it. Having no field dressing in the corner of my tunic, I got one from the tunic of the nearest dead German, but the bandage was folded differently to ours and when I tore the waterproof covering open with my teeth, most of the bandage draggled in the mud and water of the shellhole. The nearest pillbox was about 300 yards away, and was occupied by part of the 16th Machine Gun Company. I wallowed through the mud to it and their captain personally helped slash away my sleeve and put on a shell dressing.
>
> One of the men offered to accompany me to our regimental aid post, but the area was being shelled heavily and, after all, I was "walking wounded." The aid post was full to the very entrance with stretcher cases, so I sat outside on a hump of mud while the M.O. and his sergeant put my arm in a splint. Fragments of shells whizzed around ... A tag was tied to a buttonhole, giving my rank, name, number, unit, and injury. There responsibility for me ended. I was a

walking case and had to get out as best I could. A stretcher party was going out after dark and I could accompany them, but preferred to go at once and take advantage of the little daylight left.

I went first to Primrose Cottage pillbox and turned in my day's report to the scout sergeant, got my haversack and said goodbye to the boys. I went out by the way of No. 5 Duck Walk in the 3rd Division sector. The boards were slippery, and because of the hurriedly placed bandage I left the boards a little more slippery than I found them, the bleeding not being fully checked ... After tramping about five miles, I reached the 13th Field Ambulance in a ruined chateau near Potijze. It was about 7 p.m. When the M.O. saw the bleeding he insisted on my lying down on a stretcher while he re-dressed it ... Three other men with smashed bones welcomed my arrival as I completed a load for an ambulance ... At the corps clearing depot there was more bread and tea, then inoculations in the chest with anti-tetanus vaccine, and a letter pencilled on my forehead to record it. A few minutes later I was ... in an ambulance bound for the 10th Casualty Clearing Station, an hour's ride from Ypres. More bread and tea, and within half an hour I was on one of the eight operating tables.[5]

This typical Don Munday matter-of-fact account of his injury and subsequent activity minimizes what must have been a horrific ordeal. For Don this was not heroic. He was merely stubborn and would do things his way, confident in his physical stamina. Such fortitude—mental and physical—along with the stubbornness would characterize his post-service recovery and climbing exploits.

The surgery cleaned the wound of bits of metal and also set the fractured bone, including excising bits of bone from the upper ulna that had splintered as it fractured. But it did not repair the damage done to tendons and nerves. The next day, Don collected his belongings and boarded the *Princess Christian* hospital train for Rouen, a 17-hour journey. On November 2 he was sent to Le Havre and crossed to Southampton on the hospital ship *Panama* and from there to a military hospital in Manchester, where the sanitary conditions and round-the-clock nursing would give the wound a better chance to heal. Over the months the wound slowly closed up, and he was out of danger but very weak. He was transferred to Bearwood, a convalescent hospital in the countryside for Canadian soldiers.[6] Despite the care he received, the damage would remain a lifelong weakness.

He had spent a year and three months on the battlefields, had been exposed to the chemical gases unleashed by the Germans, had suffered from malnutrition and general fatigue; his fighting days were over. On November 15, 1917, while still recuperating in England, General Douglas formally presented him with his Military Medal.[7]

When the splints were finally removed from his arm in January 1918 the muscles in his forearm were atrophied, weak and tender, the joints stiff from disuse. He could not clench his fingers or move them much at all, as they too were stiff, the tendons and ligaments healed but not exercised. The prognosis was that Don was "not likely to have use of [his] arm for six months or more."[8]

Five months later, Don was still in England, awaiting the formal paperwork and transportation arrangements to invalid him back to Canada, but finally he was homeward bound. The hospital ship *Araguaya* left Liverpool on April 15, 1918, and arrived in Vancouver in May 1918. There he became a patient at Shaughnessy Military Hospital but was soon transferred to the Vancouver Military Hospital, New Westminster Section, at the Royal Columbian Hospital. There would be several months of hospital care, massage and physiotherapy, and psychological healing before he was formally discharged from the army. Injury to his arm was such that he was now considered "medically unfit for further service."

Despite this prognosis and his state of general weakness, he still had some of his old spunk and drive and, of course, an intense desire to get back into the mountains. It is amazing the activities he got himself into prior to his army discharge on September 12, 1918.

The Home Front

Phyl's married friends Margaret Lewis and Marg Worsley were also BCMC members and invited Phyl along for climbs. Phyl had met them in the Women's Volunteer Reserve Corps, organized for wartime service in 1915. The organization specialized in St. John Ambulance work (first aid and home nursing) with the intent to be of service during the war. But much to Phyl's dismay, no member of the corps ever went overseas; there was plenty for them to do on the home front.[9] "I thought I had the world by the tail and I was going to go overseas as soon as I got my certificate,"[10] mourned Phyl in later life.

While Don Munday was seeing active service overseas, Phyl was just coming into her own as a climber. Her first big climbing year was 1916. In June she was on The Lions, later Mount Bishop, then Cathedral and White (now Burwell) mountains, then Hanover and Brunswick.[11] In August she attended the BCMC camp in Garibaldi and climbed Helmet Peak and Castle Towers. With others, she watched as Tom Fyles made the first climb up The Table.

The following year she began with winter climbs to the North Shore Mountains, in January going up Crown and Dam Mountains, and on Goat in April. She was on Seymour in May and then White on the July long weekend, and up Seymour again in August, then Cathedral Mountain. On May 12, 1918, she and three male companions ate their lunch on Lynn Peaks, and a month later, along with two other women and six men, Phyl made the summit of the West Lion. This was followed by a trip to Black Mountain later in the same month.

54

Phyl trained as a stenographer, a skill that was in high demand and gave great flexibility in choosing employment. She worked in several office situations, notably in a doctor's office and an automobile dealership. In the extended climbing season of the coast, she was often off on weekend excursions. Like all proper young women, she obeyed the social conventions and was suitably garbed in public, but as soon as she hit the trailhead, she slipped behind a tree or rock and changed out of her shoes into nailed hiking boots and exchanged her skirt for bloomers, the cumbersome and voluminous knee-length pants then *de rigueur* for athletic pursuits. Phyl recalled: "On Dome [now Mount Fromme] I was climbing over a great big log, and it was on a slope, and a little bit high off the ground, and as I got over it, the elastic in my bloomer broke and it caught on a snag … I was just about four inches or more off the ground, and I couldn't reach the ground, and I couldn't get back up on the log. I had to be rescued by one of the boys. Hung by the leg of my bloomer. They never let me live that down."[12]

Bloomers were only to be worn outdoors, away from polite society; they were never acceptable in town. To keep the deception, women stashed and reclaimed their skirts on their return trip. But embarrassing situations arose occasionally. One particular incident occurred when Phyl and a girlfriend returned from a Grouse Mountain hike, running a little late and losing the light. At the trailhead they stopped to retrieve their skirts. Phyl found hers, but her companion could not. It was almost dark and the last ferry back to Vancouver was leaving soon. It was scandalous to be seen in public in bloomers, but Phyl's friend had no choice. If they spent more time searching they would miss the ferry, so down they went. Unfortunately the purser on the gangway had very clear instructions: all passengers were to be suitably garbed. In his view, bloomers were not suitable garb and he refused her permission to board. The friend spent a cold night on the dock while Phyl ferried home and brought a skirt back the next day.

Occasionally the unexpected occurred, and the weekend trip might be delayed in getting off, or their return was late. Generally weather conditions controlled when the climbers would advance for the peak, or whether they could even climb in a certain area. Forest fires were another concern, often clouding the sky and threatening the climbing party; at times a misstep or a slip meant a change in plans if injury resulted. Phyl was a conscientious worker, but at times she was late for work because of her weekend climbs. Not

Phyl James and friends on the trail, ca. 1916–18.

all bosses were sympathetic; not all bosses even believed her explanation. Such was the case in June 1918 when Phyl worked at Begg Motors. She and five others had rented a sailing yacht to take them high up Indian Arm to Bishop's Beach, the start point for a weekend of climbing.

> We went in on a high tide at Bishop's Beach way up at the North Arm and, of course ... didn't allow for the tide and ... got stuck and couldn't get away until the next high tide. That didn't get us back until the next morning, you see, the morning after we should have been back. So I missed a whole day's work. When I went in on the Tuesday, my boss was very annoyed, and he wouldn't believe me. I said: "Well, I'll show you the pictures," which I did as soon as I got them back from the printers. He believed me then, but only then. Because he knew that I was so keen on going, you see, and I think he thought perhaps I was the type that would just make excuses and get an extra day out of it. I was glad we had those pictures too. But it was a lovely, lovely weekend. It was just simply that the boat was stuck.[13]

The photographs did indeed prove the point, showing the boat high and dry on the beach. On this trip Phyl had taken her canoe, the *Terra Nova*, on board the sailboat, and when they were marooned on the beach she paddled John Fyles to the Wigwam Inn at the head of Indian Arm so he could connect with the Harbour Navigation boat and get into town.[14]

Phyl Munday and climbers on the West Lion, June 1918 (top), and the stranded launch at low tide at Bishop's Beach, Indian Arm, June 1918.

BCMC group (including Edith) in the Rogers Pass, awaiting pack horses for trip into the Selkirks, 1921.

Chapter Three RECOVERY AND DISCOVERY

DON MUNDAY MET PHYLLIS JAMES while he was still a patient at the hospital. Phyl worked as a stenographer in the administration office, and they were introduced by Phyl's friend, who was a nursing sister (and Don's physiotherapist). Phyl had heard of Don from other BCMC members, but he was overseas by the time she joined the club, so she had never actually met him. She knew he had a reputation as a skilled climber and that he was serious and rather quiet.

Not long after their introduction, Don was granted short leaves from the hospital, enough to get into town of an evening for the BCMC meetings. Phyl, who was on the executive as the librarian, encouraged Don to come with her to the meetings. At the time, Vancouver City was experiencing a strike by its streetcar drivers, and for a few weeks the only way they could get from New Westminster to Vancouver was by the Interurban cars and jitneys (private cars that travelled regular routes on the main roads, where people could flag them down for a lift to the next spot along the route). It meant a combination of walking and riding both ways. But this activity was therapy for Don, as he rebuilt his strength and his lung capacity. Although he had not been gassed directly, he had been exposed to gas in the atmosphere as it dissipated. Don weighed a mere 121 pounds at the time of his discharge. Although his health improved, he never regained full use of his left arm. Likewise the effects of the chemical gas on his lungs were never erased. For a climber, these two disabilities constituted serious handicaps.

On these excursions, talking about friends in common, climbs and aspirations for climbs they got to know one another. But for Phyl, Don was a fellow climber, nothing more. He was quiet-spoken and rather serious, not at all outgoing and sociable as she was, liking nothing better than dancing till the wee hours or arranging social events at the club. Don's reticence was understandable, given the circumstances. He was in recovery, coping with the aftermath of his war experiences—healing not only his physical body, but

Phyl and her friend Marg Worsley (on left) at Alouette Lake, 1918.

wrestling with images and memories of unforgettable horror on the battlefields. If he was a little solitary or occasionally silent, he was entitled to it.

In June 1918 Don applied for re-entry as a member in the Club and was readily accepted.[1] The timing was perfect; he agreed to stand in on the executive as director of climbs, replacing Tom Fyles who had just left for active service. The schedule of summer climbs was already organized, so his responsibilities were light until the fall season. Don had discretionary time and spent much of it writing. He resumed writing poetry, and worked at making contacts for his later journalism stints. He spent the remainder of his time at outdoors therapy, taken in snatches as he was not yet allowed to be absent from the hospital for more than one day. In August he and Phyl, along with staff and friends from the hospital, climbed to the BCMC cabin on Grouse Mountain, where they recorded their visit in the guest book.[2]

Finally, in September the Officer in Command at the hospital (on the recommendation of the doctor) granted Munday permission for a weekend absence. Undoubtedly Don was advised to enjoy his leave and to relax, take it easy, perhaps go home and visit his mother. But that was not to be. Phyl had other plans.

Earlier that year, she and her friend Marg Worsley had set out with the intent to make a try on Blanshard Peak (1,560 metres), the southernmost of the Golden Ears group, rising above the north shores of Alouette Lake. The Alouette River flows south into the Pitt River, which itself empties into the Fraser River near the small farming community of Pitt Meadows. By following the south branch of the Alouette, Phyl and Marg reached the

lake and the hydroelectric dam at the intake. There they spoke with the B.C. Electric Company man stationed at the dam, asking if they could borrow his canoe to paddle across the lake, which would put them near the foot of the mountain. According to Phyl, this simple and polite request was flatly refused. He would not permit two women to go into the wilderness beyond. Eventually he relented, but the pair had only enough time to reach the base of the mountain. They resolved to return with a male companion, knowing that the presence of a man in the party would make the gauge-reader feel more comfortable in lending the canoe. Don was the lucky man selected as chaperone. He wrote of their experiences:

> When they invited me to join them in another attempt early in September I was still a patient in the military hospital at New Westminster. The Officer in Command did not know I was spending my weekend leave climbing. The nurses—God bless them—and the staff did not always distress the O.C. with details that might have conflicted with his impression of how the hospital was, or should be, run.
>
> As we tramped the shadowy trail along Alouette River alder leaves fluttered down with grating sounds which would have kept nervous persons tense lest the stirrings meant presence of wild animals.
>
> The forest fringed lake which then mirrored the mountains beyond has since been dammed and its shores desolated by logging and fires. We slept on the lake shore in front of the gauge-reader's cabin. Order and cleanliness ruled within the cabin. The floor surely had a daily scrubbing. The gauge-reader was big of frame but no longer angular, slow of speech, paternal in his attitude, and haste had little place in his placid philosophy.
>
> We would have paid him to ferry us across the lake, thereby entitling ourselves to urge him to take us when we were ready, but we saw the idea of payment unwelcome ...
>
> Mounting westward to the ridge paralleling the lake, we had some distance through brush and stunted trees before we camped in heather by a pleasant stream ... The September afternoon was half spent before we left for Mt. Blanshard. So confident were we that we would climb the reddish tooth and return before dusk that we took only a few scraps of chocolate and no lights.
>
> As is not uncommon on the sub-alpine peaks of the range, the steep cliffs supported a good deal of matted growth not answering to

the common idea of trees. Scarred contorted trunks hundreds of years old are only a few feet in length, and probably not upright then unless huddled closed under a sheltering step of rock. Trailing branches normally much exceed the trunks in length.

Climbing over these wiry obstacles is not often practicable. Struggling through is strenuous and hard on clothing. A summit photograph shows one of the women [Phyl] with a handkerchief held curiously, but it was hiding devastation to her clothes. We got to the hitherto unclimbed summit in time to see the sinking sun cast the shadow of the mountain in a slim violet wedge for miles across forested ridges flanking the Fraser valley.

To be free of our packs gave us a false feeling of strength. We were not as fresh as we thought. We must have yielded to the temptation to stay too long on top. In the darkness we could not distinguish one essential bit of the route. There was no moon. The only place hereabouts where we could spend the night without standing up or hanging on was a ledge with a long drop below, but its less pleasant feature was stoppage of circulation in our legs due to hanging over the sharp edge.

The street lights of Vancouver blinked at us uncomfortingly. Haze drew across the sky, not even allowing us the stars for contemplation. The narrowness of the ledge hardly invited the relaxation needed for sound sleep, but we were tired enough to doze at times …

Top: A confident Phyl James poses on the summit of Alouette Peak (Mount Blanshard visible on extreme left), May 1918. Bottom: Phyl James and Don Munday on the windy summit of Mount Blanshard; photo by Marg Worsley, September 1918. Note position of Phyl's handkerchief.

RECOVERY AND DISCOVERY | 63

The homeward tramp to get the last train at Haney developed into a dull grind. Mrs. Worsley lived short of the town. A holiday weekend crowd made the train late so Miss James and I had to stand in the jammed aisle. We missed the last street car in New Westminster. Miss James took her boots off and walked in her stocking feet. Continuing toward the hospital I literally went to sleep on my feet again and again. In that law-abiding place not even a police patrol car was abroad to mistake me for a drunk and transport me to the hospital when they found their mistake. New Westminster police were like that.[3]

This joint first ascent—a precursor of many to come—was verified in 1923 when an unsuspecting BCMC group gained the summit only to discover a rock cairn that held the 1918 record. Don and Phyl made another first ascent, that of Coquitlam Mountain, later in the autumn.

Don also spent time in solitary pursuits and conceived of a practical way to rebuild his strength. He decided to build himself a mountain retreat and selected a spot on a long shoulder on Dam Mountain (1,340 metres), on the west side of Grouse. He blazed and cut a trail to the site and then built a cabin he named "Evenglow," made entirely of cedar cut and split on the mountain. On one face it had a balcony with a wonderful vantage through the trees. The cabin boasted glass windows and rustic furniture. He made a fireplace of river rock hauled up the mountain in a sling on his back. Fascinated by Don's industriousness, the local newspapers reported: "every weekend and on holidays laboriously, and with the patience of an ant ... stick by stick, stone by stone, piece of furniture by piece, he carried the makings and furnishings of a little hut up the steep mountainside to a cunningly concealed broad ledge with a wonderful outlook on the sea and land. Then he built a comfortable mountain retreat, thinking of the day when he would spend his honeymoon there."[4] Don was definitely thinking of a honeymoon, though Phyl really had no clue about this turn of thought. She viewed Don as a friend, a resourceful climbing companion, and no more. Don had his work cut out for him, but he was a patient man. He spent the next year demonstrating his worthiness not just as a climbing partner, but also as her life partner.

Opposite page: Don Munday shouldering hand-split plank for his cabin construction, ca. 1918. Above: Don on the verandah of Evenglow cabin on Dam Mountain, ca. 1920.

Courtship and Climbs

Don and Phyl and their climbing companions kept busy schedules. They used the weekends to best advantage, and occasionally took a few days extra to venture farther afield. In the second week of August 1919, along with fellow climber Tom Ingram, they embarked on a somewhat longer trip. Don was on a quest to reclimb a mountain he had ascended five years earlier in 1914 with Fred Smith, which at the time was a second recorded ascent.[5] The mountain was then called Ida, and later called Indian Chief, but today its official name is Meslilloet (2,001 metres). It stands at the head of Meslilloet Creek, which in turn flows into Indian River and the head of Indian Arm.

Don wrote at length about this trip with Phyl and Tom Ingram. Theirs would be the fourth ascent and, for Phyl, the first female ascent.

> Through the combined murk of forest fire smoke and morning fog we reached Wigwam Inn on Indian Arm by launch. We were then misdirected along a trail on the west side of Indian River which at that time could not be followed all the way to connect with a trail to an old logging camp. A sheer bluff came down to the river's edge.
>
> Perforce we waded the river. Though only waist deep it was all we could do to keep our feet in the rush of water. Just when we reached the east side a fisherman appeared around a bend with a canoe. He thereupon offered to transport our packs upstream a quarter of a mile to where a cable spanned the river near the site of a cable bridge which had been washed out.
>
> After our benefactor had left us we discovered that we had to ford it again because the last user of the cable car had tied it on the opposite side. Had the water been a few inches deeper we could not have stood against it.
>
> Some five miles from the mouth we reached the old camp. Several of the buildings were in good condition, one being occupied by Mr. Davis, gauge-reader for a company having power rights on the river.
>
> Davis placed one of the cabins and plenty of wood at our disposal, so we soon had a meal cooked and made a start at drying our clothes.
>
> Under threatening skies we crossed the river next morning on a

Cocoa break on the trail. Phyl (third from left)
is oblivious to Don's attention (far right), 1919.

foot log and climbed through big timber to Norton Lake, 2,300 feet. Here a commodious cabin of new logs has been erected at the cost of much labour right on top of an enormous boulder.

The weather remained unsettled until the morning of the fourth day. Norton Lake lies in a wooded hollow in the mountains, the vegetation coming down to the water's edge. The morning mists were clearing as we loaded our packs on a rude log raft and paddled up the lake which is about three-quarters of a mile in length.

Crossing a low divide we entered the valley of Belknap Creek which is here flowing south parallel to Indian River into which

it drains. In half an hour we came in sight of Mt. Ida's rocky gable towering nearly 5,000 feet above the head of the valley. Below us the creek muttered in a canyon ...

Under the south face of Mt. Ida the valley widens. Joseph Lake lies to the west and the two Ann Lakes directly under the peak. We followed along a brushy ridge between Ann Lakes. The green tinge of the eastern lake showed a glacial stream flowed into it, and by noon we reached the mouth of Ann Creek flowing from the north east.

As we dined we dried ourselves in the welcome sunshine, for the brush had retained a generous burden of raindrops. The creek was high now and crossing back and forth was difficult. Presently the valley widened and flowers and grass appeared, large beds of blue violets being abundant.

The valley has a wild distinctiveness that clings in one's memory. The granite breaks in great slabs, the cliffs bearing some likeness to a roof laid with disproportionately thick shingles, the edges of the "shingles" being immense overhanging faces. The eastern cliffs were cut by a splendid waterfall fed from a permanent snowcap.

Erosion was going on much more rapidly on the western cliffs and the detritus in the form of huge rocks had been flung across the valley right to the base of the east wall. Among this grew avalanche-crumpled vegetation, and the stream filled the hollows with numerous deep pools.

We therefore abandoned our attempt to reach the glacier and turned directly up the slope toward a gully that appeared to offer a route up on to the eastern spur of the Ida range. Fresh looking rock faces and newly splintered timber showed where a tremendous mass of rock had fallen recently ... This rockslide was about a thousand feet in height.

> **Food** *"You allow yourself so many pounds per day per person and, of course, the thing is the menu is very easy. You can't take fresh meat or anything because you'd no way of keeping it like that. I dried some one year but ugh! It wasn't what it was cracked up to be—because I didn't have the proper method, I suppose. So we just had bacon and ham and beans and rice and barley and cheese, those were the staples—and porridge, of course. But with the porridge it was easy because there are several different kinds and if you were going to have say, nine pounds of porridge, I'd have three of three different kinds so that you could have a variety of food."*
>
> Phyllis Munday taped interview, 1973, BC Archives.

At the mouth of the gully stood a triangular mass of avalanche snow about 40 feet thick. We mounted this; it had thawed back from the cliffs about 15 feet in a straight wall on each side, but at its upper end one might readily jump to a jutting rock. Not till we got off it here was it readily apparent that this spearpoint of snow was unsupported a length of some 30 feet or more ... The appearance of the gully had been misleading. The bed was filled with excessively loose rocks and the walls were remarkably smooth. We had to get out the rope at last. As we had packs of about 40 pounds we were somewhat handicapped.

The head of the gully proved to be a smooth walled chute 120 feet in length. We tried the north wall in various places. I was in no position to dodge one huge rock which missed my head but struck my pack so heavily it nearly hurled me down. It was now 6 p.m. Descent would have been necessarily very slow.

Discarding my pack, I wriggled up a diagonal crack in a wall and reached a slanting ledge where a block had dropped out of a buttress. The gap was just enough to admit the passage of my body comfortably as, with a single handhold, I squirmed forward with my legs dangling down in space. Once past this buttress there was a little loose rock, but in a few moments I was on top of the spur.

It now took some time to find a place where the rope could reach down to any place to which the packs could be carried by my companions. I could not see them for an overhanging rock and the friction of the rope over this made hauling the packs most difficult.

By the time this was done it was so dark in the gully that they could not see my route up the cliff, so, fastening the end of the rope on top, I took the other end down to them. At 10 p.m. we camped in luxuriant heather on the edge of a cliff. There was sufficient wood but no water. The moonlight revealed a distant snow patch from which I carried a lump big enough for our needs. The array of glacial summits along the upper Coquitlam valley shone in the moonlight.

It was midnight before we got to bed under a fly-proof tent, thanks to which we slept rather later in the morning ... It was in the middle of the forenoon before we got on our way again. Daylight examination revealed that the previous day had played such havoc with our clothes that two of us had to remain in our sleeping bags till the damage was repaired.

RECOVERY AND DISCOVERY | 69

Proceeding westward, we encountered a curious succession of wide shelving ledges and overhanging walls, most of the ledges being too steep and smooth to stand on. With some difficulty we mapped out a feasible route to the snow above. Striking rocks again, the going was good. Climbing in full view of a vast expanse of nameless mountains, we had an ever changing outlook as we ascended, and fine masses of gleaming cumulus clouds added to the charm of light and shade to the snowfields.

At 2 p.m. we reached the eastern summit of the range, about 6,350 feet. The snowfield on its northern slope is extensive and feeds a glacial system that is remarkably complex. In its extent the glacier is divided by a bold ridge, half the glacier continuing north to form an important source of the Coquitlam River, the other half turning eastward down a narrow trench to the head of Ann Creek; this glacier divides sharply north and south, draining respectively to the Coquitlam River and Ann Creek. It is further complicated by a small flow of ice from the east so that a cruciform pattern is produced.

We camped in a heather patch 50 feet below the summit. After lunch Mt. Ida was still in heavy cloud and we merely made a trip to explore the snowfield.

Toward sunset the clouds drifted away leaving Mts. Tantalus, Garibaldi and Mamquam clear in the northwest and north ... To south-eastward "The Great White Watcher" of the Indians—Mt. Baker to more unimaginative usurpers of the land—might have been an immense rosebud against the violet sky ...

The heather was white with frost at daybreak. Everything below 3,500 feet was submerged in a sea of rolling cloud ... Having breakfasted with the slowly dissolving mists before us, we shouldered our packs and crossed two ridges to the pass leading to Meslilloet Glacier which lies parallel to the north face of Mt. Ida. Leaving our packs here, we skirted the edge of the snowfield to the foot of the peak which looks well from this side. The rock is firm and for climbers of ordinary ability roping is hardly necessary although a cliff of imposing proportions is traversed. The actual summit at 7,000 feet is an odd rock on which two persons may perch at one time.

This was the fourth recorded ascent ...[6]

When Don wrote this account he included a small aside: "In the course of this trip, Ingram noted two closely parallel sets of footprints across a snowfield and entirely in jest announced to us that he had seen signs of a wedding; he was surprised when he learned that he was a true prophet." [7]

In August the same year, Don organized a climb to Mount Baker (3,285 metres) in Washington State.[8] This dormant volcano rises majestically above the Cascades and on a clear day dominates the skyline looking south from Vancouver or east from southern Vancouver Island. It was on this trip that an incident occurred that further convinced Don that Phyl was the one for him. Don, Phyl and Tom Ingram were climbing across the lateral moraine of the Roosevelt Glacier.[9] They had unroped at the edge of the ice as the slope appeared to present no real difficulties. A single step away from reaching the vegetation on its edge, Don got into trouble.

> When I put my full weight on a safe-looking point of rock it simply dropped away beneath my foot, somehow giving me an outward toss which at least allowed me to turn over in mid-air in an effort to land on my feet. During that small interval I had ample time to estimate my chances of escaping a helpless slide into the black chasm between the glacier and the lateral moraine. No guidance of mine placed my feet on the only spot where they could hope to hold. It did not wholly surprise me that the woman in the party, Miss Phyllis B. James, landed a foot below me at the same instant with the intention of trying to check my fall. Instead of this, her footing broke away at once. With the ground crumbling under my feet, I caught her arm, giving her the moment or two of support she needed to rake out tiny ledges with her nailed boots.[10]

For Don, Phyl's actions bespoke how closely attuned they were. "Even at that time we relied on each other for rightness of action in emergencies, often without audible language between us." [11] Don maintained that there was "a certain measure of telepathic understanding; later, as husband and wife, this became more pronounced though not to a stage of definitely controlled interchange of thought. In the wilderness such swift understanding is a great safety factor, and I am quite conscious sometimes when her judgement supports an unspoken decision of mine in trying situations." [12]

By nature, Don was taciturn and uncomfortable with extended conversation. His face was not expressive, and it was difficult to read his thoughts. His outward appearance was the very opposite of Phyl's; she could bubble over with enthusiasm and openly expressed it. But behind Don's facade was a romantic soul who composed poems about the beauties of nature and was a keen observer of all living things.

Some of his drafts of poems survive. Of varying quality, they strive to bring his intangible feelings into tangible form. These are the first few lines from an untitled work.

> The smoke of forest fires screens
> The wearying city far below
> An upper world is ours today,
> A world apart, a world aglow
> Where every bush is varying flame
> That in transcendent pattern blends
> About the boles of evergreens
> On which the Autumn vainly spends
> That selfsame call that in our hearts
> So keen and dominant to-day
> Drives out the darker moods of life
> Implants instead sheer Beauty's sway[13]

Don's war diaries also provide clues regarding his earlier loves and delineate his thoughts on both the joy and pain of relationships. He had impulsively married while in England awaiting shipment to France. The marriage did not last the war, and Don was bitter. In his war diary he wrote: "Clarity comes from spiritual beauty such as I found in the face ... of the last woman I loved, but there it flickered out and left her just nothing more than a pretty statue and more dangerous." But regardless of this insight, he confessed: "My thoughts will return to where my heart is still ... "[14] And the following year he wrote: "Flora leaves memories of things evil and bitter ... to the man to whom you brought the flower of love."[15] Once sadly disillusioned, Don was careful about his emotions. In Phyllis he saw someone who could share his love of the outdoors, and who was assertive and caring. He saw a soulmate.

Don's persistence and gentlemanly ways eventually advanced his case. Over the course of 1919, the James and Munday families came together for social and recreational opportunities. On a February trip to the BCMC cabin on Grouse, Phyl's father and sister, along with Don's brother, climbed with them. Don and Phyl's enthusiasm for climbing encouraged Esmée (Betty) McCallum, Phyl's sister, to join the BCMC and qualify as a graduating member in 1919, while that same year, Bert Munday fulfilled the requirements to became an active member.[16]

Before the end of the year, Don and Phyl became engaged and the following February they were married. The ceremony—as was customary at the time—was at 9 o'clock on Saturday morning, February 4, 1920. The day dawned with fog so dense that Phyl left home an hour early for the church, to ensure she would not be late. But despite the worries, everyone arrived on time, Phyl's sister Betty (who herself had married a young soldier in 1914) stood with her, and Don's brother Bert was best man. "The bride was dressed in a serviceable brown traveling suit" noted the newspaper columnist reporting on the occasion, who also wrote that "the young couple were in receipt of many handsome presents including a beautiful cabinet of silverware from the staff of the *B.C. Veteran's Weekly*, a silver chafing dish from the B.C. Mountaineering Club, a set of electrical appliances" and many other gifts.[17] After the ceremony, the family members returned to Phyl's parents' home at 520 Burrard Street for the traditional wedding breakfast. The happy couple came in through the front door, amid a flurry of best wishes and congratulations. They exited secretly via the back door, having changed from their wedding attire into their outdoors clothes, and left on a climber's-style honeymoon. The guests were left with breakfast but no newlyweds.

Don and Phyl headed for the streetcar, and then the eleven o'clock ferry across Burrard Inlet to North Vancouver. From there they caught the Capilano streetcar to the end of the line and hiked through the forest to Don's cabin on Dam Mountain where they would spend the next week high above the city and high above the fog, in the world that they loved best.

The newspapers had been covering the two climbers' various pursuits over the years and noted: "The young couple are concluding

Honeymoon to Be Spent on Mountain Top

Well - known Vancouver Couple Were Married This Morning.

MARRIED at 9 o'clock this morning at Christ Church by Rev. C. C. Owen, Miss Phyllis James, daughter of Mr. and Mrs. A. F. James of 520 Burrard street, and Mr. W. A. D. Munday, news editor of the B. C. Veterans' Weekly, and son of Mrs. J. Munday, 224 Twenty-ninth avenue east, left immediately after the service to spend their honeymoon on Mount Dam, on the North Shore.

In climbing the mountain side several thousand feet the young couple are concluding the romance that started with mountaineering some years ago. Both are enthusiastic mountain-climbers. Mr. Munday, who is second vice-president of the B. C. Mountaineering Club, has the distinction of having made the first ascent of certain peaks of the Garibaldi and other mountains. In several of these he was accompanied by Miss James.

In company with Mr. Munday and another companion, Miss James was the first person and the only one since to climb the south peak of Golden Ears Mountain. She made the first ascent of Mount Coquitlam in 1918 and made the fourth recorded ascent and the only ascent by a woman of Mount Indian Chief. Mr. Munday was the first to climb Mount Hanover several years ago.

the romance that started with mountaineering some years ago." And of the choice for their honeymoon retreat: "Friends of Mr. Munday, who are acquainted with his descriptive writing and songs, state that they are not surprised that he had chosen to give such a picturesque setting to this connubial Alpine romance."[18]

Both Don and Phyl had popular followings, due in the main to the social columns in the local newspapers. Their exciting and busy lives made fascinating reading, and the papers duly documented Don building his cabin on Dam Mountain and then rejoiced in their marriage. Don often wrote up their climbs, and as a freelance journalist, did what he could to sell articles to newspapers and magazines. Phyl was a busy and outgoing Girl

Guide leader, and her name was frequently in the newspapers as well. When the two of them were married, the story and their media appeal just grew.

Several months after the wedding, Don and Phyl embarked on an ambitious journey on the Canadian National Railway to the Rocky Mountains. Neither had climbed in this area of the province before, but they were inspired by accounts of mountaineering in the newly created Mount Robson Provincial Park. It was like nothing they had done before. Never mind that they were attempting exploration in unfamiliar territory, in mountains higher than those ever climbed near home, that they were armed only with a map and notes taken from mountaineering accounts published in the *Canadian Alpine Journal*, carrying Don's compass to find their way, and packing all their gear. Never mind that after disembarking from the train near Robson Station, they were unable to arrange for pack-horses and had to carry their 65-pound packs from the train station by trail to Berg Lake. It wasn't daunting; it was adventure.

Despite a high snow pack, they made ascents of Mount Mumm (2,962 metres), Lynx Mountain (3170 metres) and Resplendent Mountain (3,426 metres), the latter a first ascent by a new route via the northwest arête. A sudden weather change on Resplendent forced them to race for their lives to a rock rib when snow on an ice slope began avalanching. Elsewhere, they enjoyed the abundance of wildlife, spending many moments with their binoculars tracing the ascent of sure-footed mountain goats and sheep. It was this 1920 trip that changed their perspectives about game hunting. Don, like his comrades, often carried a rifle to hunt game such as rabbits or goats to supplement the climbing diet. No longer. After this the camera would be the Mundays' only way of shooting game and their trophies would be photographic ones.

It was also on this trip that Phyl changed her mind about her boots, more specifically, the soles. She had been carefully assessing Don in his new boots. For years climbers wore leather boots with edge nails —a special type of soft metal nail with a long spike—on the soles. Edge nails were ordered in bulk and then each climber applied them to his or her own boots, first by drilling holes in the soles and then pushing the edge nails through the sole from the inside, and clipping them over so the two portions of the edge nail were just on the counter of the boot. The nails were placed in pairs around the edge of the welt of the sole and acted like crampons (but were

The honeymooning couple, 1920.

Boots *"The boots were good leather boots. We always had them well made, and they had the edge nails in them in those days. It wasn't until 1920 when Don first wore tricounis, and I didn't trust them. I let him wear them for a year, and when we were in Robson I found that he was much superior to me ... so the next year I bought tricounis and I've never looked back. Now of course, they don't even wear the nails, they have the Vibram soles on the boots which are very good, really, except if you get on a snowless glacier, when it's all just ice ... then you have to wear crampons if it's steep. So we didn't need to carry crampons most of the time in the earlier days because of the tricouni nail. [The tricouni] was a very good nail, it was good on rock, and also good on ice, and just dandy in the woods. The edge nail was slippery, of course, on the ice, but otherwise it was good."*

PHYLLIS MUNDAY TAPED INTERVIEW, 1973, BC ARCHIVES.

actually now a part of the boot sole). They were particularly good on logs and slippery surfaces, but on the ice, they slipped.

Don had purchased the new tricouni nails, which—like edge nails—were pushed through the leather soles. Unlike the edge nails, they could not be pushed through pre-drilled holes, and this made them much harder to apply. Once they were pushed through, instead of clipping them over on the edge of the sole, the prongs on the tricouni nails were shaped so that they spread when driven in, and thus locked the nail securely. Don had found them excellent for rock work, but it was in the Rockies on the ice that Don's tricounis really performed. Watching Don beside her on the ascents, Phyl was finally convinced of the merits of tricouni nails and vowed that when they returned to Vancouver, she too would switch over.

A New Club

Although the B.C. Mountaineering Club name sounded reflective of the province, the climbs were almost always on the coast and membership principally comprised Vancouver area residents. The Alpine Club of Canada (ACC) drew members from around the province (and indeed, around the world) and concentrated on the Rocky Mountains for its official climbs and camps. Don and Phyl were intrigued. Several of their friends in the BCMC were already members and had attended the famed annual camps in the Rockies. Don and Phyl wanted to broaden the geographic area of their climbing to the Rockies and joining this club would facilitate that goal.

Phyl at the summit cairn, Lynx Mountain, 1920.

Don and Phyl's extended honeymoon to Mount Robson Park in 1920 was pivotal. The elevations of Lynx, Mumm and Resplendent exceeded those of any coastal mountains they had yet encountered, and they found their fitness and mountaineering skills were ready for the test. They were confident and comfortable on the climbs.

On this first trip to the Rockies they went entirely on their own, armed with information gleaned from articles in mountaineering journals and stories and advice from friends. It was a rather bold move as they were miles from the support network of the BCMC and their climbing circle. But the trip was a success, and triggered a desire to see more of these mountains.

On September 25, 1920, they both applied for membership in the ACC. The process required applicants to be proposed by current members and to list at least two witnessed mountain ascents as verification of their climbing abilities. Members Thomas Ingram, R.C. Johnson and Elizabeth

B. Harman, friends and also fellow members of the BCMC, proposed Phyl's application. She listed her recent ascents of Resplendent Mountain (the ascent via the northwest arête which established a new route) and Lynx. Her husband was listed as witness. Don's application was proposed by Elizabeth B. Harman, Thomas Ingram and Edith M. Henley, and he listed two early ascents, that of Mount Garibaldi in August 1912 and Mamquam Mountain in July 1913 (interesting choices, as neither were his first ascents of these mountains, but they were both climbs in which Munday's sister, Pansy, and Loretto Hanafin made the first female ascents).

Don and Phyl were both accepted as active members on October 4 and now belonged to a truly international group of climbing enthusiasts. The Club was formally affiliated with the prestigious Alpine Club in London, England,[19] thus cementing and encouraging friendly relations between mountaineers in the two countries. Membership entitled Don and Phyl to receive the annual *Canadian Alpine Journal* and the more frequently published smaller *Gazette*, and also to attend the annual camps. The ACC had regional sections throughout Canada, and Don and Phyl allied themselves with the Vancouver group, quickly becoming involved in activities, meetings and climbs. They now participated in two locally based but distinct clubs and served on the executive of each for the next 10 years.

Don served as editor for the BCMC newsletter, *The B.C. Mountaineer*, from 1923 through 1926. He led many club climbs and served as vice-president. Phyl also led climbs and was club librarian for a few years, beginning in 1918, and a stalwart organizer of dinners and dances.

Within a short time the couple's participation in the local chapter of the ACC led to national involvement. Don was appointed to the national executive in 1926, and in 1932, when Arthur O. Wheeler formed a committee to study glaciers and glacial action, Don was one of its members and on trips into glacier country, his pack always contained a tape measure and paint to mark the toe of the glacier. The goal was to systematically record the measurements of glacial tongues and their movements over a period of years. For several years Don also served as western vice-president for the ACC and contributed articles, records of climbs and book reviews to the *Canadian Alpine Journal*.

In 1928 Phyl was appointed as the photographic secretary and she continued in this capacity for over a decade. This position had an ongoing

Don and Phyl, Capilano Creek, ca. 1920.

responsibility to coordinate the annual photographic competitions, arrange exhibition of members' photos, coordinate jury selection for the competitions and ensure the safe receipt and return of the photos submitted.

Soon it was a stretch for them to fully commit to both the BCMC and the ACC. From 1930 onwards, Don and Phyl only maintained membership in the ACC. Their outdoor activities, however, continued as before, with their trusted climbing friends, regardless of membership affiliation.

The Twosome Becomes a Threesome—Edith

On March 26, 1921, Phyl gave birth to a daughter, Edith Phyllis, and the climbing life just carried right along. Whereas most women of her time would have retired from strenuous pursuits or community involvement to tend to an infant, Phyl just picked things up where they had been prior to the last few months of pregnancy. She asked for and received a seven-week leave of absence from her Guiding responsibilities. This was her first hiatus from Guiding since she began as a Girl Guide herself in 1910.

At eight weeks, the infant was carried up to Evenglow Cabin on Dam Mountain for the first of many weekends, and at 11 weeks, she made her first ascent, to the summit of Crown Mountain (1,503 metres). The newspapers loved that one: the Vancouver *Province* printed two photos showing Edith, one with each parent at the summit.[20] Edith was also taken to Mount Bishop, Hollyburn and The Lions (although not the top on this climb).[21]

Years later Phyl recalled: "When she was so little, we carried her in a hammock strung around Don's shoulder, and he steadied her little head with his arm. Carried her like that until she got big enough." Next Don fashioned a carrier that fitted over his backpack. It "had canvas on it, a big canvas band, so that when she was put into it, it could come right around from her hips to under her armpits, so that she didn't slide down it ... so that she could go in, fully dressed, and be covered up with the canvas, and it didn't matter whether it rained, or what it did, she didn't get wet. And that's the way we carried her until she got too big for it. And he made also a hood to it, so that if it rained, we could pull it over her head, and then mosquito netting."[22] The carrier was adjustable so that as Edith grew and her neck muscles strengthened it could be fastened at more of a vertical and less horizontal angle. This way Edith could look around her and watch her mother, who followed on the trail right behind.

Don and Phyl holding daughter Edith, 1921 (top), Phyl and Edith on top of Crown Mountain, June 1921 (left), and Don supporting Edith in sling, Crown Mountain, June 1921.

RECOVERY AND DISCOVERY | 81

"One way to acquire sure-footedness on wilderness trails is to put a baby—your own baby—on your back in addition to your pack," wrote Don many years later. Apparently Edith slept five hours at a stretch on the trail, and when awake she crooned softly in time with his pace.[23] In fact, it is this humming and cooing that endeared Edith to many of the Mundays' climbing companions. By all accounts Edith was a happy and contented baby, easily transportable, and not much of an impediment to her mountaineering parents. This was a blessing, considering their unusual and committed lifestyle, and leads to some speculation about the direction their climbing activities might have taken had Edith not been so portable during these early times. Nevertheless, the extra provisioning—the cloth diapers, and change of clothes—all required space and maintenance. "And thus it was," Don wrote, "she became an unconsulted, though not unconsidered, member of our party in a forty-mile trip along the almost forgotten section of the old Lillooet trail between Vancouver and Squamish."[24]

On the July 1st weekend in 1921, the young family embarked on this hike along Seymour Creek and down the Stawamus Valley into Squamish, returning to Vancouver via Howe Sound on the Union Steamship.[25] It was a bit of an experiment to see exactly how it would be to pack Edith—who was growing—and supplies on an extended basis. Don described the first part of the trip.

> Reassured by scattering rain-clouds, we left home about noon, crossed to North Vancouver, and reached a point about two miles above the falls on Seymour Creek—a dam has since then changed all this. Just before we reached Burwell Creek where we camped, we passed three surveyors on the trail. So engaged were they in politely hiding their interest in the size of my wife's pack that they quite missed noting the precious freight topping off my load ... from a deep bed of fir boughs we watched the sunset-tinted storm clouds clearing from the black and white heights of Mt. Bishop on the one side of the valley, and Mt. Cathedral on the other ... chorusing song-birds woke us ... It was good to be alive [on] such a morning, even with the self-imposed bondage of a pack ... Too soon we came to thickets of salmonberry bushes still wet with raindrops. Soon even our boots were full of water. With a baby on

Phyl washing baby Edith in a homemade cedar washtub in front of the fireplace in Evenglow cabin on Dam Mountain, 1922.

your back you cannot put your head down and bore into a thicket. The only thing to do is to feel for the trail with the feet."[26]

Soon the valley contracted to a stupendous defile through which the creek fell steeply between cliffs high above them. Windfalls blocked the trail again and again. Recent torrents had washed away sections of the trail, and they began to worry about making their destination, which was a cabin at what was then known as the Bank of Vancouver Mine.

> Unable to bridge the stream, and knowing the trail shortly returned to the western side, we battled our way along a rockslide (talus) of dangerously loose fragments amid which grew luxuriantly devil's club, salmonberry and musk currant. Even without a baby to consider, it verged on the impassable. We finally jumped into the creek and waded along the shore.
>
> Daylight dimmed. The trail grew rough. Patches of snow appeared, and we dared not go farther in search of dry wood ... everything here seemed utterly sodden ... In spite of our wet clothes and the biting wind we slept. Baby was snug and dry in her own nest. We breakfasted lightly on boiled barley and raisins before starting the 700-foot climb to the mine cabin which stood across the creek. The only bridge was an uprooted tree four inches thick, bare of bark, springy, and sprayed upon by a waterfall.[27]

When they reached the cabin of massive hewn logs, they found it was in a state of decay, but the interior was in good order. As a late breakfast and early dinner cooked, Phyl spent time with Edith. "It was wonderful because they [the cabins] had these huge stoves that the cooks used to use for cooking for the miners ... these monstrous big bread pans ... and so that was marvelous for bathing my baby in the morning ... which I did. Along came three, I guess they were geologists, from the mine. They had come over through a pass and they were absolutely stunned when they saw a small baby in a bread pan ... on the oven door."[28]

Leaving the cabin, they climbed 400 metres to Loch Lomond, the source of Seymour Creek. The lake was still frozen and the snow one metre deep along the shore. On the descent, they splashed their way down the

Edith and her parents at camp in the Selkirks, 1921.

trail, windfalls still obstructing their way, into Squamish, where the sun came out in a brilliant welcome.

The hike must have proved satisfactory, for later that month they met up with other BCMC members and took the Canadian Pacific Railway from Vancouver to Glacier Station near Rogers Pass in the Selkirk Mountains, where the annual BCMC camp was to be held.

It was a novelty for the BCMC to locate the camp away from the coast, and the decision to do so may have been undertaken at the suggestion of the Mundays, who had ventured away from the coast the previous year. Don and Phyl had had a taste of climbs in Robson Provincial Park, and they were anxious to sample a little more of the interior climbing country. Camp director Tom Fyles (also an ACC member) directed the BCMC advance party as they selected the sites. For the first week the group camped at an elevation of over 2,000 metres near the Hermit Hut below Mount Sifton,

close to timberline. The second week, they pitched the tents in a sheltered site not far below one of the snouts of the great Asulkan Valley glacier, near to Glacier House, the Canadian Pacific Railway hotel. Ascents were made of Mount Sir Donald and the chief peaks of the Hermit Range but weather broke before the Dawson Range "could be attacked."[29]

For the Mundays this trip was a rather different experience with four-month-old Edith along. Phyl hardly climbed at all. Don managed the first climb. He and six others ascended Mount Rogers, the highest peak in the Hermit Range, via the south arête, an almost all-rock route. The party descended by the Swiss Glacier which "afforded a splendid glissade."[30]

Don did not climb Mount Tupper or Mount Grizzly, and when it came time for Hermit Mountain, the family climbed with their companions only partway on the Tupper Glacier, to about 3,000 metres and then left the party. Of the six or so peaks tackled during the second week, Don only ascended Mount Sir Donald, which was, after all, "the big event to which all looked forward."[31] There were seven in the Sir Donald party, which was thought to be the largest party to make the ascent at one time. The route selected was not the "classic" route popular today via the northwest ridge on blocky quartzite, but via the southwest ridge, which was much more precarious and involved loose rock. The party left the Vaux Glacier

Glacier House, famed Canadian Pacific Railway hotel in the Selkirk Mountains, 1921. Right: Don and Edith, 1921.

and climbed through the couloir and up to the southern ridge. The summit view was disappointing because smoke from forest fires obscured even the nearest mountains. The size of the party and hazards from loose rock made it a slow climb; they arrived at 1:45 p.m., some eight hours after leaving their high camp near the base of the mountain.

One day prior to breaking camp, while others attempted Lookout Mountain, Don and Phyl, along with Miss Stewart (the youngest and least experienced of the club members at the BCMC camp), took Edith over the Asulkan Pass (2,341 metres) and then returned. It was a round trip of 13 kilometres and enough to stretch their legs and see the panoramic vistas of the Dawson Range. Inspiration for another

Clockwise from top right: Descending along ledge, Mount Sir Donald, 1921; Don carrying sleeping Edith in his homemade backpack, Asulkan Pass, 1921; Don tending to Edith while Phyl and the other climbers eat a meal, 1921.

RECOVERY AND DISCOVERY | 87

time. But soon it was time to return home. Camp broke up, they carried packs across a fork of the Asulkan Brook to the waiting packhorses, and the rain came down. Huddled under the sheltering roof of the Glacier Station, their last night was dry at least. The train stopped at 5:30 a.m. and all boarded, bound for Vancouver.

The Mundays (and their climbing companions) adjusted to the restraints placed on their activities by the presence of an infant. An obvious change was the climbing itself. Don was able to climb, but Phyl could not, physically linked as she was to the feeding habits of her daughter. Edith was content to be carried in Don's homemade backpack, but as soon as she was hungry, she had to be removed and fed. It was not possible, practical or safe to attempt to climb with Edith. Instead they hiked and explored, testing the limits of what was doable. In camp, Edith was often passed around from one person to the next, to give Phyl two free hands for meal preparations or other activities. Photos taken at the time show various people holding Edith.

Edith's presence changed the dynamic of the group. Here was a diversion from the singularity of the climbing mindset. Edith came with her climbing parents, and it was expected that she—and her parents—be accepted. It was a test of friendship and an introduction to a new way of thinking. In the 1920s it was unusual for a woman with an infant to continue her extreme sports activities. Motherhood was looked upon as the next phase in female life, and it often signalled an end to many recreational pursuits. Neither Phyl nor Don accepted this view. They continued to participate in strenuous activities outdoors with friends rather than being tied to a nursery—a bold move and a public statement that family responsibilities and commitment to climbing could coexist. It was a shift in perspective that was accepted yet not followed with such commitment by their peers. Over the next few years many BCMC members who climbed together married. Tom Fyles and Margaret Gladstone, both on this trip, married the following year. But Edith remained the only baby accompanying the group.

Edith's presence on climbing trips was also appreciated by those outside their inner circle. Gustave Gambs (an ACC member) was camped near the BCMC group and was on the Tupper Glacier the same day as the Mundays. He personally thanked Phyl and commented on "the so unique experience of hearing a baby cry on a glacier." [32] Non-climbers were also intrigued. Edith's presence at the Asulkan campsite was a story that quickly made its way to the tourists at the grand 90-room CPR hotel Glacier House. Edith was so well behaved that no one staying at Glacier House would

Left: Don (with Edith on his back) and Miss Stewart on Tupper Glacier, 1921.
Right: Don carries Edith on a vertical climb, Selkirk Mountains, 1921.

believe there was a young baby camping in the valley. Surely a baby cried? Curiosity got the better of many guests, who clambered up through the alpine meadows to the camp. Several brought cameras. Edith was a novelty, but also a lesson in options.

Eventually, though, Edith got too large and wiggly to be carried, and a new phase in their climbing activities began. Edith learned self-sufficiency at an early age; by the time she was five she regularly hiked the 2½-hour trip down Grouse. "She always had an imaginary pack train, and she'd talk to these horses as if she was a seasoned old packer ... and pick up a stone every now and again, and throw it ahead of her and call out her horse's name, and tell him to get going. She really used to enjoy it."[33] But she was not always able to go with her parents on extended or high climbs. At the organized camps, there were occasionally other children, but more often than not Don and Phyl did not want to take advantage of friendships by assuming that their climbing companions would help care for Edith. Instead, they took turns participating in and leading BCMC hikes; one would go and the other stay home. Edith also had her grandmother or aunt to take care of her, which allowed her parents to plan at least one major climb together each season.

Edith's lunchtime break in the snow, 1921.

Chapter Four CLIMBING ON
THE COAST

GETTING OUT TO THE MOUNTAINS most weekends, away from Vancouver and the urban life, was integral to the Mundays' psyches. They were social people who had a great group of climbing friends, so the outdoors was a place for camaraderie and company, not just an escape. The Mundays varied their activities by participating in a range of club-sponsored events, but sometimes they chose to retreat to Evenglow Cabin by themselves on weekends.

Edith was often with them on the recreational jaunts with friends, but when it came to the serious expeditions she was left with family or friends. Without such a support network Phyl may have had to stay behind, as would have been expected in her role as a mother. More probably, given their commitment to climbing with each other, Don and Phyl would have planned a less active agenda. As it was, the Mundays packed more climbing into the decade of the 1920s than almost any other climbers.

At the Head of Pitt River

The August 1922 BCMC annual camp on the shore of Garibaldi Lake was ill-timed for the weather, forcing climbers to cut short their expeditions. Such was the case for Don and Phyl, who had planned "a backpacking trip for 15 miles above timberline to the neighborhood of an imposing black peak eastward of Garibaldi Lake." They now re-evaluated their options. It was well into the second and last week of the camp before the weather briefly cleared and they joined forces with three others—Neal Carter, Harold O'Connor and Clausen Thompson—for a daytrip "across the headwaters of the Pitt River."

Top: Don adzing plank inside Evenglow, ca. 1920.
Bottom: Don's mother in front of the fireplace, Evenglow, ca. 1923.

Most of the other climbers planned to participate in a climb up Mount Garibaldi, so getting a good start in the morning for the Munday party was not straightforward. The communal hand-assembled club boats were busy ferrying members to Sentinel Bay on the end of Garibaldi Lake, the start of the traverse to Warren Glacier and south to the mountain. So it was not until almost 8:00 a.m. that the five companions "landed on the terminal moraine of Sentinel Glacier."[1]

Don described the day's adventure in an article appearing in the *Canadian Alpine Journal*. This was Don's first submission to the *CAJ*, and the opening paragraph included an explanation of the uniqueness of coast climbing and informed members (most of whom were fixated on Rocky Mountain climbing) that although the altitudes of the mountains on the Pacific Coast are lower than those of many peaks in the Rockies, in some sections of the Coast Range "an 8,000-foot mountain may possess all the glacial features of 10,000-foot peaks in the same latitude in the Rockies." The words that followed illustrate his point effectively.

> We climbed the glacier eastward to Pitt Pass, one of the three glacial passes at the head of the Pitt. Then we mounted the northern slope to Sphinx Pass at the western base of the peak of that name. Two and a half miles across the neve of Sphinx Glacier brought us to the rock ridge south of Copper Peak [now Mount Carr] at an elevation of 7,900 feet. (Garibaldi Lake is 4,600.) From here, for the first time we got a partial view of our goal. Beyond Gray Pass were Crosscut Ridge and three higher unnamed peaks.

Don's writing *This description of mountain literature, on page 45 in the BCMC's* Northern Cordilleran, *published in Vancouver in 1913, is one that Don surely took to heart. It fits his personality, his literary style and his quest for accuracy.*

"The first essential in mountain description is accuracy; the second, lucidity. You do not know into whose hands those pages of yours may fall. Take no poetic license with either route or landmarks. The life of some eager but untrained climber may depend upon his being able to follow other guidance than that which your record affords. The man of science will thank you for your faithfulness; but, wanting that, he will toss aside as worthless the most elegant piece of rhetoric that ever came from the human pen. The fellow-climber and the naturalist are the only critics to whom you are responsible."

In the descent to the pass we made a traverse of an excessively steep ice-slope to negotiate the bergschrund. A series of huge crevasses below finally forced us off the glacier altogether; the rocks on the south proved simple enough. Gray Glacier flows northward from the pass ...

From the pass our climb began. It was now 1:30 p.m. The heat and light were intense, nearly three-quarters of the surrounding country being covered with snow and ice. The neve ahead of us was not unduly difficult. The pinkish granite of the summit ridge was much shattered. In the light of overseas experience, Thompson and I saw something appropriate in the name Parapet Peak. Visibility was perfect, and we longed for time to push north and east among unexplored, attractive glaciers and heights.

Southward lay a slightly higher peak; to descend to the col seemed unreasonably simple. We started down at 3:15. The arête quickly developed into a palisade of smooth slabs, not utterly impossible, but plainly impracticable. The neve was gashed badly, and in addition possessed a schrund all along the base of the arête; into this chasm we descended to outflank a crevasse, got out with some trouble to a ledge under an overhanging part of the cliff, and from a kneeling position on this narrow shelf had to leap across to a lip of snow. To perform the maneuver, packs and ice-axes had to be hoisted with the rope.

Below this no serious difficulties were met to the col, the summit of Mt. Isosceles being reached at 6 p.m. The aneroid indicated a height of 8,025 feet. In the lengthening shadows the great ice-falls on the northern slopes of the Mamquam Range and in other directions glowed intensely blue; food and films were exhausted, and time did not permit a detailed study of the canyon-cleft ranges.

Cliffs on the west face furnished agreeable scrambling; a friendly snowball bridged doubtfully the astonishing deep schrund. Skirting the cliffs of Parapet we returned northward to Gray Pass as cliffs, and ice-falls above them, prevented a direct course down to the glacier on the south side of the pass. Down this unnamed glacier we hurried till it became too shattered, then traversed above timber line across the east and south faces of the Sphinx, dropped down to Phoenix Glacier, climbed it in the dark to Pitt Pass, where, with an acetylene lamp I signaled our coming to camp with such success that a supper-less member of the Garibaldi party met us with a boat below Sentinel Glacier at 10 p.m. A feature of the trip was that we traveled on five different glaciers; in addition there was the second trip the full length of Sentinel Glacier ... The peak at the south end of Crosscut Ridge is the only unclimbed peak within a day's trip of Garibaldi Lake, but the next day we did not feel like tackling such a distant mountain, so went to Mt. Castle Towers across the lake. The next day we broke camp.[2]

Don and Phyl had been members of the ACC for only two years. Their climbing credentials were not demonstrated outside the Lower Mainland, and they had yet to attend an ACC camp where others could observe their fitness and mountaineering abilities. Don concludes his article by adding: "The fact of a lady being a member of the party may not be a fair indication of the strenuousness of the trip."[3] In later submissions (especially after Phyl's ascent of Mount Robson), such a qualifier was not given or required.

Fitzsimmons

In 1923 alone the Mundays made three major forays. At the beginning of June Don and Phyl made a trip to Avalanche Pass southeast of Alta Lake near Garibaldi. They made a reconnaissance of the district, selected a site for the BCMC summer camp at the head of one of the branches of

Fitzsimmons Creek and marked it on their map, so the information could go out to members in the next newsletter.[4] This advance trip was also an opportunity for them to visit their friend Neal Carter, who was spending the summer in Garibaldi Park on a water-power survey.[5] His descriptions of the alpine areas were hard to resist. Ever the mountaineers, they put their imprint on the area, by making the first ascents of Blackcomb (2,440 metres) and Overlord Mountain (2,634 metres).

A geological survey party under Dr. Camsell visited claims up Fitzsimmons Creek, and their photos of the district further east aroused our interest ... We were met at Rainbow by Mr. N.M. Carter, a climber then engaged with a party making a survey for a proposed hydro-electric project. The party proved most hospitable, and the next morning we accompanied them when they went to work in the tangled flats and swamps of Fitzsimmons Creek, a tributary of Green Lake.

They showed us the not obvious beginning of the trail up the creek ... It climbed high above the turbulent creek and several times we turned aside to look down the canyon walls fantastically stained with blue, green, red and other mineral stains. There are many mineral claims up the creek, hence the trail ... About seven miles [out] ... it began to zigzag up beside a gorge where a creek cascaded for a thousand feet. As we neared the mouth of the hanging valley at 4,800 ft. the forest trees presented almost an uncanny aspect in the dull light, the trees being uniformly small, slender and close-set, and hung thickly with streamers two feet long of blackish or yellowish-green lichen.

We soon struck patches of soft snow. It was sodden with rain and we often sank knee-deep. Alpine marsh marigolds actually thrust their lavender-tinted flower buds through six inches of snow. At 5,300 feet the valley widened to a broad basin between ridges promising great peaks lurking behind the rounded skylines.

As we were carrying a generous week's supply of grub, we welcomed the sight of a little log cabin at last in the middle of the valley at about 6,000 feet. An omelet and other culinary triumphs did much to erase the effects of the ten or eleven mile grind. The cabin itself offered a puzzling problem. It had obviously been recently reconstructed out of old materials. The explanation given later by the

Alta Lake, Rainbow Lodge and Mount Whistler.

prospectors who owned it was that a wind storm of cyclonic character had torn the original building to pieces.

The valley has gained the name of Avalanche Pass. Snowslides from the eastern slopes sweep clear across to the western slopes where the clumps of standing trees are banked with shattered trunks deposited there ... We walked a quarter of a mile south of the cabin to the rim of the pass. Before us suddenly was revealed the 3,000-foot icefall of the Cheakamus Glacier glowing ethereally blue in the soft shadows of ascending columns of cloud through which glinted long shafts of golden evening light. Descending 5,000 feet from the summit of Mt. Castle Towers, it is by far the most magnificent glacier in Garibaldi Park. Its snout is 250 feet above Cheakamus Lake ... the lake is four miles long and averages a mile in width ...

Reluctantly crushing avalanche lilies and other early flowers underfoot, we mounted eastward to the crest of a ridge which extended our view eastward of the splendid array of glaciers feeding Cheakamus Lake. On the north side of Fitzsimmons valley three bare spearheads of granite rose gaunt and severe in the shadows. Distant ranges in the northwest seemed to rise to elevations of more than 9,000 feet.

Prospectors declared nobody had ever been eastward of Red Mountain, a richly coloured peak about 8,000 feet high ... The much twisted form of Fitzsimmons Glacier swung around behind Red Mountain and emphasized the mountain's vivid colour.

At the head of the glacier towered defiantly the sheer cliffs of a nameless mountain which seemed the lord of the region. A long heavily corniced ridge led up to the summit from the west. The name Mt. Overlord seemed appropriate for this peak, which we judged would prove to be over 8,500 feet in height.

We pitched the tent instead of sleeping in the cabin as the latter showed signs of being infested with mice and packrats. We got off at 6:30 a. m. The day promised to clear although the barometer remained low. Ice formed during the night in running water.

Three lakes lay in the valley down which we descended to Fitzsimmons Glacier. The largest was nearly a quarter of a mile in length. We descended a thousand feet and then climbed to the crest of the huge lateral moraine near where it takes form as the glacier passes the base of the northern precipice of Red Mountain.

It was still a little early for a second breakfast, but the glacier offered no inviting stopping place so we ate a little here ... Roping together we went down to the glacier. The crevasses were somewhat complex and troublesome owing to the reverse curve described by the glacier. Thin snow bridges finally gave place to a more secure depth along the winding central trough between two icefalls whose top-heavy impending pinnacles looked impressive while we were in their line of fire.

The extent of the upper snowfield was unexpected. We gained it by one of several sagging bridges across an immense crevasse along its lower margin. Half a mile to the south stood the rocky outpost forming the key to the corniced summit ridge. Later comers termed this point "Refuse Pinnacle" from its shattered condition ...

The clouds shut in, making it hard to keep direction across the nearly level snowfield. Fog is thought of by the average person as something dark and chill, but this was oppressively warm and blindingly bright. The night frost had crusted the snow too lightly to carry us so that we broke through knee deep at every step.

We found the pass in due course and wallowed through avalanche snow to a jutting rock from which we gained the southern side of the outpost peak. Most of its snow had slid off the ledges into a wild hanging valley 2,000 feet below; the basin had two outlets to the Cheakamus valley far below.

We were forced to traverse this slope of the peak for a considerable distance, crossing a succession of steep crumbling rock ribs, loose scree and sodden snow. In fact we

Packs *"Don made our packs. We didn't like the Trapper Nelson [then the norm]. Because if you were going over logs in the bush, you've always got those two 'spikes,' as I call them, below, to hook into it, if you want to jump or slide off the log, and then, if you're going through bush—trail-less bush—and you haven't got your pack built higher than the two pieces of the side ... high enough ... you hook into the bushes. And Don made our own pack-boards ... And then, I made the packs to fit them. He put screw-eyes down the edge of the pack-board, and eyelets in the pack ... Then we had a heavy wire that you could slide down through the eyelets which kept the pack on the pack-board. I made just a flap on the pack, and the eyelets, so that we could slide it off, if we needed to. We could use the pack-boards, then, for any other kind of backpacking. It made it very good. There were no strings and things around to catch."*
PHYLLIS MUNDAY TAPED INTERVIEW, 1973, BC ARCHIVES.

moved mostly one at a time. When not too busy we caught alluring glimpses through rifts in the clouds of the glacial peaks as far southeast as Mt. Mamquam.

A small glacier capping the southeastern shoulder of Overlord seemed deceptively close in front, always appearing to be just past the next rib. As we might be at least an hour from the peak, at 11:20 a.m. we stopped on a small ledge to eat. A sudden flurry of snow soon hurried us on.

Scorning the still distant ice, we mounted the crumbling rocks and outflanked the more formidable crags encountered on the way to the serrated and corniced skyline. We reached it at the only point where a gap existed in the cornice which faced away from us. A cloud rift revealed the summit ahead.

Once more dazzling vapor closed in. At the distance of ten feet the lip of the cornice was actually indistinguishable, yet it was our only guide. To keep within sight of it meant traveling almost in the irregular crevasse formed along the ridge by the cornice as it sagged preparatory to avalanching to the glacier a thousand feet below.

Through the brilliant obscurity we plodded upward, coming out on broken rock 100 feet below the summit. Here a squall of snow struck us. The actual summit was a little rusty-red platform in the angle of the sheer northern and western walls. I stepped aside to let my wife mount it first, but she hooked her arm in mine that we might reach it together ...

Owing to the great quantity of snow still on the mountains at this time of the year, the fragmentary views from the summit were splendid in character, particularly toward a group of five peaks to south and east that were connected with Overlord by a high snow pass. This was the head of a broken glacier in the furthest extension of the Fitzsimmons valley. The Fitzsimmons glacier is probably the main source but it parallels the creek for most of its length and then enters some miles down the valley from the pass.

We spent two and a half hours on the peak. Descending the summit ridge to the break in the cornice, we worked some distance down icy ledges of a loose slatey formation. Below this was snow covered ice menaced by the sodden cornice about and recently raked by slides. There were a few crevasses above the bergschrund and we required an hour to descend this 700 feet. Then rejoining our morning route, we went down the glacier without incident.

The next day was definitely showery. We spent it ... by the fire ...
Next morning we started down the trail in a light rain ... The descent
to Alta Lake took four hours. We had previously arranged to start that
afternoon with Mr. Carter in an attempt to climb Wedge Mountain in
a day and a half, but he did not return to camp until evening.

This consequently left us with an idle day on our hands on the
morrow. Mosquitoes proved such a pest around the lake that about
8 a.m. we set out in desperation to climb a mountain to get away from
them. Going up Fitzsimmons Creek a short way we turned north along
a trail to some mining claims and from them headed directly up the
bluffy slope into the dense low-lying motionless clouds. The mosquitoes
kept pace with us till we reached timberline where we struck a blazed
trail of whose beginning and end we could not guess.

Our objective was the most westerly of the prominent peaks of
the Spearhead Range. The trail crossed our route. We had little hope
of finding our mountain in the clouds, and for two hours amused
ourselves by building a raging fire whose warmth offset the chilling
vapor as we waited in a vain hope of a little break in it.

Despairing of any change in the weather, we pushed on up across
snow patches and boulders and finally struck a rock ridge that we
thought we recognized from views from Alta Lake. It soon narrowed
to a shattered ridge of dark rock dipping sharply on the left where we
caught glimpses of the neve of a glacier.

The summit seemed always just a little ahead, but each point
always revealed one more just beyond. The silence, the breathlessness
and the obscurity made it almost eerie to be going on thus. Eventually
the ridge pitched off steeply in front of us and we clambered down a
way to make sure this was the opposite side of the mountain. Then we
climbed up and built a small cairn as there was no sign of previous
climbers. We suggested the descriptive name of Mt. Blackcomb. The
elevation was apparently about 8,000 feet. The time was 2 p.m.

From its position the mountain ought to give a pleasing view of
the valley below, the Spearhead Range's large northern glaciers and the
mountains to north and west. As it was, we saw nothing, so the trip was
barren indeed—one of the disappointments to which climbers must
reconcile themselves as best they may with recollections of times when
they persisted thus and were rewarded at the summit with a dramatic
parting of the cloud screen to disclose some splendid panorama.

Picking up the blazed trail, we followed it towards Fitzsimmons Creek without much trouble as the blazes had for the most part been laboriously hacked at frequent intervals ... We had rough going in places before we came out on the Fitzsimmons trail about two and a half miles from Alta Lake.[6]

1923 and Big Plans

In 1923 the Mundays found themselves in a position to change and manage their lifestyle. A businessman by the name of Arthur Shewan Williamson contacted them with a proposition. He had read the newspaper articles about Don building Evenglow Cabin and had followed the couple's mountaineering exploits. Williamson was involved in several business pursuits—he had interests in both mining and real estate—but for one specific scheme, he judged the Mundays would be perfect. He was a principal investor in and the general manager of a concern called the Alpine Scenic Highway Company, which had purchased most of the plateau of Grouse Mountain and land on its western and southern slopes. The idea was to build first a bridle trail up to the plateau, and then a toll road for automobiles.

Earlier schemes to build inclined railways from the top of Lonsdale Drive to the summit had been postulated as early as 1909, but had come to naught; the intervention of the First World War and the subsequent economic uncertainty postponed or cancelled most large-scale development schemes.[7] But the idea resurfaced after the war, and W.C. Shelley, president of the Alpine Scenic Highway Company, proposed not a railway, but an automobile toll road, which would wind its scenic way from North Vancouver to the Grouse Plateau. A hotel for tourist accommodation would then be constructed on the plateau. The lodge would also have day facilities for hikers and horseback riders, who could ascend the mountain on a new bridle trail that would be graduated in the ascent so horses and novice hikers could get up the mountain without too much exertion.[8]

This scheme was a shock to the climbing community. For all the years since the establishment of the BCMC in 1907—and even before—climbers had been the principal users and creators of trails on the mountain. They had built their club cabin on its slopes. To have Grouse become private property with controlled access had not been foreseen.

Williamson asked the Mundays to become involved as employees of the company. It was a wise move to have prominent climbers associated with the business. He hooked them by offering an opportunity that seemed tailor-made to their lifestyle. Don would be paid to build the new bridle trail to the plateau and could then rent horses to clients wishing to use the trail. The trail would terminate on the mountain plateau, and on this plateau— the future site of the tourist lodge—Don would oversee construction of a log cabin, bigger than Evenglow, that would serve as a temporary facility until the lodge was built. The Mundays would occupy the cabin as a home, and from here they could greet visitors, offer food and refreshment, and make a living. The Mundays quickly accepted. To live in their own cabin high above the city was a dream. To be offered the means to earn money on the mountain itself and not have to return to the city for employment made it all possible. In the July issue of *The B.C. Mountaineer*, Don alerted the climbing community to the plans.

Innovations on Grouse

About the beginning of August a new trail up Grouse will be completed by the interests who intend to place a hotel on the plateau. The route taken will be from the Lonsdale car terminus eastward to St. George, thence up the open slopes of Dome Mountain, green timber being entered at 2500 feet and Mosquito Creek crossed at about 2800 feet. From thereon the trail will bear westward toward the end of the old trail on the bare rocks overlooking the city. The gradient is so remarkably easy throughout, and the character of the route so pleasant, that the old Grouse trail is likely to go into the discard as soon as the new route becomes generally known. The new trail is primarily intended for saddle and pack horses, so it will be well suited for foot traffic. The intention is to keep the trail open for horse traffic all winter. This service is being handled by Mr. Don Munday. Horses will be available from the Lonsdale car terminus about August 1 ... The entire mountain top is now private property ... A refreshment stand will be placed beside the lake; drinks, fruit, meals, etc., will be served daily, summer and winter. Mrs. Don Munday will be in charge. This will be a permanent feature although begun in temporary quarters. Doubtless, climbers will be pleased to know that these services will be handled by fellow-climbers.[9]

The company optimistically announced that the trail would be completed and open to the public by Sunday, August 12, 1923.[10] Don and

R.C. "Johnny" Johnson formed a partnership to run the livery located on Lonsdale near Boundary Road; the horses were tethered in an orchard.

Simultaneously, surveyors from the firm of Hawkins and Horie marked the right of way for the toll road, working through the summer and early autumn. The road began from Centre Road, Lynn Valley, and was to be "6 miles long, cleared to 66 feet wide" (and thus opening up the vistas) running diagonally from the base of the mountain to the property near the summit. Meanwhile, Don began to cut the trail, working ever higher up the mountain. It was long, hard work. The family now lived on Kings Road, quite near the trail head. Very soon it made little sense for Don to come home at the end of each day—hiking down the mountain just added to his time—so Phyl erected a tent in the trees, near the small lake on the plateau. Here she and Edith spent their days. She called it Alpine Lodge.

Sporting a rough wooden sign, Alpine Lodge was the first commercial establishment on the mountain. Phyl sold cool drinks to thirsty hikers and made sandwiches and snacks. Her steady customers were the surveyors (who stayed at this camp; Phyl now had five men to cook for)[11] but daily custom made the venture worthwhile. Always a social person, Phyl enjoyed the visitors and extolled the virtues of mountain activities.

> **Don and his health** *"There were some things that he couldn't handle too easily, but he was a very determined person. He never let it deprive him of doing anything, and he worked at it constantly. He had a roll of paper and he used to keep his hand in his pocket, rolling this paper all the time, to exercise the hand muscles and the arm muscles. The hardest thing for him to do was to tie his boot laces and to carve meat. But other than that, he never let it bother him at all."*
> PHYLLIS MUNDAY INTERVIEW, 1973, BC ARCHIVES.

The work on the trail progressed; Don was confident that the trail and the wooden cabin on the plateau would be completed by winter, so they took a little time off to continue their mountaineering pursuits, venturing with a friend into the Cheam mountains southwest of Hope to make a first ascent of Mount General Stewart. Williamson did not mind the time they took for climbing; in fact, he encouraged them to visit the Cheam area. The publicity their climbing exploits received in the local newspapers linked them with the Grouse Mountain development, so their minor celebrity status worked to advantage for the business.

Don (on left) and companions on Foley Peak climb, 1924.

The Cheam Mountain Range

Mount Cheam rises steeply above Bridal Falls, beyond the flat delta land of the Fraser Valley. This dramatic landmark is visible from 30 kilometres distant and has long been accessed by climbers. Surprisingly though, the cluster of nearby peaks—the Cheam Mountain Range—despite their relative closeness, were largely ignored by early Vancouver climbers, intent as they were on climbing north and east of the city. It was not until 1923 when the Mundays forayed into the area that attention was drawn in this direction.

The four peaks east of Cheam are known as the Lucky Four Group, named collectively after a nearby copper mine that opened in 1917 and was active for some years after. Three of these peaks—Foley, Welch and Stewart—bear the individual surnames of the principals of a railway construction company that was once the largest in North America. This company built the Fraser Canyon section of the Canadian National Railway and other rail lines and was also involved in the Lucky Four copper mine.[12] It was to these mountains that Don and Phyl directed their attention, in particular to Mount General Stewart (now Stewart Peak), reputed to be the most challenging, having the hardest approach from the northern face that

featured great cliffs with glaciers at the foot. Miners and trappers declared the mountain to be inaccessible. Proving it was conquerable seemed a perfect challenge.[13]

The Mundays and Bev Cayley travelled to the small town of Hope at the head of the Fraser Valley. They were there at the invitation of A.S. Williamson, who was also a superintendent for the Lucky Four mine. He arranged their visit to coincide with his travel to the Lucky Four. On this trip he escorted not only the three climbers, but also a mining engineer, Mr. Nelson, and a surveyor, Mr. Horie.

From Hope, they crossed the river by automobile to Laidlaw, and then rented packhorses to travel through the timber to Jones (now Wahleach) Lake, at the north end of which was a hydroelectric dam, maintained by a BC Electric Company employee who was also a climber. From his cabin it was another seven miles to a small and rudely constructed cabin perched at the timberline. This was the cabin used by the miners of the Lucky Four Mine, itself located near the glacier toe, just northeast of Foley Peak. The cabin was Williamson's destination and the stopping-off place for the Munday party. They arrived by 6:30 p.m. and settled in for the night as best they could, electing not to sleep in the rudimentary (and as they found) unfinished cabin, but in their tents. The next morning they left Williamson at the cabin and headed off toward the Welch Glacier. This was the last point at which Williamson was able to follow their movements, as soon they disappeared over a fold in the glacier; it would be 13 hours before he saw them again.

It was nearly midnight when Williamson welcomed them back to the cabin and heard of the successful first ascent of Stewart (2,230 metres).[14]

Williamson was very glad to welcome them back to the cabin at nearly midnight, and to hear of the successful ascent. By now he was impressed with his choice of Don and Phyl for the Grouse Mountain venture. He was obviously also impressed with their daughter, for although she was not with them on this trip, he was well aware of her adventures. In honour of her mountaineering experience, he insisted on calling an unnamed peak in the range "Baby Munday."[15]

Excited by the opportunities presented by these mountains, the Mundays returned the following April, pushing the climbing season just a little. In the company of fellow BCMC members Bill Wheatley, Dudley Foster, Eric Fuller, H. O'Connor and Bev Cayley, they climbed Foley Peak (2,307 metres). This was the first complete ascent.

106

As they had done earlier, they approached the area from Vancouver by boarding an evening train up the valley. Four hours later they arrived at Laidlaw, where they spent the night. They left the next morning for Jones Lake and followed the trail—this time on foot—along the creek. The trail ascended some 700 metres over its 16 kilometres, but the journey was more than a little challenging as they were packing in through an unexpected and heavy snowstorm. Three and a half hours later they arrived at the lake only to find that the trail ahead presented even more of a challenge, for the winter's windstorms had left havoc on the forest floor—fallen timber, uprooted trees and debris—all hidden beneath the newly fallen snow. Snowshoes were useless and had to be dragged through the windfalls. The remaining distance took six more hours of scramble and pluck.

As before, the climbers' destination was the unfinished cabin built for the Lucky Four Mine at timberline beneath the mountain. Upon arrival, they found that the roof was covered in deep packed snow. They had to tunnel through the snow to locate and clear the stovepipe hole, then light a fire in the inadequate wood stove. Drying wet clothes and keeping warm proved nearly impossible, but at least they were sheltered from the weather. The next morning at 9 a.m. they set off snowshoeing on the four-foot-deep new and loosely packed snow.

Don wrote the following account for *The B.C. Mountaineer*:

Snow clouds were gathering deliberately from the northwest, but the peaks remained clear. The crest of the ridge, 6,800 feet, was reached shortly before noon, permitting entrancing views eastward, through shifting clouds, of a world of nameless peaks. Foley was obviously the only peak of the range even remotely within the power of the party this day under winter conditions, and the chances seemed slim indeed. Before the half mile along the ridge was covered, snowshoes had to be exchanged for boots, owing to the narrowness of the corniced crest.

On the Lucky Four Glacier the snow lay 5 feet deep. The angle soon became 45 degrees, and steadily steepened. The eastern arête on closer approach proved out of the question owing to the iced rocks. The northeast face, the only one of the three that was accessible, was smothered with loose snow. Its condition in many places gave cause for grave concern, but never quite reached the point where going on meant unjustifiable risk. The arête was gained about 300 feet below the summit, and then success was assured.

For the most part the climb was still on the face, now steepened to about 65 degrees, being rocks overlain[sic] with mixed ice and snow. The south face is nearly perpendicular, the arête too sharp to carry a cornice. Clouds had closed in at last, snow falling, the wind rising.

The three faces of the slender pyramid meet at the summit which was a tiny platform of ice from which one member of the party claimed to be able to look down all three sides of the mountain at once. The time was 3:10 p.m. It was no place to be caught in a storm, and an immediate descent was begun. Once off the arête the wind was not so biting, but an added difficulty was finding the steps which were completely hidden with the snow now streaming and hissing down the great face. New steps might have been made but a safe route was not to be abandoned lightly. The descent to the glacier was nearly as slow as the ascent.

Changing back to snowshoes was necessary on the ridge: a blizzard was sweeping it, and the temperature dropping rapidly—an experience to remember. Even with the snowshoes, going downhill was laborious. The cabin was reached shortly after 6 p.m.

Morning broke brilliantly, displaying the range at its best. The delicacy of the lines of the wind-sculptured snow on the precipices was unforgettable. Seldom are peaks of this order so well placed for viewing them to advantage. Reluctantly the party started home at 7:15 a.m.[16]

A few months later, the Mundays returned to the area, this time with Charles Townsend, and again encountered wintry conditions when they attempted to ascend Welch Peak (2,440 metres), the highest in the trio of mountains.

Snow fell as low as 3,000 feet in the valley of Jones Creek. At Timberline Cabin, 4,600 feet, the total fall was about 10 inches, and at 5,500 feet nearly 18 inches. A mile of mountain side with steep grass slopes, coarse rockslides, moraines, and glaciated granite slabs exposed by the retreat of the glaciers, were not improved by the masking loose snow. Two starts were made on successive days when the weather gave false promise of clearing. A height of rather less than 7,000 feet on the Welch Glacier was reached once. This glacier is steep, hard and smooth; step cutting could only be done after scraping the deep snow off the ice. Fog, snow and wind made things thoroughly disagreeable.[17]

A few weeks later, others took up the challenge, and the peak was captured by a different trio of Club members—A. Cooper, B. Spouse and Fred Smith. The following May, the Mundays, Bev Cayley and 17 other club members climbed Mount Cheam, led by Eric Fuller, who had climbed it several times previously.[18] Vancouver climbers were now enthusiastic about the area.

Grouse Mountain

As the autumn advanced, the cabin construction began in earnest. It was a much larger venture than Evenglow Cabin, comprising three bedrooms, a kitchen, a large dining room and common area. A covered verandah allowed a magnificent view of the 600-metre drop from the plateau. As before, Don had to carry all the building supplies up by hand (or by tump line), but this time he could use pack horses, although in most cases he found the loads to be more awkward than would comfortably work on horseback.

By November the cabin had walls and roof rafters. The reduced hours of daylight affected how much work could be accomplished, and the cooler, wet weather was a warning that time was running out. Still living in the tent, Phyl and Edith had to keep moving to stay warm. Phyl sawed and split firewood for the winter, hoping to get in a good supply before the weather broke. But in early December a cold front arrived and deposited more snow than Grouse had seen that early on in years. Living in a tent with a two-year-old was suddenly very complicated indeed. In an interview many years later, Phyl recalled exactly what went on when the snow fell. "Tenting in winter at an elevation of 3,800 feet is by no means a pleasant experience. We battled many a raging storm ... Don spent every daylight hour working on a substantial log cabin, while I sawed and chopped firewood, cooked the meals, took care of my baby, scraped snow off the tent and helped him between whiles."[19]

In fact, life got a little dangerous. The snow did not stop. The Mundays had to set their alarm clock for every hour during the night so they could get up and scrape the snow off the tent roof. Phyllis recalled one occasion: "I woke with a start and as I put my hand up I felt the tent practically right down on us. We hurriedly put an apple box over Edith, hoping it would give her air if the tent came down. With great care we squeezed out of the door and gently took the snow off in such a fashion that we would not leave the tent roof unevenly weighted."[20] This was the last straw. Friends rallied round and came to assist Don with the cabin, but it was a race against nature.

The middle of December came with the weather getting worse and the snow deeper, so we knew we must soon move under a solid roof, or be buried under the wreckage of our tent. Even with two friends to help us, the situation was fast becoming desperate unless the weather relented. Part of the cabin was roofed, but lacked floor and windows, and the walls were still unchinked.

We watched the sky anxiously but a big halo around the sun told us another storm was approaching. By night the mountain top was enveloped in a raging blizzard. The heavily iced edges of the fly whipped and crashed against the roof of the tent till it seemed the canvas could stand the strain no longer. The wind roared down the hollow of Grouse Lake like the rush of an avalanche.

We worked all that night. The usual five minutes walk to the cabin now took 1/2 an hour or more with 50 pound bundles of floor boards on our backs. So heavy was the snow that a new trail had to be broken every trip. The only light was a feeble electric torch, and though we knew every foot of the ground there was a real risk of becoming lost.

One man laid flooring and one packed it from the tent, while I alternatively helped with both jobs. The other man worked without rest shoveling snow from the tent where my baby was peacefully sleeping through it all. Wind and snow blowing in from the un-floored part of the cabin frequently put out the light there, the air being full of snow dust.

Just before dawn the storm abated a bit and we all indulged in a short rest. Daylight brought a dull but stormless day so it was imperative that we move before the next storm set in. The snow was higher than the top of the tent.

The door was used as a sled for the first load: the frozen canvas fly to nail over the unwalled section of the cabin. The snow was so loose and deep that moving things on the hurriedly built toboggan was only a little less laborious than backpacking it, and a toboggan trail had to be shoveled for 400 yards along the deep slopes.

Our baby thought this wonderful world of snow must have been made purely for her own pleasure; she thoroughly enjoyed trip after

Clockwise from top left: Edith outside tent after the big snowfall on Grouse Mountain, December 1923; Don and Edith beside Alpine Lodge, Grouse Mountain, 1924; Don carrying hood for stove, 1925; Edith and Phyl with packboard loaded with a wooden chair and ferns.

CLIMBING ON THE COAST | III

Don and Edith outside Alpine Lodge, December 1923.
Inset: The ice-encrusted interior of the unfinished Alpine Lodge, December 1923.

trip from tent to cabin. Her joy relieved the strain on us, for we were all decidedly tired and the trips had to be made.

By 10 o'clock that night all the important things such as the stove, entire food supply, bedding, clothes and household equipment were safe under a solid roof, the very words "solid roof" meaning everything in the world to us at that time.

To me at least this crude home seemed a palace even though walls, floor and ceiling were solidly coated with ice and snow. I knew we were safe from storms. Before we turned in that night for an untroubled sleep, everything had to be carefully covered with tarpaulins to keep them dry, because the stove was doing noble work thawing the icy roof. For nearly three days the dripping continued and as fast as the ice thawed off the logs, we chinked the crevices thus opened.

Barely had we moved into the cabin when the mountain was lashed by another furious storm, making us very thankful we had grasped the only opportunity to move. The horrible experiences of that tent in its secluded hollow were left behind. We were now out on the very edge of the world, 3,000 feet sheer above the floor of the Capilano Valley, out where you felt you could look out and face the world ... [21]

It was no wonder that Don, as editor of the *Mountaineer,* included the following statement in the January edition: "No Apologies. The Editor makes no apologies for the lateness of the December issue—when snowstorms come with the ferocity and frequency that marked most of December, life in a tent on Grouse Mountain Plateau is highly strenuous. But those days are gone forever—and log walls and a sound roof defy the wildest whims of winter, and the snow shovel may be laid aside in favour of a typewriter." [22]

By the time the cabin interior was dry and the logs chinked, the rest of the construction essentials had been taken care of by Don and the two loyal friends who had helped them move. It was now just a few days before Christmas, and Phyl was on a mission. Leaving Edith in the care of the men, she set forth down the path toward the city. When she returned, she had small gifts, a turkey and fixings for Christmas dinner. Don cut down a balsam fir and they decorated it with ornaments carefully packed up from Vancouver. Two rare photos from this time survive, one taken inside the unfinished cabin showing the tarped bundles, the unfinished roof and the melting snow, the other showing the table set for their Christmas meal, complete with ferns for the centrepiece.

The table set for Christmas dinner in a thawed-out Alpine Lodge, 1923.

Christmas dinner aside, it was basic essentials only at the newly constructed Alpine Lodge. There was no generator for power, no running water or water tank, no garbage disposal or septic tank. A large stove did double duty for cooking and heat, while the lack of plumbing necessitated an outhouse. In winter their water came in the form of solid ice cut from the lake, which was hacked into manageable chunks and laboriously melted before it could be used. Cooking water did double duty, as did wash water. There could be no waste. An adequate supply of firewood was also a challenge, as the wood was stunted and limited on the plateau. Don often packed up firewood that he cut lower on the mountain. Later as Phyl wrote, he "carried all the pipe from town up the mountain to bring water to the cabin from Grouse Lake. He also carried up my sewing machine, and of course, all our supplies of every sort that had to be backpacked."[23]

Alpine Lodge was their home, but it was also a business and the reason they were there in the first place. They never knew when a knock on the door would signal a visitor. There were no defined days off, as thirsty hikers could show up seven days of the week. The sign outside the cabin

The Mundays outside Alpine Lodge, 1925; an advertisement in *The B.C. Mountaineer.*

read: "Meals, Refreshments, etc., at all hours. Special prices to members of the B.C. Mountaineering Club and the Alpine Club of Canada. Under the management of Mr. and Mrs. Don Munday. Permanent Quarters now under construction on Plateau." [24] Another sign listed "hot drinks, coffee 15 cents, soup 20 cents, sandwiches 20 cents, meals 1 dollar." [25] In the summer they catered to thirsty hikers and in winter they rented toboggans and warmed chilled hikers.

The life was hard and labour-intensive (and aggravating at times when unappreciative customers complained about the simple menu), but the business enabled them to live where they loved year-round, high above the city every day of the year. Outside the lodge, Phyl nurtured a garden of wildflowers brought back from climbs and carefully transplanted into natural crevices in the rocks.

For months, in a marvellous commitment to volunteerism, Phyl had hiked down to North Vancouver one afternoon each week to attend Guide meetings. "For some time after we moved into our cabin I went down to town to my Guide Company, returning after the meetings. Away up the trail with just the light of my bug (candle pushed up a hole in the side of a jam can), my trail light. An owl used to talk to me. Every time he called I'd answer and so it went on until I came out of the woods to the open plateau. Don always had a lamp in the window for me. The light of Home, Sweet Home."[26] After the first winter, though, the logistics were insurmountable. "With deepest regret I had to ask for a year's leave of absence, the first since starting the [Guide] Company in 1911, with the exception of seven weeks in the spring of 1921. It hurt me very much to leave the girls ..."[27]

Phyl in her captain's uniform with Edith, Grouse Mountain, 1925.

Phyl missed Guiding terribly, but it did not take her long to realize that she was not alone in her situation. Other girls and young women lived in equally isolated conditions, in logging camps or mining towns. This realization led her—while still resident at Alpine Lodge—to form the first Lone Guides Company, which united girls in remote areas through a progressive newsletter sent by the mail. This was Guiding that she could accomplish from her mountaintop location. Phyl would remain in charge of Lone Guides until 1945, long after the Grouse Mountain years.

Edith was home-schooled, and by the time she was five years old she could read and write and knew the names of every bird based on their song or flight path. She knew no other life but the indoor–outdoor life on the mountain. She was the pet of all who visited Alpine Lodge and embodied an idea novel for city-dwelling folks—that a child could grow up on a mountaintop. "Little Edith Munday, five years old ... This small mountain climber has already gained prominence for her exploits and makes the ascent from North Vancouver quite frequently in two 1/2 hours. She has appeared on the silver screen in Fox News and is quite a favourite with visitors."[28] The Mundays' cabin became a destination for BCMC members on the weekends. They squeezed into the big common room where they listened to the news of the world on the wireless and played the gramophone.

As residents on the Grouse plateau, the Mundays by default became the emergency responders for lost or injured hikers. Once Phyl piggy-backed a 14-year-old injured girl down the mountain. Many times they were called upon for bandages and solace. On a clear crisp Saturday afternoon in March 1925, a cry for help drew them from the warmth of their cabin to the outside. A panic-stricken teenaged boy quickly blurted out his story. He and a friend had been playing, sliding down a frozen slope. His friend had hit an icy patch and gone over an edge. Don and Phyl clambered down through the snow and located the boy, some 600 metres below their cabin. He had fallen a great distance and was unconscious, but alive. Between the two of them they managed to manoeuvre a sled down, strap the boy on and haul it back up to their cabin. Their prompt action saved his life.

Don then raced down the mountain into North Vancouver to find a doctor willing to climb back with him. The boy—Sid Harling—was in no condition to be moved, and Phyl did her best to warm him. She covered him in blankets and heated water on their wood stove, filled empty jam jars with the water and placed them all around him. In the end, Sid Harling stayed with them for three weeks until he was sufficiently recuperated to handle the trip down Grouse. Phyl's first-aid training was essential. When news of the rescue hit the newspapers, the Mundays became local heroes. The Girl Guides Association of Canada presented Phyl with their highest honour, the Bronze Cross for valour.

Treasure-Seeking Climbers

Arthur Shewan Williamson, a man who played a big part in the Mundays' ventures over the next few years, was mightily impressed when he saw them in action on the high slopes in 1923. Ever the businessman, it seemed to him that their mountaineering skills might be put to yet another practical purpose—to aid the mining industry. He told them of his hopes to find the entrance shaft for the first producing silver mine in the province, the Eureka–Victoria, which had not operated for almost half a century. In 1868 the mine produced $400,000 worth of silver from mainly superficial workings but ceased production just a few years later. The site was known to be high on Eureka Mountain (now Silver Peak, 1,949 metres), 13 kilometres from Hope. Some of the veins of ore were quite visible in the granite strata, but miners had been unable to locate the original entrance. If it were found, mining operations could commence at the old workings; if not, a new site would be selected anyway. From Williamson's perspective, no harm would be done in having Don and Phyl take a look.

What better excuse would a climber need to volunteer? In mid-July 1924, they arrived in Hope and were taken to the current mine camp (located on the spot of the historic Eureka–Victoria camp) high on the north side of Eureka Mountain. Stretching out across from the camp lay a magnificent panorama of the Hope mountains, the Fraser Canyon and Holy Cross Mountain, about two kilometres to the south. The miners briefed Don and Phyl on what exploration had already taken place, but as Don later commented, "It is typical of this class of men [miners and prospectors] that they shun broken glaciers and precipices."[29] To the Mundays the most logical plan was to climb to the top of Eureka, for this would give them the best vantage point for the reconnoitre. Attended by mining representative Andrew Dixon, they ascended via the west face, only to be challenged by a huge chock stone wedged in a gash formed by the corrosion of the ore vein known by the miners as the old "Victoria South." It was a moderate climb to the summit and mainly rock work. This experience suggested to them that the task that lay ahead—exploring to search for the old mine works—required only rock scrambling. They did not believe that their ice axes would be needed, so Dixon was sent back down with them. This was to prove an error in judgment.

The initial foray was on the opposite side from their ascent, the eastern face. The Mundays searched and found the continuation of the "Victoria" vein, noting its course on a hand-drawn map, fixing its location with reasonable certainty. But as they made their way across the mountain, they encountered "Snowslide Gulch," an area of high avalanche frequency and challenging to traverse. High up in the cliffs above the gulch glittering in the light, they saw what appeared to be another vein of ore, and this inspired them to press on, even without ice axes. Traversing carefully 65 metres along the face of the icy south cliff, they encountered an area where finger holds provided the

Don gathering mineral samples near the old Eureka mine site, 1924. Without an ice axe, he had to kick the samples out of the cliff side.

only route. Without axes to cut out larger holds in the ice, there were no options. It was risky and difficult but eventually they crossed.

About halfway up the gulch, as they made their way above the ice pack, they closed in on their "New Discovery" vein, cropping out in the face of a great rock wall. Climbing now switched to rock scrambling on the agglomerate rock—glassy and hard, slippery with running water. Reaching the top of the wall, Phyl lowered Don by rope over the cliff where he pounded out ore samples with his hands and feet. Again, an ice axe would have been most useful. At 8:00 p.m. they were back on the summit and there spent the night. The next day Don once more dangled over the cliff and pocketed whatever loose samples he could, and then they made their descent of the mountain.

A few days later, when the samples were assayed, it was apparent that Don and Phyl had indeed found very high-grade silver ore from the 60-metre-long open "New Discovery" vein. What had been merely an exercise inspired by curiosity turned out to be of economic advantage for the mining concern. Within weeks the company began driving a tunnel deep into the mountain, the object being to get under the veins hinted at on the mountain surface.

Newspaper coverage of this latest episode of quirky and daring adventures contributed greatly to the growing legend of this dauntless climbing couple.[30] The news broke just days before what would be the story of the year—Phyl's ascent of Mount Robson. And Don, of course, as editor of the *Mountaineer*, couldn't resist his own poke.

> It is somewhat unique in the history of mountaineering for climbers to be asked to turn their ability along that line to use for the benefit of miners, but this was done recently by the owners of the Eureka-Victoria Mine which is about 8 miles southward from Hope. Mr. and Mrs. Don Munday were the climbers. Eureka Mountain is about

6,100 feet high, the mine camp being at 5,000 feet on the north slope and commanding a magnificent view up the Fraser canyon from Hope, and of the surrounding mountains, the nearest, Mt. Holy Cross being probably close to 7,000 feet. The south peak of Eureka Mountain is unclimbed. The rock seems to be something of a geological puzzle, and agglomerate or conglomerate composed of a variety of small stones cemented together so solidly that the mass usually breaks through them rather than around them ... The ore vein which they particularly wanted to explore contained silver, and was visible high in the cliffs in the centre of "Snowslide Gulch," so named because of an avalanche which so nearly proved fatal that further exploration was left to mountaineers. The gulch is comparable to Crown "Crater," but is on a much grander scale, with added difficulties ... This was on the southeast of the mountain and two traverses of the mountain were made in the day, necessitating some stiff rock climbing.

The miners were skeptical about what people calling themselves mountaineers could do, but it may be fairly said that their unbelief disappeared when they saw the ore and learned how it had been obtained—chiefly by dangling over a cliff on the end of a rope.[31]

Always the promoter of climbs for the club, Don concluded the article with a tantalizing suggestion: "To the eastward of Eureka are a number of attractive peaks which appear to be close to good trails; several must exceed 7,000 feet considerably. No record exists of their having been climbed."

Don and Phyl's practical utilization of mountaineering to aid other pursuits had economic potential, a fact not missed. Living as they did on the modest income from Don's journalism and their income as caretakers of Alpine Lodge, the idea that mining ventures might compensate for information on geology and mountain access opened up future possibilities for them.

Don and Phyl with Gustave Gambs, Abbot Hut, 1925.

Chapter Five   THE ALPINE CLUB OF CANADA

Established in 1906, the Alpine Club of Canada (ACC) sponsored annual summer camps held at different locations in the Rocky Mountains. Members could come for a few days or a few weeks. The club scheduled its annual general meeting to occur at the camp—which was probably the most practical way of ensuring that members from across Canada would be in attendance. There was tradition and structure. Tents and basic gear could be provided at the camp, and everyone's meals were cooked by hired staff and served in large open mess tents. Each night there was a fireside singalong, storytelling and recounting of the day's activities. Climbers were expected to sign up for specific climbs according to their skill levels. Professional guides, and later club-sanctioned member-guides, led groups through alpine meadows, along glaciers or up mountains. The camps drew international participants in addition to the Canadian members.

The Robson Ascent

The 1924 annual Alpine Club of Canada camp was held at Mount Robson Provincial Park from July 22 to August 4. BCMC members set out as a group on the Canadian National Railway from Vancouver. They disembarked from the train at Robson, the closest railway station, in a jumble of packs, boots, blankets and cameras. It was more than 40 kilometres from the station to the camp at Robson Pass. Joining Don and Phyl were Bev Cayley, Ivan R. Miller, A.H. Bain and Edith M. Henley. Edith Munday, now three years old, stayed at home with her grandmother.

Once at the camp they mingled with the 170 others—among them representatives of the English, American, French and Swiss alpine clubs; the Scottish Mountaineering Club; the Appalachian Mountain Club; the

Mount Robson and the Tumbling Glacier, Mount Resplendent visible in background.

Cascadians; the Sierra Club; and the Royal Geographical Society. It was an extraordinarily large camp, and more were expected in for the annual general meeting on July 31. That would be followed by the unveiling of a special monument to commemorate the completion of the surveys delimiting the boundary between British Columbia and Alberta. The newly erected monument stood just a few hundred metres from the camp, at the summit of Robson Pass.

The weather for their stay was mixed. Extraordinarily fine days were interspersed with rain and low clouds. The views of the surrounding mountains—especially of Robson itself—were often obscured, which was a disappointment to many who had come to the region for the first time. An unexpected bonus, however, was the almost complete absence of mosquitoes. This was even remarked upon in the official summary of the camp as an "an unusual charm."[1]

The Mundays planned a full schedule. As per ACC policy, a list of organized climbs and hikes was posted on a bulletin board. Each activity included a specific group leader or guide and was rated for its difficulty, and described generally so that members could select activities appropriate to their skill level. Members could sign up for those they were interested in, and providing the numbers signed up did not go over the posted

A campfire scene at the 1924 Alpine Club of Canada camp.

maximum, everyone could go. During the camp, BCMC members climbed Mount Robson, Lynx Mountain, Resplendent Mountain, Mount Ptarmigan, Calumet Peak, Mount Mumm, Moritz Peak, and Gendarme.

Many individuals signed up for an attempt at Mount Robson (3,954 metres), for this really was the plum climb and the reason why the camp was situated there that year. The notice board read: "Members will, of course, understand that the attempt is only open to those of tried skill and endurance and cannot be made by promiscuous parties or novices ... Moreover, the services of the Guides for such purposes will be limited, as there will be a wide range of mountain area to work over and a great many people to cater for ... It must not be forgotten that on dangerous and difficult climbs only a limited number can be taken on a rope."[2]

The mountain had not been climbed since its first ascent at the Alpine Club of Canada camp in 1913.[3] At that time, members Albert McCarthy and William Foster, with Austrian-born guide Conrad Kain, tackled the mountain from its east face (now known as the Kain face). The 1924 camp had been selected by ACC President Arthur O. Wheeler to enable a second attempt by club members, and he had hired Kain to once more guide members on the summit quest. It would be Wheeler who would decide, based upon all the names on the sign-up sheet, how many parties would make the attempt, and who would be selected. Don and Phyl, and presumably Bev Cayley and other BCMC members (who were, like Don and

Phyl, also Alpine Club members) signed up. It was worth the shot, they all thought, although being from the west coast, and new to ACC camps (it was the Mundays' first), their mountaineering skills and credentials were little known by Wheeler and others in the ACC Executive.

The original climbing sheets from the annual camps are preserved in the ACC records. For 1924 the activities of Don and Phyl are clearly documented. On July 23, in company with six others, they went on an expedition to Mount Gendarme (2,927 metres) via Inderbinen Pass.[4] The ascent was complete. The next day, with Don acting as guide, Phyl plus six women and three men climbed Mount Mumm (2,962 metres). It was on their return from this climb that Wheeler pulled Don and Phyl aside and informed them that they had both been selected for the try on Robson. They had made the cut. For Phyl, it was unexpected. Wheeler, the autocratic and paternalistic president, was well known for his gender bias.[5] Prevailing impressions at the camp had been that women would not be allowed to attempt Robson.

Phyl recorded: "... it was with amazed joy that I heard from Director A.O. Wheeler's lips that I was chosen to accompany my husband on the second 1924 party."[6] They were absolutely delighted—for they truly were a climbing twosome, and it would have been wrenching for one to go without the other.

The first party consisted of prominent club members Malcolm J. Geddes, T.B. Moffatt and Harry Pollard and American climbers J. Monroe Thorington and A.J. Ostheimer. They, along with Kain, had already embarked for the High Camp, and for the first attempt on the summit. The Mundays were to be in the second party, along with Andy Drinnan and Fred Lambart. After what they hoped would be a good night's rest, the second party planned to leave from the Robson Pass camp the following day. Shortly before leaving camp they found their numbers increased by the addition of Miss Annette E. Buck, J.T. Porter and a second guide, Joe Saladana.

The *Canadian Alpine Journal* of October 1924 contains an article by Phyllis Munday titled "First Ascent of Mt. Robson by Lady Members" and it gives a fair account of their climb. What it lacks, however, is the passion and immediacy of her first draft (preserved in her personal papers now housed in the BC Archives) and the extra spice of Don's own recounting in

Alpine Club of Canada members who made successful ascents of Mount Robson, 1924. Rear (left to right): Malcolm Geddes, T.B. Moffatt, Fred Lambart, Andy Drinnan, Joseph Porter. Front (left to right): Joe Saladana (guide), Don, Phyl, Albert McCarthy (ascent 1913), Annette Buck, Harry Pollard.

The B.C. Mountaineer. For it was an ascent fraught with drama and danger, punctuated by human error. Events on the ascent convinced Don and Phyl that never again would they be separated on different ropes. "Robson was the first serious climb on which my wife and I were not members of the same rope party. We vow it will be the last."[7]

It began easily enough. Don wrote: "Camp at Robson Pass was left about 9:30 a.m., the trail being followed down the valley nine miles to Lake Kinney, a descent from 5,450 to 3,200 feet. Here packs were laden with food for the High Camp at 6,500 feet on a shoulder of Robson south of the Great Couloir of the west face. The climb was hot, steep and dry, camp being reached shortly before 8 p.m. Three tents, food and other equipment had been placed on this high shelf, the highest point a comfortable camp could be placed, but not really high enough from the purely climbing point of view."[8]

At High Camp they prepared supper and settled in to await the return of the first party. It was mere minutes later that two of the first party appeared on the trail, on their way back to camp. But there were only two, what about the others? After a moment of worry, it soon came out that these climbers —Thorington and Ostheimer, both experienced mountaineers— had turned back. As the two climbers devoured what was to have been the Mundays' meal, they told of how thousands of tons of ice from Robson's immense ice cap had crashed down over the climbing route soon after the rest of the party had surmounted the wall. Thorington and Ostheimer had turned back below this ice wall, declaring it unjustifiably hazardous. Presumably the others had gone forward.

Everyone settled in for the night, just a little anxious about what the next few hours would bring. In the wee hours the following morning Conrad Kain's well-known yodel signalled the return. He had safely completed his second ascent of Robson and guided Geddes, Moffat and Pollard on their first. Kain would now turn around and attempt the mountain again the next day with the Mundays. But for now he needed rest, so he crawled into his tent and spent the day resting and sleeping. (A day, incidentally, spent by Don and Phyl in complete frustration, as it was perfect climbing weather and they were itching to be off.) The following morning, at 3:30 a.m. on July 27, he roused them and the Munday party moved off. Wrote Phyl:

> We were off to test the perils of the climb for ourselves.
>
> At about 8,000 feet we gained the ridge behind the little black peak of the west face, in time to see the ice-front of the southwest face

discharge a mass of ice down cliffs where exceptionally big avalanches are sometimes hurled 5,000 feet into the valley of the Little Fork. Nearly a thousand feet higher the same glacier has broken through the ridge to fling ice down bare cliffs for 6,000 feet almost to the trail along Lake Kinney.

What concerned us more intimately was that we had to cross the cliffs for nearly 100 yards directly under the glistening and shattered wall which, 100 feet in height, hung far out over the way we must go.

From this and the greater wall somewhere above, tremendous avalanches had fallen just after the previous party passed—some assurance that less remained to threaten us. A few stray blocks came down with crashing reports as they shattered on the rocks, but we passed safely.

More good rock climbing followed for about 2,000 feet, the shining white peak in sight most of the time, and seemingly close at hand. So far we had performed so that Conrad had not roped us, but now we had to work across the cliffs 200 yards under the upper ice wall, and then actually climb its 150-foot face. The wall extends for more than a quarter of a mile, sloping diagonally upwards ...

The ice-cliff, amazingly overhanging, fantastically sculptured, grunted uneasily. Conrad coached both rope-parties carefully; we gathered up the slack of the ropes, and worked out along a protruding shelf. Perhaps a fairly steady head and foot is needed for one to trot rapidly along a ledge with 8,000 feet of thin air immediately below; nevertheless it is fairly certain that no one in the party actually saw just then the void below or the ice menace above.

In one place the ice sloped back slightly, and here Conrad decided to force a passage, and plied his ice axe vigorously, working out diagonally far beyond the base of the ice wall—surely the dizziest place imaginable, but obviously the only way. Cutting small handholds, he stood on one foot and chopped the final step to surmount the crest of the ice, over which he disappeared. I had anchored him with the rope around my ice axe thrust in a hole in the ice. Now it was my turn to follow. Without a professional guide I had scaled as difficult ice walls before, but never with such an excess of nothingness under my heels, or so much impending above.

The second rope followed and we strode gladly up and across the upper glacier, with the gleaming summit cornice in full view against a blue-black sky such as is never seen at lower altitudes. The glare of the noon day sun was felt even through snow glasses. The snow was soft, and the second rope, led by Joseph Saladana, went ahead to break trail for a while. Unusual warm weather on the mountain had "rotted" the snow and ice, with the result that in crossing a crevasse Joe suddenly plunged out of sight, getting a severe shaking up and dropping his ice axe. Before Conrad could reach the scene my husband had taken charge of the situation and Joe, bleeding about the face, was on the surface again. However, an hour was spent recovering the axe from the bottom of the chasm, 50 feet below. This delay proved serious as it practically robbed us at once of any chance to reach the summit and return to camp before dark.

In a few minutes we reached the top of the south ridge at the base of the final wedge. The slope above is unlike anything elsewhere in the Rockies—an absolute chaos of ice blocks on a slope of not less than 45 degrees; domed with snow, and bristling with gleaming icicles, they were a never to be forgotten sight, fairylike perhaps, but sinister, hostile, menacing. Even in the bright sunlight, we shivered if we stopped. When a cloud crossed the sun the cold was intense.

Around, between, under, the ice blocks we climbed, the rotted snow often subsiding beneath us, necessitating the use of the rope to get the rest of the party across the holes. Sometimes we crawled on hands and knees across doubtful places or even lay down and wriggled. Utmost care was required to avoid giving some of the shattered masses just the jar which might set them going, probably to disrupt the whole slope.

Conrad was thoroughly anxious about the slope below the great cornice which with a smaller secondary cornice upon it, caps the highest rocks of the mountain. Excessively steep, and without cohesion, the steps broke away repeatedly, but the slope as a whole held. An avalanche here would have shot us down 3,000 feet, then over an enormous cliff of ice to the lower glacier ...

The second rope waited under the big cornice while we cautiously made our way up a wall of crumbling ice, then up a ridge where the ice was torn apart ...

"Well, lady, here is the top of Mt. Robson," said Conrad, taking in the slack as I came up beside him and looked down both sides,

On the rocks, Robson climb, 1924.

seeing Berg Lake a mile and a quarter below, the camp tents were mere specks in Robson Pass ... The time was 4:30 p.m.[9]

Phyl's account describes the lost ice axe but avoids mention of a second incident on the ascent, one that could have had more devastating consequences for them all. It occurred quite soon after the recovery of the axe while Kain was again in the lead. In the *Mountaineer*, Don did not hesitate to recount: "While he [Kain] was busy cutting steps the tail-ender on his rope ignored his implicit orders as to the mode and time of crossing the rotten bridge, and fell in as Conrad had predicted; No. 3 on the rope was not in position to stand a strain he had no reason to expect at that moment; fortunately No. 2 [Phyl] was well braced; otherwise all four almost surely would have gone into the crevasse. The danger was created by the human element."[10] He was more explicit in an unpublished manuscript:

> Conrad, relying on his party's obedience to his careful instructions, was intent on cutting steps on a steep slope above an ice-bridge nearly as fragile as a greenhouse roof. His back was to them and he had thrown down about 24 feet of rope slackly between himself and Mrs. Munday.
>
> The woman who made the fourth on the rope now ignored orders to move only one at a time and to drag herself prone across

this essential bridge. Consequently she dropped into the crevasse and jerked the unprepared man above her from his footholds. We four on the other rope watched helplessly while my wife unaided braced herself to hold the double weight. Conrad snatched in the slack frantically, knowing he could not possibly check the three if they fell together any distance. But my wife held them and the second man regained the footholds before Conrad took in all the rope.[11]

The loss of time caused by both these incidents meant that they now must spend the night on the mountain, which they did, huddled at about 9,500 feet, on a rock ledge. They roused the next day at 3:00 a.m. and reached High Camp two hours later. That afternoon they returned to the main camp, and telegraph messages were sent off to the newspapers in time for an article to appear the following day in Vancouver and other places announcing the successful ascents and, importantly, the first female ascents.

In later weeks, Don felt he had to set the records straight in regards to the female ascents. As Phyl and Annette Buck were on the same rope it was assumed by the general public that they were on the summit simultaneously. Robson's summit was too small to allow more than two people at a time, so Kain brought the climbers to the summit in their rope order, first Phyl, then Lambart, then Annette Buck. Here is what Don had to say.

> ... a correction of the impression being spread in Canada by American publications and news services that an American woman was the first woman to reach the top of Mt. Robson. Mrs. Don Munday was the first, preceding the other woman by some 15 or 20 minutes; while those who know Mrs. Munday realize she is not the one to wish to press unduly the distinction, the first person is first, and this is so well recognized in well-informed mountaineering circles that on a first ascent, for instance, the guide steps aside just short of the highest point to let one of his party be the first to reach the top.[12]

Phyl and Don spent a day quietly in camp and then on July 30 ascended Mount Calumet (2,977 metres) with other club members. The annual general meeting was held the following day. It was there that club members learned more of the details about the unsuccessful attempt on

At 12,000 feet on Mount Robson, 1924.

Mount Everest and the deaths of British climbers Mallory and Irvine. By early August BCMC members returned to the west coast, in time to head straight up to their own club camp in the Spearhead Range.

Into the Cariboo Mountains

The Mundays contributed to general knowledge about the topography not only of the Coast Mountains, but also the Columbia Mountains, specifically the Cariboo, or McLennan Range, west of Jasper. They had passed through the area in 1920 on their honeymoon trip and the mountains they saw from the train made such an impression on them that five years later, when they read about recent climbs in the area, they were inspired to visit for themselves. What sparked their interest was an article in the English *Alpine Club Journal* written by American climber Allen Carpe. A synopsis of this article was also published in the ACC *Gazette*.[13] Carpe, an experienced climber, along with R.T. Chamberlin and A.L. Withers, penetrated these interior mountains in 1924. This party made a first ascent of a mountain they called Titan (renamed Mount Sir Wilfrid Laurier in 1927). Boasting an elevation of 3,520 metres, it is the highest peak of the interior ranges. Carpe told of the heavily glaciated peaks surrounding Titan and the challenges available for climbers.[14] He also stated that these mountains held the headwaters of the North Thompson River.

Winter was always the time to dream and scheme. Don and Phyl prudently arranged their own visit to the Cariboo Mountains as a first stop on their way to the 1925 ACC camp at Lake O'Hara. In late June 1925 they disembarked from the Canadian National train at the station a mile or so beyond Tête Jaune junction, each weighed down with supplies. Don carried a 70-pound pack, and Phyl a 55-pound pack. At the station they met Mr. J.W. Switzer, the postmaster, who kindly invited them to sleep that night in the "lobby" of his post office while he returned to his ranch some miles distant.

The next morning they were off, armed with copies of the maps submitted to the authorities by Carpe. The Mundays' strategy was to follow Carpe's route and penetrate through to the mountains—some 30 kilometres distant—heading toward Mount Titan by following Sand (later renamed Tête) Creek to its source, a glacier listed by Carpe. Melting snows engorged the valley with runoff water, and the 24 kilometres was rough going.

Don and the postmaster in front of the Robson Station post office, 1925.

According to Don, "two and a half days were needed to cover this distance, a whole day being required to make the final three miles."[15]

Neither did the weather cooperate. It blew fierce gales almost continuously, and as they soon found out, both camping and climbing were constant struggles. Don's report in *The B.C. Mountaineer* gives a sense of these conditions.

> Terrific winds were the rule—a wind break of boughs had to be built to protect the tent at base camp. Unsettled weather prevailed ... On account of the size of the glacier at the head of Sand Creek (which emerged through a mighty arch of ice) the trips are very long, making it necessary to move camp two miles up the glacier to 7,500 feet to Kiwa neve, half circling Titan to the west face, where ice demanded an hour's step-cutting in a gale in which there was actual risk of being blown off the mountain.
>
> Throughout the region crevasses were found exceptionally treacherous owing to the frequent snowstorms and fierce drifting—one glacier shelf below Holway Peak repeatedly flung a snow-plume half a mile across Stripe Glacier when the wind blew in earnest. Much time was lost unraveling a crevasse between the two peaks of Titan.

Phyllis wearing snow goggles and zinc oxide ointment for sun protection, on the summit of Sir Wilfred Laurier, 1925.

> Snow-glasses were a necessity to protect eyes from flakes of surface ice, as big as one's hand, skimmed off the snow and whirled high in the air by the wind.[16]

They summited Titan and from there figured a strategy for their next ascent, the unclimbed peak of Carpe's "Mount David Thompson" (later renamed Mount Sir John Thompson), a little to the south, but a storm then drove them down to timberline where they "bivouacked two nights under a tent pitched as a lean-to on ice axes at 7,300 feet on a gale-swept spur [of the mountain]." The weather did not improve. Difficult as it would be to move on, they could not stay bivouacked much longer. So they were up early planning to depart when "an extra blast of sand and mica dust made Mrs. Munday peer over the windbreak. 'We'd better get out of here!' she exclaimed and scraped our untouched breakfast back into the pot. The west wind raged across the head of Sand glaciers; from the upper plateau wind drove falling snow half a mile horizontally, as from a giant nozzle, before dropping it on the trunk glacier." [17]

At 2 a.m. they packed up and started uncertainly under a threatening sky. Racing clouds smothered all the summits. It would be a hard slog to Mount David Thompson.

> The ground was frozen an inch deep; snow raced bitterly across the glacier even in the very lee of the 3,000-foot precipices of Mt. Titan; by 5 o'clock we reached the McLennan River divide at nearly 10,000 feet. In the next hour we covered three miles, descending 1,500 feet and climbing 5,000 feet across the chief of the three McLennan glaciers which unite at their snouts.
>
> Here we touched rock again for a few yards, then descended a mile, losing 1,000 feet elevation along the David Glacier. The north ridge of David Thompson is not a practical route though not actually impossible. The east face is not climbable; the south is possibly the same but was ruled out by distance. The whole northwest face is ice to the summit ridge and subject to ice-falls. A subsidiary northwest ridge of ice offered the best chance but promised much step-cutting and had one bad place, which proved very bad, a great section of the slope subsiding visibly and repeatedly under our feet during the process of cutting footholds. [18]

Don complained that his ice-axe blows only opened a crack. He merely nicked the ice, "leaving Phyl to chip out a little more. Her hands bled with the ice I hailed down upon her, but she would not pause to put on mitts. We had 800 feet of step-cutting, the upper part being thinly covered with snow. Upon rounding a boss of snow at 12:20 p.m., we suddenly gained the summit ridge." [19] This was a first ascent.

The summit was "a sinuous knife-edge of snow soaring to a tiny peak on which only one person could stand. Visibility was splendid." It was from the summit that Don and Phyl enjoyed a totally unobstructed view of the valleys and rivers below. They could see that the mountain's glacier-fed rivers did not—as Carpe had stated—drain into the Thompson watershed at all. Accuracy of mapping was important to Don, who commented: "we were able to correct other topographical errors of the Carpe-Chamberlin party which made the first ascent of Titan last year."[20]

"At about 30 feet below the summit we left our record in a cairn dizzily perched on the very edge of the precipice. We then hurried down. The climb to David Pass was in deep, sodden snow. The McLennan neve was worse. Crevasses were troublesome on the 1,500 foot climb to Promise Point." There they found water, the first drink in 15 hours. "Camp was reached at 7:20 p.m. The total time was seventeen hours, in space of which we had ascended and descended 10,000 feet and traveled fifteen miles."[21]

The final week's climbing was curtailed abruptly because of an accident. As Don led the way through the bush at lower altitude, he swung his axe from side to side, lopping off branches to make it easier for the packs. One swipe dislodged a wasp nest and the insects swarmed him. Instinctively he reacted and launched himself feet first down a steep side hill of scree and thick bushes in an attempt to escape the wasps. Momentarily blinded, he flung up his arm (which held his very sharp axe) to protect his face. Little did he realize that Phyl, seeing him slide and not knowing the reason, had herself launched forward to save him from sliding into the torrent far below. "Her devotion was ill-rewarded," Don wrote, for his axe neatly connected with Phyl's thigh and cut through to the tendon.[22] They were still seven miles from the station. As Don recorded in his phlegmatic way: "We had to camp instead of going through to the railway that night."[23] Apparently the cut healed in a few weeks and Phyl suffered no permanent ill effects. But it certainly would have been a challenge to be thus injured and still have to pack out to the train station.

As was typical, Don wrote about their trip, providing an official record for the *Canadian Alpine Journal* and creating more lively narrative accounts for publication in newspapers and magazines. For Don, the official record was serious business and must be as accurate and as informative as possible. Articles written for the *Journal* augmented mountaineering knowledge and served as references for other climbers who ventured after. Thus, his account detailed their day-by-day movements, drawing on the daily notes that they had made on the trip.[24] For the mountaineering record he corrected what he believed to be the misinformation published the previous year. Never one to mince words, Don was blunt; Carpe—based upon his own description of where he travelled—could never have actually seen all the watersheds he marked on his map and his "conclusions are mistaken ones." The source of the North Thompson River was not the mountain Carpe had not climbed but tentatively named "Mount David Thompson." Munday included his own map with the article, superimposing Carpe's delineations to show the inaccuracies.

It was extremely important for Don that when climbers published accounts they be as accurate as possible and not assume or extrapolate. If you didn't see it, you didn't map it. To rebuke a fellow climber, and a contemporary, was far different from correcting the historical record, such as entering an area sketchily delineated on pioneer maps and creating a more accurate map. Rigid in his views, Don did all he could to ensure his own accounts were completely accurate and not left open to misinterpretation. He expected the same standard from others, knowing as he did how frustrating it was to rely on a map and find it inaccurate. Once something is published, it becomes fact, and for mountaineers, incorrect "fact" can be dangerous.

> **Ropes** *"How about your mountain ropes?"*
>
> *"Oh, they were the old regular hemp ropes, with a little red cord running through, indicating that it was a proper alpine rope. Nothing like the light ropes that they use today, but they were good ropes in their day. I've still got two or three of them."*
>
> PHYLLIS MUNDAY TAPED INTERVIEW, 1973, BC ARCHIVES.

Don's article spurred Carpe to revisit the area in 1927 and publish again.[25] In 1939 another American climber, R.T. Zillmer, endorsed Carpe's 1924 conclusions, which prompted Don to respond in a 1940 article where he very clearly demonstrates that he has done his homework and spent time in archives and consulting the historical record. He argued that Carpe was far from being the first white man to penetrate the Cariboo Range, that the Canadian Pacific Railway surveyors had clearly been there before and the documents they created—the annual reports, survey notes and maps—showed this undisputedly. The Zillmer-Munday feud continued via articles and letters in both the *Canadian Alpine Journal* and the *American Alpine Journal.* In 1941 Zillmer maintained "Mr. Munday's controversial spirit gets so much the better of him." He requested that the published discussion be terminated as he had no wish to be drawn into further argument. He had "only the highest regard for Mr. Munday's work." No doubt also, having experienced Don's tenacity in presenting his opinions

THE ALPINE CLUB OF CANADA | 141

Don in tent, on the Premier Group trip, 1925.

regarding "accuracy in all matters concerning the mountains," [26] Zillmer knew that the polarized positions would never see compromise.

Nomenclature complicated the discourse. Carpe and Chamberlin applied tentative names to glaciers, valleys and peaks as a means of reference. The Mundays used these names and added a few more of their own, but just a couple of years later, new and formal names were applied by government. The official naming of geographical features is a legal responsibility of the Geographical Board of Canada. Suggestions for names are referred to the Board, which may, or may not, adopt the recommendations. Often formal naming occurs many years after informal names have been applied and in use, thus supplanting common usage. It makes it confusing for mapmakers, confusing for people searching for published information and confusing for the historical record.

The Diamond Jubilee of the Dominion of Canada occurred in 1927 and this event seemed a logical time to celebrate 60 years of nation-building. A cluster of superb glaciated mountains in the Cariboo Range were selected to be formally named "The Premier Group" to commemorate past prime ministers of Canada (those not earlier recognized in mountain names). Mount Titan became Mount Sir Wilfrid Laurier, Mount David Thompson became (confusingly) Mount Sir John Thompson and Mount Welcome

In the Premier Group, 1925.

became Mount Sir Mackenzie Bowell. Britain's prime minister at the time was acknowledged when Challenger became Mount Stanley Baldwin. The Mundays' Mount Hostility became Mackenzie King, and on it went.[27]

Lake O'Hara Camp

Pitched on the Alpine Club of Canada's own land on the south shore of Lake O'Hara, the 1925 camp sat amid the glory of the mountains, on the British Columbia side of the continental divide. From Abbot Pass west, rivers drain into the Pacific; from the east, into Hudson Bay. According to the official report, the weather for this camp was bright with no snowfall, and the rain fell primarily at night. This was the first year that the stone hut on Abbot Pass (2,925 metres) was used as a stopping place for longer excursions, built by the Swiss guides of the Canadian Pacific Railway only three years earlier. Over 140 attended the camp (among them 26 BCMC members).[28]

The Mundays hiked in from Field via the Dennis and Duchesney passes to Lake O'Hara. At the camp they began by signing up for what would become a classic hike, a two-day trip via Paradise Valley. Presumably the axe wound on Phyl's leg prevented her from more strenuous undertakings until she healed. On July 30 they ascended Mount Odaray (3,159 metres) but it was another five days until Mount Huber (3,368 metres), their next climb.[29]

On the last day of the camp, three climbers sat in the corner of the hut on Abbot Pass overlooking Lake Louise on the col between Mounts Victoria and Lefroy. Gustave Gambs had just returned from Mount Lefroy on the one side of the pass, while Phyl and Don, "cut loose on their own" by director A.O. Wheeler, had just set the new record that day for the south summit, via the southeast ridge route up Mount Victoria (3,464 metres). Their ascent was clocked in at two and a half hours.

Reluctant to leave the mountains, the threesome schemed, resolving to meet two days later in the little town of Field and climb in the Yoho Valley. They parted and Don and Phyl headed back into camp, for the next day they planned to tackle the formidable Mount Hungabee (3,492 metres), the highest peak at O'Hara. Phyl's ascent would be "the first time a woman had attempted it without the services of a Swiss guide," wrote Don, noting that as they departed the hut, guides Ernest and Edward Feuz "shouted their good wishes for our success."[30] Despite its huge rock walls, they found it to be a leisurely climb. "It being so warm on the summit no extra garments were needed in spite of a wind ... No particular difficulties were met at any point."[31]

Following the climb, they hiked out of camp to the railway line, then travelled the remainder of the way to Field by train. Meeting up with Gambs, the threesome hiked up the Yoho Valley to Takakkaw Falls, then on August 12 spent a leisurely day on the summit of Mount Daly (2,166 metres). They then moved to the head of Little Yoho Valley, but at this point the weather broke. Stormbound, with both their vacation time and grub nearly at an end, they waited impatiently. Signs of improvement in the weather tempted them. Conscious of the date and the commitments that awaited them at home, Don, Phyl and Gambs consulted the map Don had brought. It was considered the most comprehensive and official map, but as they would find out, it was not the most accurate in dealing with the backcountry topography. The shortest and most direct route back to the CPR line seemed to be via Emerald Pass to Emerald Lake. And so they resolved to tackle it. This journey, unnecessarily complicated because of misinformation, was one they would recall for some time to come.

Misinformation seemed to be the theme for them in Yoho Park. Don was not silent upon their return. In the *Mountaineer* he railed against the problems they had encountered in various areas of Yoho; the first being on their way in from Field to Lake O'Hara.

Perhaps some members have already discovered the numerous topographical shortcomings of the map of Yoho Park, but possibly it might not be out of place to put climbers on their guard against being misled by the trail indicated as running over Dennis and Duchesnay Passes from Field to Lake O'Hara. There is a fine trail to the fossil beds on Mt. Stephen. Crossing a hanging valley, we then climbed a notch in the high ridge behind Mt. Stephen, encountering an ice patch raining down rocks which forced a climb of unpleasant cliffs. The valley north of Mt. Odaray grants an impressive view of that mountain, but lack of a trail as shown lessens the pleasure of the last part of the trip. There are twice the number of lakes shown on the map along the route.[32]

And then other difficulties arose on the various climbs from camp. "Horseshoe and Wenkchemma glaciers are mis-mapped, numerous other glaciers omitted altogether, and a trail shown as crossing the most difficult break in the Hungabee-Temple ridge [does not]."[33]

But it was the trip through Emerald Pass that was the last straw. It involved "more concentrated mountaineering than the writer ever wishes to cram into half a dozen trips in future," Don wrote. The chief problem was that the pass contained three glaciers, although none were indicated on the map. Even today, trail guides omit references to this route, as it is not easy or preferred.

We broke camp in the rain. Packs averaged 30 pounds in weight, but my wife carried more than this I found later, she scenting trouble from afar and wishing me to be less encumbered should step-cutting be required. In falling snow and with snow underfoot, we plodded up the west moraine of the glacier on the Yoho side of the pass. Much of its slope, saturated by the storm and undermined by shrinkage of the ice, was tumbling down boulders nicely timed to suit our passage ... the first pass was reached without undue difficulty. Completely hemmed in by dense cloud at this critical turning point, we consulted and insulted the map. With the limit of vision cut down to a few yards and the storm apparently renewed with increased intensity, we were still unanimous for going on. The second glacier sloped away in front of us, while to our right seemed to be the head of a valley which "didn't belong."

I led out onto and down the glacier to find out the how and where and why of it. On reaching the opposite side we argued the point as

Climbers on the summit ridge of Mount Victoria, 1925.

to where the glacier ought to be inserted on the map and on these assumptions set out to find the missing half of Emerald Pass, frequent checking by compass being needed. Snow was much deeper on this side of the range, being halfway to the knees. We headed up the glacier but the ice soon became too smooth and steep to climb without cutting steps, and this would have been prohibitively slow from the necessity of clearing the snow off first. Moreover, some sort of icefall barred the way above this slope.

But the icefall also indicated an easier gradient above it, and the slopes of Mt. Marpole suggested a way to outflank the icefall ... Here I made an excuse for my wife to lead—by no means a new experience for her. The safest place was in front, for the more the slope was disturbed the greater the risk of its sliding off bodily of the glacier a hundred feet below ... Clawing our way upward, sometimes on all fours, we reached and passed the level of the icefall. Marginal crevasses still cut us off from the invisible but presumably less broken centre of the glacier. However, the going was improving somewhat ... A momentary movement of the storm clouds revealed the glacier sweeping upward, ever-steepening, wall-like, to meet sheer precipices of Mt. Marpole. Retracing our steps, I resumed leadership and attacked the problem of the icefall ... Between great chasms, one continuous fragile fin of ice two hundred feet long offered direct passage through the maze. But when I came to scrape the snow off it to cut steps I found its breadth reduced by half owing to a foot or more of snow plastered on the side of it ...

Every foot of the way had to be sounded carefully with the ice axe. Few of the concealed crevasses were even a foot wide at the top, but nearly all were of the type dangerous because of thin lips of ice treacherously overhanging the great caverns below ...

At 1:15 p.m. we paused a moment on the actual crest of Emerald Pass, the cliffs of The President and Mt. Marpole dimly visible on either hand ...

The third glacier likewise ought to be simple under favourable conditions, but snow in the pass was knee-deep, and we descended into an intricate maze of irregular crevasses, the worst of the day, an experience none of the party will ever forget ... [34]

A close call capped their day. The tail ender on the rope was swept from the footholds on an icy snow slope, causing the rope to jerk and the second climber to be dragged down. "No. 1 barely had time to give the rope a half hitch around the shaft of the axe and drive it in with all his might. There was forty feet of rope between members of the party, but axe and rope both held under the terrific strain." [35] Adrenalin high, they continued on.

A few hours later, just as the daylight waned, the lights of Emerald Lake Chalet came into sight and soon a bridle trail was found. At 9:00 p.m., after fifteen hours in the snow, three exhausted climbers reached the doors of the chalet, only to be refused food service; only iced drinks were offered. Disheartened, and cognizant of the irony, they hiked on to Field, where two hours later they dug into a well-deserved meal.

Geikie

"A tremendous grim wall it is, seared and fissured by ice-filled couloirs, and surmounted by two fine towers sprinkled with new snow." [36] Thus historian and climber J. Monroe Thorington described Mount Geikie (3,270 metres) as it appeared to him in 1925 from above Icefall Lake. Even today it has been described as a "big bulk of a mountain" and "the dark horse of the Canadian Rockies." [37] The mountain was first ascended in 1924 and this climb described in the *Canadian Alpine Journal* of the same year, perhaps prompting the decision to situate the 1926 ACC camp in the Tonquin Valley in Jasper National Park. Don and Phyl attended the camp, their third. In addition to the main camp, two subsidiary camps—some miles distant— had been pitched to allow ready access to different peaks. One camp was at Surprise Point, the other in Geikie Meadows.

The Mundays now felt more confident of themselves in relation to other members, knew the routine and were active participants. Don confidently offered his services as a guide for the August 3 attempt on Mount Bastion, which qualified as a "badge climb." But the next day brought frustration. The annual general meeting of the club was scheduled for August 4, and that bit into the Mundays' time schedule. They had signed up to make an attempt on Mount Geikie in two days' time, but to get to the mountain, they first had to travel from the main camp to the Geikie Meadows camp. To Don's consternation, he was required to attend the meeting, as he had been nominated for a position on the executive. He and Phyl impatiently waited for the meeting to end; meanwhile, the Reverend R. Sharpe from

Cleveland, along with H.F. Thompson from Regina, had left before the meeting and had a head start.

Don wrote: "Our start from camp for the Geikie Meadows camp was delayed in the first place by our attendance at the annual meeting of the Club, and secondly by a question which arose as to who should take part in the climb of Mt. Geikie. Messrs. Sharpe and Thompson had gone on ahead, and it was nearly 6 p.m. when Miss Esther Thompson, H.J. Graves, my wife and I started down Tonquin Creek." His impatience shows in his words: "Our directions proved insufficient at several places along our route, sometimes so that we lost time by looking for the precise route when it did not really matter much, and again lost time by pushing ahead when it would have paid perhaps to make a thorough search." He details the hike leading pack horses from the main camp to the Meadows camp, the base for their attempt on the mountain.

> A prominent blaze marked the crossing of Tonquin Creek. Convenient stepping stones allowed us to cross without wetting our feet. On the far shore we sat down and ate some sandwiches. We then got off on what was probably an old caribou trail. The timber was small and rather thick. When we came to a little stream we followed it up till we found where the trail crossed it, and it soon led us out above timberline in sight of Geikie Pass, and of Mt. Barbican.
>
> Just below the crest of the pass an ice patch was nearly thawed bare and already was plainly an unpleasant place for the pack horses. From the crest we looked far up toward the headwaters of the Fraser. To my wife and I, it was a memorable moment. For several years we had looked down from our home upon the mouth of the great river, and now at last we beheld its uttermost sources among the crags of the Rockies.
>
> Our party, looking across the scene, agreed it might have been more fitting to have named a mountain more closely connected with the river's source, Mt. Fraser, than the one bearing the name at the head of Geikie Creek which is a tributary.
>
> Immediately below us and stretching several miles to our left ran the gently sloping bench of Geikie Meadows. Parts of it were thinly wooded with the treeline outposts of their kind. The sun was down and the last of its wild tints touched the racy clouds. Story shadows lurked already down in the valley.

A campfire session at the Tonquin Valley camp, 1926.

The trail angled easily down a slope of shale and then disappeared in the wide green slopes. Having been especially warned not to keep too low, we naturally then kept too high. Far ahead we saw the basin that had been described as a dried-up lake and to which we had been told not to descend. Therefore we kept close along the foot of the slopes of loose boulders under Barbican. It was noticeable that these areas were "creeping" downhill. The movement, a slow one, doubtless occurred when the clayey soil was wet. The earth was distinctly ridged in advance of the rockslides.

The dusk slowly shut in upon us. The gloom seemed to accentuate the loftiness of the encircling heights. When the slope became more rugged we angled down toward the forbidden lake basin among the tree clumps. As best we could in the darkness we scrutinized every foot of the ground as we went down. At the edge of the lakebed we turned up the hill again. Later we learned we must have been within a few yards of the beaten horse trail, but the soil was too hard and dry for it to be visible at that short distance in the dark.

When we got up among patches of steep and slippery boulders Graves insisted on relinquishing leadership in my favor although we were agreed as to the probable direction of camp. The black bulk of Geikie still dimly indicated the general neighbourhood of camp, but we feared that everyone might have gone to bed. If no light were burning we might pass fairly close without seeing it.

It was probably a strange experience to Miss Thompson to be prowling around thus in the dark on an unfamiliar mountainside without a light, food or bedding. Of course, if it came to the worst, we could halt and light a fire and wait till daylight. There was no lack of dead wood. We pushed on over rounded ridges, somewhat puzzled at not hearing horse bells if we were anywhere near the camp.

Suddenly we looked directly down into a shadowy hollow which seemed to contain a lake which had no business being there. In it seemed to be dimly reflected a snow patch. But a glance across beyond the lake promptly showed there was no snow patch to be reflected. Our eyes were playing us tricks. The snow patch was an unlighted group of bell tents and the lake a flat meadow. But the rest of the camp was nowhere in sight.

Graves sent a shout ringing through the night. It was answered immediately from the left and above the tents. Picking our way down a steep slope to the tents, we then saw the rest of the camp on a higher bench, and a light glowed cheerfully in the cook tent. Better still, we found the cook on the job with the kettle boiling for tea, and a hot meal ready to serve. And he was in a perfectly good humour in spite of the time being 10:30 p.m.

When we gathered around the table in the light of several lanterns, Miss Thompson looked out into what now seemed by contrast to be intense darkness, and said, "It's a good thing we got in before dark." We laughed, but the surrounding blackness gave her a feeling that we had accomplished something out of the ordinary in keeping going under such conditions and in hitting the camp with such precision.[38]

The following day the party rested in preparation for an early morning start on the mountain. This Geikie camp was placed on the site of the one from which C.G. Wates, Malcolm Geddes and Val Fynn had made the first ascent in 1924, and from which just days earlier Andy Drinnan and Lawrence Grassi had made the second ascent, working out a new route.[39] A nearby tree trunk bore a pencilled inscription to this effect.

Don documented the climb.

We left at 3:30 a.m. under the guidance of Hans Fuhrer whose cheerful grin had popularized him at the Alpine Club camp. We followed more or less six horizontally across the Geikie Slide until we came around into the basin of the blue Inkwell which had no visible outlet even at high water. At the other end of the lake a little glacier was nearly hidden under rocks. Most of these seemed to be discharged from the cliffs west of the prominent snow couloir which runs up to the southeast ridge and even at this early hour they dropped with regularity.

The snow was hard and as we kept close to the wall on the left we often met icy patches at the edge. We mounted almost to the point where as seen from the lake the couloir turns out of sight behind the lofty tower.

The rocks were steep with much debris on the ledges. We followed closely the route suggested by Fynn ... Before we reached the prominent horizontal ledge under the reddish-yellow cliffs there was one awkward swing around a bulge for anyone possessing only moderate length of arm and leg. As an eight-foot reach was perfectly ample for Hans, our rope sometimes had difficulty in keeping up with him, the more so as we often had to wait to avoid being in the line of fire of the inevitable rocks dislodged. The leading rope consisted of Hans, Miss Thompson, Thompson and Graves. Sharpe led the second rope with Mrs. Munday and I.

Just below the ledge some smooth slabs called for considerable confidence in the adequacy of minute hand and footholds. In places the cliff roofed the ledge and left little more space than one could crawl through with a rucksack. I was the last to pass along and unavoidably delayed my rope when a big slab of roof settled down on my back and pinned me to the ledge which was no wider than my body at this spot. By some squirming I quickly worked it sideways and sent it crashing down the precipice.

On rounding a sharp corner we came upon some bits of paper left behind by Drinnan and Grassi. We were now in the prominent broad couloir which leads directly up under the summit. There was always more or less choice of a route, but as must always be the case in climbing of this character, the party below must delay and must endure considerable anxiety because of falling rocks. Here the leading party drew well ahead of us. Again on the broken wall close under the summit, Hans' long limbs proved their worth and there was a short

pitch that demanded considerable care on the part of the second rope, there being no really secure anchorage for a considerable distance below the leader as he negotiated the troublesome corner. The first rope reached the summit nearly half an hour in advance of us.

Somewhat to our disappointment camp was not visible, the slightly lower summit hiding the view in that direction. Threatening clouds flying low ... were eyed anxiously. The time was 1:30 p.m., and even without a fresh snowfall we were none too sure of getting off the mountain that night. Almost at once the clouds cloaked the summit, shutting off a view that at best had been shadowy and restricted.

After gulping down a little food hastily while snowflakes hissed around the summit snowcap, we commenced the descent. Even the long-limbed Hans asked for the assurance of a rope anchored above when his party had preceded him down the first little wall. Then, as there was decidedly limited standing room below, he continued down and left us to help the shorter-limbed Sharpe down the same place. Some snow among the rocks here added a little to the difficulty.

The snow squall soon passed, the thunderous heart of it being more in the direction of Mt. Fraser. The descent continued without special incident until we neared the horizontal ledge. At the place in question we had almost caught up to the first rope. They were just starting down the left hand of two small parallel chimneys when Sharpe trod on a broad shale-covered ledge which all before him had used in turn. There was nothing to suggest that the rock under his feet was not an integral part of the mountain until with an ominous grinding it slid out from under him, turned slowly over, then with increasing bounds rushed down past my wife and I toward the other party. They saw it coming but were helpless. The rock was fully six feet long and four feet wide.

The suspense was terrible. The rock crashed on to the point between the two gullies ... before toppling slowly over into the vacant chimney. It was one of those occurrences for which a climber ought to be spiritually prepared; the peril was not in the slightest degree attributable to human carelessness.

Immediately after the first rope descended the worn slabs below the horizontal ledge, a short sharp shower of rain made them so greasy

Phyllis and fellow climbers on the windy summit of Mount Geikie, 1926.

that every member of the second rope probably recalls their descent with a vividness that the members of the first rope may not appreciate.

Hans outflanked the awkward bulge below this. The descent of the final wall leading down to the gully was made in the twilight, it was a grimy business owing to the shower of debris accompanying each as we descended in turn.

It was with distinct triumph that I felt the snow underfoot, some of us at least being confident of our ability to negotiate the gully in the darkness. Before we had all got out nicely to the length of our rope a tremendous report sounded high above us. Almost before the first hollow echo replied from the opposite wall, the fragments whistled down amongst us, sending up great spurts of snow.

One chunk hit almost between my wife and Sharpe who were not five feet apart. Fortunately my wartime experience bade me duck as for a bursting shell. As it was, the fragment flattened my hat against my skull as it went over my head. A few smaller rocks came down from time to time tearing by unseen and mainly holding to the middle of the couloir. It was largely a case of feeling for each foothold in the snow, and there was little effort to force the pace once the maximum amount of darkness reigned. By this time the cloud hung low above our heads.

When we got clear of the couloir we lit our insufficient number of lights and picked a way down the unstable morainal debris to the Inkwell. Perched there on the rocks we opened our packs and pooled the edible contents. Cans of peaches and pineapple had been intended for a triumphant feast on the summit, but no one now regretted that they had been carried to the top and down again.

The distance across the Geikie Slide seemed long and presently Hans headed straight down toward Geikie Creek, mistaking a steep declivity for the slope of the draw coming out of the basin between Barbican and Geikie. As he was too far ahead to carry on a coherent conversation, I told Graves of the error and that my wife and I would continue across the slide to camp.

This we did, in a very few minutes coming to a twisted pine whose outline was clearly remembered ... Having picked up this definite landmark we went on and reached camp shortly before midnight. All was in darkness there, as was to be expected. Our last scrap of candle—a whole one had been dropped out of reach among the rocks—burned out just as we stepped into the cook tent.

The fire was still glowing redly in the stove and the kettle almost boiling. While my wife examined the generous variety of food left ready by the cook, I secured candles and went back to guide the others in by placing a light where it would be visible down the draw. It was about 12:30 a.m. when they arrived.

Hans felt rather badly about his mistake, but the leader who has never gone astray has not led much or has not led where the way was not obvious. There are times when a leader is so engaged in overcoming a wearying succession of little obstacles that there is a real difficulty in giving the required attention to that of keeping the right direction.

For my part, I offered Hans an apology for the lack of discipline shown by breaking away from the party as I had done. The usual results of a party separating are highly unsatisfactory even when all members are well able to take care of themselves.[40]

The ascent—successful despite the stormy conditions on the summit, which denied them time—made the history books because Phyl and Esther Thompson were the first women to summit Geikie. The newspapers in Vancouver carried the story of their 21-hour climb under the heading "Mrs. Munday Climbs Geikie: Vancouver woman one of two who are first to ascend Jasper Park Peak."[41] For the Alpine Club, the camp was considered one of its most successful, marked by this ascent and a first ascent of Turret Peak, long considered a mountaineering challenge. For Don and Phyl, Geikie was not a favourite; the steep slopes and the quantity of loose rock near the base created conditions that were far different than those on the coast. Phyl especially was known to remark that she was "not a rock monkey"; she preferred the challenges presented by the varied conditions of ice and snow.

> **Photographs** "We spent most of our time in the winters, Don with his writing and me doing the photographs— printing. He did all the developing of our photographs and I did all the printing of the prints ... Don built his own enlarger out of water-pipe and old camera and so on."
>
> PHYLLIS MUNDAY TAPED INTERVIEW, 1973, BC ARCHIVES.

THE ALPINE CLUB OF CANADA | 157

High camp for Waddington. Looking to Franklin Glacier from Fury Gap, 1928.

Chapter Six   MYSTERY MOUNTAIN YEARS

"**P**HYL'S EYES SHONE AS SHE handed me the binoculars and pointed to a tall mountain nearly due north through a new cloud rift. The compass showed the alluring peak stood along a line passing a little east of the head of Bute Inlet and perhaps 150 miles away, where blank spaces on the map left ample room for many nameless mountains."[1] Thus Don Munday hooks the reader's attention in *The Unknown Mountain*, a classic of mountaineering adventure. The scene was on Mount Arrowsmith on Vancouver Island in the first week of June 1925. The Mundays and their good friend Tom Ingram had ventured from the mainland on the CPR ferry, which landed them at Nanaimo. From there, a small bus drove along the Island Highway through Parksville to the Alberni Highway. They alighted at Cameron Lake. On the lakeshore they set up camp, and then began their ascent of Arrowsmith, the climb made in a day from the lake. Although they found the trail "of an easy gradient and in fair condition in most places," the time up:

> was exceeded on account of a heavy fall of snow obliterating the trail. Thick weather continued until the tip of the so-called first peak was reached, but here a momentary glimpse of part of the mountain gave us partial bearings, sufficient to negotiate the wall of fine cliffs facing toward Arrowsmith ... A wait of about an hour and a half on this peak was finally rewarded by a dramatic sweeping away of the clouds from Arrowsmith, the last to clear. Everywhere snow was avalanching from the mountain. Drifting had been so furious that the actual snowfall was a matter of guesswork—we sank often to the waist. The rocks were free of snow, afforded splendid climbing. The summit of the north peak was reached at 3 p.m.
>
> An hour and a half was spent enjoying the glorious prospect ... The lake was reached about 10 p.m.[2]

The Mundays with their friend Tom Ingram (centre) pose beside the bus that would take them from Parksville to Cameron Lake, on their Mount Arrowsmith trip, 1925.

This climb was to be a farewell climb for Ingram, who at age 53 considered his active climbing life to be coming to a close and invited Don and Phyl to accompany him on this final excursion. Arrowsmith was chosen not just on a whim, but for a practical reason. Recent government land survey parties, in particular one led by R.P. Bishop[3] in 1922, reported that mountainous terrain north and west of Garibaldi most certainly appeared to be a vast sea of mountains, whose altitudes exceeded those farther south, such as those in the Tantalus Range and within the climbing sphere of Vancouver-based climbers. The remoteness of this area and the fact that it was unsurveyed and uncharted terrain, merely added to the curiosity. By climbing Arrowsmith, "the highest point of the section of the mountainous sky-line of Vancouver Island visible across Georgia Strait from the city of Vancouver,"[4]

MYSTERY MOUNTAIN YEARS | 161

Don, Phyl and Tom Ingram thought they might have a good observation point from which to view this unknown section of the Coast Range.

What they saw on that splendid June day was inspirational. They "beheld the glittering Coast Range sweeping northward till lost in ultimate distance somewhere in the vicinity of Bute Inlet, as indicated by the compass." Amid the clouds appeared very briefly "the black bulk of a massive mountain, too rugged to be whitened by the storm and apparently the monarch of its district. It was readily picked out by the naked eye."[5] Could this be the particularly high peak specified by Bishop?

Don confessed: "There and then we determined to satisfy the whim to push our horizon further still. Thus it was that in September [1925] we went to the head of Bute Inlet."[6] For of course, their summer climbing season was already well committed. It would not be for another three months that they were free to take up the quest.

Not surprisingly, Tom Ingram delayed his imminent climbing retirement and accompanied Don, Phyl and their friend Athol Agur on the great adventure. In Vancouver they boarded the Union Steamship SS *Chelosin*, accompanied by supplies, food, and climbing gear. The *Chelosin* unloaded them at a cannery near the entrance to Bute Inlet, and from

there a trapper, Jack McPhee, took them in his gas engine-powered 16-foot rowboat to Ward Point. Five people, four packs and freight filled the boat to capacity and then some. Ward Point was as far up the inlet as was manageable. It was McPhee who advised them on the next phase, suggesting Mount Rodney might provide a vista inland.

> From sea-level we climbed 5,500 feet on the north shoulder of Mount Rodney. We had heavy packs, the day was hot, no water available, the final three thousand feet loose or overgrown rockslide, hence the crest was reached long after dark. Rain started at daybreak next day, but on the afternoon of the following day the easterly (highest) peak of Mt. Rodney was climbed over broken rockfaces, the upper part of the glacier and the pleasant rock of the steep pyramid. The view left nothing to be desired.
>
> The height of the nearer peaks averaged about 8,000 feet ... glaciers clung everywhere, sharp rock peaks abound and the valleys are deep and narrow. The big peaks of 10,000 feet and over around Chilko Lake were too distant (40 to 60 miles) to be as imposing as we expected ... [we] made almost a complete traverse of its eastern peak in order to reach the next peak south which we suggested should be named "Blade Mountain." Its two glaciers and an intervening rock shoulder were quite interesting to negotiate, drifted deep fresh snow adding to our troubles. The 600 feet of snow-masked rock arête of the peak proved a sporting finish, in a wintry gale ... Another storm in the night kept us awake clearing the tents of snow. In the morning we started down for sea level ... Many of the glaciers in this region descend below 4,000 feet elevation, and winter avalanches actually plunge into the salt water.[7]

Mount Blade (2,470 metres) and perhaps Mount Rodney (2,390 metres) were first ascents.[8] From these summits a route toward their "Mystery Mountain" presented itself. A huge trench (which they later realized was that of the Homathko River) appeared to lead northward for 40 kilometres or so from the head of Bute Inlet. "A vast expanse of glacier seemingly closed the end of this great corridor, and out of the whiteness sprang a range of splendid rock towers. Wintry cloud roofed them. Piercing this in

Athol Agur, Tom Ingram, Don and Phyl, heavily laden, board the MV *Chelosin*, 1925.

lonely majesty towered the nameless sovereign of an unknown realm."[9] Here then, appeared the logical route to their Mystery Mountain. But the route was not without its own challenges, as they were to learn the following summer. The dense vegetation at the lower elevations (because the valley was on the seaward side of the coastal range) would cause immeasurable packing and transportation difficulties. A few days later, they were back on *Chelosin* and filled with plans for a return visit and a serious expedition.

A New World

Don and Phyl spent the winter of 1925–26 in preparation, not only assembling their supplies and food, but also obtaining information from the Geological Survey and researching historical maps and charts. They wanted to be well prepared for the next season's explorations. In early May 1926, Don and Phyl returned for a brief reconnaissance to get first-hand information about the Homathko Valley and thus better prepare for their expedition. They had brought with them a small rowboat and "kicker" gas engine. A big gas boat towed them closer to the mouth of the Homathko and then the trapper McPhee led them several kilometres upriver to a huge logjam, the limit of navigation. High tide affected the water level greatly, so they both took notes of the route McPhee followed as he manoeuvred around unmarked hazards.

Several days later they were home and packing supplies. On May 22, an advance party of Don and R.C. "Johnny" Johnson left Vancouver with most of the equipment and food required for the expedition. It was important to get the supplies as far as possible up the Homathko River before spring thaws added volume and danger to the waters. They relayed supplies back and forth to a trapper's cabin. It was miserable weather: the rains drenched them and the wind threatened navigation. One rain-filled night the river rose 15 centimetres. The rapid and dramatic response of the river to changing weather conditions became an important factor when moving supplies and themselves upriver.

Supplies stashed, Don and Johnny met the others at Orford Bay. Waiting on the wharf stood Phyl, Tom Ingram, Athol Agur, Don's brother A.R. (Bert) Munday and five-year-old Edith. This was to be the first of several summers when Edith would stay in the care of acquaintances while her parents climbed in Waddington country. She was not amused.

164

What to do about Edith?

During the Waddington years, when Don and Phyl were gone for six to eight weeks at a time, Edith spent summers in the care of friends at various locations on the coast. In 1926 five-year-old Edith stayed with Mrs. B. Ellett and her grown daughter at McPhee's Landing, Bute Inlet. This was the first of yearly extended separations for the family, and undoubtedly it was not easy for any of them. Phyl felt Edith's absence greatly. Don managed rather well to capture the excitement of their reunion. "Before the boat touched McPhee's Landing Phyl leapt ashore to Edith, our daughter. We spent a delightful time all trying to talk at once, trying to read a big budget of mail, tell of our trip, and do justice to the incredible supply of huckleberry pies provided by Mrs. Ellett."[1]

The following year the Mundays began the first of many summers venturing into Waddington territory via Knight Inlet. In the spring of 1927 they met Americans James and Loretta Stanton at their isolated home at Knight Inlet. The friendship that developed between the Mundays and the Stantons made it possible for Edith to stay with Mrs. Stanton in 1932.

Edith was not amused at being left while her parents climbed, ca. 1927.

Phyl's climbing diaries reveal her conflict about parenting and climbing. On the inside cover of each diary, Phyl carefully pasted a photo of Edith so that she could look at her during their absences. The diaries are sparse and briefly document daily activities, but occasionally Phyl recorded her inner thoughts, perhaps as a comfort. On September 15, 1927, the last entry in the diary reads: "Oh so happy to have my girlie. God Bless her. She is so well and happy ... The end of a long, strenuous, weary, wonderful, lovely, magnificent and glorious trip. Climbed the mountain but not the final tower. Disappointed but all worth while ... Better luck for the peak next year."

The following year on June 12: "So hard to part with my happy little girl. Oh God, take good care of her for us." And in 1930 on August 2: "all I want now to make it perfect is Edith."[2]

As a youngster, Edith could not understand why she was left often with people she hardly knew, in places she often didn't like, for such long periods.

She knew her parents climbed mountains. She had the years on Grouse Mountain to know what it was like living in the outdoors. She went with her parents on hikes and shorter excursions, but she was lonely and miserable separated from them for the extended summer climbing trips. At one time she reckoned that her parents must love the mountains more than her, for why else would they leave her for so long? But as she matured and began to climb with them on bigger trips, she understood that it wasn't a case of her parents loving the mountains more, but that her parents loved her differently than they loved the mountains. It was a revelation that she could live with.[3]

In 1934 a friend of Phyl's from Guides took Edith under her wing. She believed that Edith was growing up too wild and needed more structure in her life. This friend, Norah Denny, was also the headmistress at Queen Margaret's School just outside Duncan on Vancouver Island. She arranged for Edith to become a boarder at the school. Edith attended from 1934 until her graduation in May 1938.[4] Although she was apart from her parents while she attended school, Edith was able to continue in Girl Guides, which made her very happy. She had first joined her mother's Brownie pack in 1928 and "flew-up" to Guides in 1932. The school under Norah Denny had a very active Guide company and Miss Denny channelled Edith's enthusiasm into productive and rewarding

The Munday family, ca. 1935.

challenges. In 1938 Edith took on her first Brownie pack as a Tawny Owl, and in 1942 became captain of the 2nd B.C. Lone Guides Company. Guiding would be a mainstay in her life, as it had been for her mother.

The summer she was 16, in 1937, marked Edith's debut on the climbing team. That year, the Mundays undertook the longest ocean trip yet in their homemade boat, Edidonphyl. They travelled for 10 days up the coast—a distance of 600 kilometres—from Vancouver to Bella Coola. Overland, they searched for a great peak that had shone out to them while they were on Silverthrone a year earlier. Together with Henry Hall, the three Mundays hiked from Bella Coola through some of the most magnificent country they had yet seen, and they found and made a first ascent of the mountain they named Stupendous (2,682 metres). Phyl was so proud of Edith—the way she paced herself and handled the ever-changing obstacles of the route. Edith's fortitude was a natural inheritance from her gifted parents. The Mundays spent some time at Stuie Lodge, built by Tommy Walker, a professional guide and outfitter. During their stay, the Governor General of Canada, John Buchan, Baron Tweedsmuir, visited. As Walker was then unmarried, he asked Phyl to stand in as the hostess for a formal reception at the lodge, which she did, somehow managing to find a dress suitable for the occasion!

In 1938 Edith persuaded her parents to incorporate some horseback riding time into their annual climbing trip. Edith wanted to go back to the Bella Coola area, as she had enjoyed herself immensely the previous year. In May 1938 Tweedsmuir Park (an enormous recreational reserve) was officially created, and Stuie Lodge, now renamed Tweedsmuir Lodge, was no longer a fishing resort. Phyl and Edith, along with about 10 female companions (including some of Phyl's long-time Guiding friends, such as Amy Leigh), rode from Bella Coola into the park, taking several days to camp, hike and explore along the way. They met up with Don at the end of the ride. From there, the Mundays, Henry Hall and others tackled some of the minor summits to the north of Mount Saugstad.

In 1944 Edith married. She was 23 years old, and her husband, Flight Lieutenant R. Gallon, was soon overseas. Edith moved to the United Kingdom, where she lived for many years until returning to B.C. in the early 1970s. She was an enthusiastic traveller, eventually owning her own travel agency, and like her parents, she loved the outdoors, camping and nature photography.

The Munday party on *Chelosin*, heading to Bute Inlet, 1926. Left to right: Johnny Johnson, Athol Agur, Tom Ingram, Bert Munday, Phyl and Don Munday.

A week of back-breaking relays moved the supplies up the river. They followed historical maps—the only ones available—retracing the steps of Alfred Waddington and his survey crew some 60 years earlier and Canadian Pacific Railway surveys from 1872 and 1875. It was a desperate attempt to move up and inland before the spring freshet entirely overruled river travel, for the Homathko was swelled by a number of glacier-fed creeks. Whitemantle was the first and Scar followed shortly after. Each creek was crossed with great difficulty compounded by the engorged conditions. They felled trees to cross, and skidded cedar logs out of the woods to brace their crossings. Thirteen days later they "had traveled about 30 miles from Bute Inlet by the windings of the river, and estimated we had averaged a distance of 100 miles per person—three loads relayed one mile means covering five miles of ground." Don noted: "At no time had the woman in the party carried the lightest load."[10]

"Getting up to timber-line is usually hard work in valleys having the coast type of vegetation." With this opening sentence, Don neatly reduces the drama, danger and frustration of their Homathko River bushwhacking, an activity so exhausting yet so essential to their attempts to penetrate from the ocean. It was a necessary phase; alternative transportation did not exist. There were no roads, no railways, no passable trails; access via plane or helicopter was still in the future. They worked their way up Coola Creek, finding a good site for a camp at about 135 metres above sea level. Astonishingly, they met the snout of the Waddington Glacier not far from camp at an elevation of only 470 metres.

Heavy loads of ice-climbing equipment, clothing, food and shelter now had to be carried up the glacier; they cached a minimum of food and non-essentials near the camp for their return. They moved up the glacier as it curved west and northward, climbing out of the confining valleys and into the open expanse of glacier, icefalls and vistas. The Whitemantle Range hung high in the clouds south across Scar Creek. They worked their way up the glacier, gaining in altitude, moving through the shining new world of ice, snow, whiteness and monumental summits. Swirling mists obscured their long-distance vistas, but three times, in the direction of the head of Waddington Glacier, they thought they glimpsed a shining peak higher than all the others. They named the saddle at the head of the glacier Mystery Pass, not just because of the uncertainty that lay there, but because the inclement weather conditions obscured their vision of what

Crossing Scar Creek going in to Waddington, 1926. Don holds the rope tight for Phyl.

"Big glacier creeks were the big problem coming in off the snowfield, and they were big creeks. You could hear them roaring as you were coming to them in the valley, and you knew very well that you were going to have problems. We tried to wade a couple of them, roped together, and it was hopeless. The speed of the water was simply turning the rocks over under your feet ... [On Scar Creek] there was one old tree practically across, a dead one, and we finally managed to lug a couple of others across it, and Don fastened a climbing rope on a tree and held it as a guide-line. Coming over a thing like that with the force of the water jiggling the logs ... your bridge was not only just swaying, but it was jiggling as well, with the speed of the water. When you come over that with about 60 pounds on your back, you're not as agile as you would be on the flat. Anyway, we eventually got all our loads over, and went on to the next creek, and then we finally went up a valley beyond Scar Creek ..."
PHYLLIS MUNDAY TAPED INTERVIEW, 1973, BC ARCHIVES.

Ice-Flooded Valleys on the Way to "Mystery Mountain." Coast Range, B.C. Photo Don Munday

lay ahead. They could not see and the powdery metre-deep snow challenged progress. "We wandered not too uncertainly among big snow domes and looming rock towers; always thigh-deep in snow, and from which one often must work the legs free, and baffled by the blinding obscurity of bright cloud." [11] Packing snowshoes or skis through the Homathko Valley had not seemed practical, but how much easier the conditions on the snowfield would have been with these pieces of equipment.

Phyl suffered from snowblindness, an incredibly painful condition generally caused by ultraviolet light in bright or glaring conditions. The weird, bright, foggy mist and white snow were the cause. Cold wet teabags placed over her eyelids eased the piercing ache somewhat. But the pain came from light, any light, even the light experienced with closed eyes. There was nothing to do but endure it. Phyl, of course, soldiered on, carrying her own pack; Tom Ingram led her by the hand. Finally they rested for two days, Phyl waited for her condition to improve, and Bert Munday rested a pulled leg muscle. The others explored, confirming the best route forward to their mountain, which was still not clearly visible. A thorough check of their food revealed barely enough for four more days. There was no hesitation; they had come this far and would not turn back until they had made one last attempt to reach Mystery Mountain. Emerging on the upper part of what they named Bert Glacier, they made their way slowly near "a splendid double-topped mountain," now named Agur Mountain, but conditions did not warrant an ascent.

Don climbed minor peaks and took panoramic photographs, carefully noting direction and details in his notebook. This would all form the basis for mapping. He was luckily able to capture images in and around the clouds. Finally, "through Mystery Pass peered unmistakably the slender final spire of Mystery Mountain." [12] It was enough to spur a last effort, and they were off.

"Billows of a sea of ice."
Franklin Glacier between elevation of 4500 and 5500 feet, on way to "Mystery Mountain," Coast Range, B.C.   Photo A.R. Munday.

On June 23 they broke camp, Ingram and Johnny leaving at 8:00 p.m. in order to break trail to the top of the icefall of Bert Glacier, almost a kilometre above camp. The rest followed, reaching Bert Pass at 12:50 a.m., which they measured at almost 3,000 metres in altitude. They descended into the upper valley of the Waddington Glacier, which continued northward to Mystery Pass. Far to the east, across the Homathko valley, they discerned part of a great Homathko field of ice or snow. Such a great icefield had never been guessed at by others. Don postulated that it might cover 300 square miles.[13] Again, photographs were taken and notations made. Finally, they "surmounted the 9,500-foot pass at 5:15 a.m. An involved network of glaciers below linked the lesser mountains with the mighty bulk of 'Mystery Mountain' which at last stood revealed from base to crest—an upstanding symmetrical form culminating in a great slender tower tipped with snowy plumes."[14]

They were unsuccessful in completing an approach to the base of the mountain, although they travelled a long way toward it, always diverted by avalanches (which resounded in very close proximity) or insecure snow bridges or far-reaching crevasses. The Munday party named many of the peaks and glaciers as they passed by and took photographs and measurements, enabling their mapping. Spearmen Peak, Arabesque Peaks, Mounts Combatant, Tiedemann, Asperity and Serra—all seemed to exceed the heights of most Rocky Mountain peaks.

One avalanche rumbled too close by, literally trickling out mere metres away from them. It was time to turn around, time to return to the coast. They had been gone five weeks. They had done all they could on this first expedition and had accomplished much in the way of understanding the frozen highways on which they must travel to reach Mystery Mountain. For them it was truly a fabulous discovery of a vast country, filled with high peaks and enough climbing to last them for years to come.

Endless Explorations, or A Mountaineer's Playground

The year 1927 began with sadness when in February their good friend Athol Agur died in an avalanche on Grouse Mountain. Johnny Johnson, who was with him, narrowly escaped the same fate; only a tough little cypress branch that caught and hooked his boot saved him. Despite extensive searches, Agur's body—carried down and buried in the avalanche—was not found for several months, until midsummer.

Neither Johnson nor Don's brother, Bert, was able to commit to climbing with Don and Phyl, so they went alone, leaving Vancouver on the SS *Venture* on May 30, headed for Glendale Cannery, near the head of Knight Inlet. The plan this season was to tackle Mystery Mountain from Knight rather than Bute Inlet in the hopes of finding easier and closer access. They had brought on board their rowboat with its gas motor, and from the cannery they headed toward Kwalate Point and the river of the same name. An American couple had settled there, not far from the site of a First Nations village that had long ago been obliterated by a tidal wave. The Stantons were to provide advice, friendship and general assistance over the next few years.

Having travelled the length of the inlet, Phyl and Don ascended the Klinaklini River on June 4, veering off into a channel that allowed them to beach their boat on a gravel bar. Next came bushwhacking up the steep ridge above the river to see how the land lay. They were rewarded for their efforts. "Mystery [now named Franklin] Glacier curved back impressively before us for about 18 miles, a dim, white, secretive aisle between dim, white ridges merging into a ceiling of pallid cloud. But the ice lay perhaps 3,000 feet below us; plainly the Franklin River valley offered the logical approach to the glacier. We could not identify with any assurance the bases of the hidden mountains at the head of the glacier, as those seen a year before."[15] So back they went to Knight Inlet, east around Dutchman Head, and to the mouth of the turbulent Franklin River.

Wind, deluging rain and extreme tides contributed to the navigational complexities. This was no easy entrance, but by June 10 they were camped on a sandbar more than 10 kilometres up from the inlet. It was less than an hour's tramp to the glacier, which descended to a surprisingly low 200 metres above sea level. At this level it was about a kilometre wide and tortuous to travel. Confident that this glacier would be their entry into the hinterland and the high mountains, Don and Phyl backtracked to the

Stantons, and then back to the *Venture* and then returned to Vancouver, their reconnaissance successful. They came back in mid-July accompanied by Phyl's sister, Betty McCallum. This would prove to be a less than wise choice, for although Don's brother had worked out well as a companion, Betty was not endowed with quite the same resolve. Previously a member of the BCMC, Betty was more of a weekend climber, not used to the endurance required for high mountain travel and great distances. On this trip she tried her best, but the conditions were beyond her capabilities or her inclinations. She soon knew it.

By July 26 they were camped in the valley below the Franklin Glacier. They named it "Last Valley Camp." They spent the next few days cutting trail across the moraine ridges and getting supplies up to the edge of the ice. Conditions proved perilous as the moraine constantly shifted, undermined by the river, making footholds unstable. Two days later they established "Goat Camp" at about 540 metres. From here the view inspired them: "far up the vista of shadowy valley [Mystery Mountain] glowed alone in evening splendour with purple rock and crimson snow—like a torch to inspire our long course up the glacier."[16]

Phyl and Don relayed supplies up onto the Franklin Glacier. "Phyl carried a net weight—exclusive of containers and packboard—of 70 pounds," related Don in his matter-of-fact account.[17] They pushed on, but the going was tough and slow, the glacier broken by icefalls, ridges, crevasses and troughs between. The temptation was to go around, and travel not on the glacier but on the moraine. They brought the supplies

Phyl on moraine of Franklin Glacier with her 70-pound pack, 1927.

MYSTERY MOUNTAIN YEARS | 173

In January 1928, at the suggestion of A.O. Wheeler, Don wrote to the Royal Geographical Society, London, to propose that he write a paper on the subject of exploration in the Coast Range in the vicinity of Mystery Mountain. The secretary wrote back expressing interest in the article and urging Don to join the RGS. "In the hope that your great interest in geography and survey may lead you to think of joining this Society I send you the necessary papers." * Before the end of the month, Don had followed this suggestion; the two people who supported his application were writer-naturalist Julia Henshaw and A.A. McCoubrey (then president of the ACC). By the time he returned from Waddington in August, a letter of acceptance was waiting for him.

Fellowship in the RGS was awarded to those involved in geographical endeavours, who had a proven record of advancing geographical knowledge or who had brought geographical issues to a wider audience. Don's research, his authoritative articles in the Canadian Alpine Journal *and, of course, his own explorations contributed to his acceptance. Fellowship entitled Don to place the initials FRGS after his name, which lent an air of legitimacy to his pursuits and to his authorship.*

* Royal Geographical Society Archives, London.

up near a lovely waterfall surrounded by heather, lupines and other alpine flowers. On August 2, with the supplies all relayed to this campsite over the eastern margin of the glacier, they agreed to a few days of rest and exploration. They mounted a ridge they named Marvel behind the camp, and from this altitude they determined that the Franklin Glacier was joined higher up by another, which they named Corridor Glacier. This arced back toward Bute Inlet and the Ice Valley they had travelled the previous year. Mystery Mountain dominated the panorama. At this proximity it was "revealed as less simple and compact in structure than we had supposed, but at this distance some details quite important to us remained unsuggested."[18] This undoubtedly referred to the complicated structure of the mountain, with its succession of icy gullies and rock ribs, and to the compact but loose structure of the rock, which would soon prove to be difficult and insecure for climbing. The mountain was composed of a succession of western sub-summits clearly visible along the long ridge.

The panorama also told them that there were no trees between Mystery Mountain and where they stood. As Don later recounted: "The mountain stands in an area of 400 square miles devoid of even scrub timber, making it impossible to establish a base camp within striking distance of the mountain."[19] This meant revising considerably the supplies they would bring. The choice was either to carry large quantities of wood for fires to cook their food or to pack mainly cooked foods and a smaller amount of wood. They elected to bring a small bundle of dead branches and mostly cooked foods as they headed to the mountain.

Moving forward, they scrambled up the moraine slopes to gain a rocky point on the west side of the Franklin Glacier. This spot they named Icefall Point. Here they camped and cached their food before continuing. They crossed another glacier, naming it Dais, after which came Regal Glacier. From Regal Glacier they aimed for the southwest flank of Waddington. "Icy snow on this shadowed slope gave good footing for our crampons ... Finding a course through the labyrinth of crevasses proved engrossing,"[20] wrote Don in his understated style. But soon they "gained the crumbling rocks" some 160 metres below the crest of a ridge of magnificent peaks. Here they took off the crampons and climbed to 3,660 metres. Still ahead Epaulette Glacier shone on the westerly shoulder of their mountain. They bivouacked back on a spur of Mount Cavalier that night, but after breakfast, with both food and wood consumed, they headed back to Icefall Point and the food cache.

Two more exploratory trips provided further information. What would be the route to the summit of their Mystery Mountain? Up Corridor Glacier they advanced to the Buckler Glacier, thinking that a way might be made through to the easterly slopes via Spearmen Peak. "Buckler Glacier's icefall formed a splendid spectacle. But a route through was intricate ... Hundred-foot ice-cliffs, cleanly sliced, defended the upper terrace under the rock walls, unless we risked passage under the bulging front of a still higher glacier."[21] That glacier had recently loosed an avalanche.

Working their way toward the southeast ridge, "the cliffs of Spearmen Peak proved uncompromising. Phyl bruised an arm severely by thrusting it out to deflect a rock Betty could not dodge. Not far above this a rock hit Phyl squarely, and blood welled at once through the scarf she wore round her head. Bandaging was out of the question where we were, but she insisted on going on."[22] Soon they lost the light and were forced to retreat, returning to their bivouac at 3:45 a.m. They had been gone over 24 hours.

The unpredictable but frequent rock falls complicated the climbing. Don's account of the incident conveys little drama, but a later interview with Phyllis reveals just how precarious the situation actually was. She described the hand holds—mere finger holds, actually—just cracks and not much more. And then:

A rock came from somewhere up above, goodness knows where, and managed to use my head for a target. For a minute I thought I was going to black out and then I realized that Don and I were on this [ledge]. My sister was further back ... and was all right but Don and I were right on this face. And if I fell, I'd pull him off. All of a sudden, luckily, it struck me: if I fall, I'll pull Don off. I can't fall. It's amazing, I didn't fall. I just hung on with these four little fingers on each hand until I'd sort of got the dizziness over.

Don, of course, there wasn't very much he could do either because he was just a little higher than I was but not above me so that he could hold. You see, a fall when you are going across a face, you haven't got the same chance of belaying like you have when you are one above the other. But all went luckily. We had to come down, of course, because blood was beginning to ooze all over the place.

We got down further and there was a sort of sloping rock with a great big lovely puddle of water in it and I could lie there and my sister sloshed off the blood. But it was no real damage because a scalp bleeds very heavily usually if it's damaged. And it probably looked a lot worse than it really was but it was uncomfortable at the time.[23]

The next plan was to try the opposite side of the mountain, the northwest ridge from Fury Gap. Reaching Fury Gap (2,900 metres), they climbed beyond it, westward to the base of Mount Chris Spencer in order to study Mystery Mountain from this angle. "Mystery Mountain is composed of about twenty peaks over 10,500 feet, and for a length of about five miles nowhere drops below that elevation; the northerly face carries an irregular summit ice-cap."[24] It was daunting. No sightline showed a clear route. One thing *was* clear: complicated glacier and ridge travel would get them closer.

Early the following morning they set off to attempt the northwest ridge. They mounted easy but slippery lichen-covered rocks, then traversed snow along the Scimitar Glacier flank, with the Tiedemann Group in the distance on one side and Mystery Mountain on the other. At 6 p.m. they were at about 4,235 metres and 166 metres above them was Mystery Mountain. Don described the moment: "A slender white fang leaned feebly lighted against a starry sky. We struggled on to its base ... We certainly could not cut steps ... up that tower and get down before dark. The waning moon aided little in such weather. Rising wind already blurred the downward guidance of our footsteps." It became a race against the weather. Before they made it back to camp, their carbide lamp failed completely. "We stumbled, tumbled and mumbled for about a quarter of an hour in the bellowing gloom ... The night burst into crashing flame. Rain as though forced from a giant nozzle—snow—then hail, flailed us, while the wind literally pinned us against the rocks during its fiercest gusts. The stabbing brilliance of lightning, the pitilessly swift intermittence, the fierce glare flung back from snow-whitened rocks, combined to make vision almost agony. Our instinct still was to struggle downward."[25] Years later Phyl recalled:

> It's really wild when it's like that, and [there are] all these tongues of fire on the rocks and tongues of fire on our ice axes, buzzing. Just like a blowtorch almost, with sparks of fire coming off the tip of my ice axe. We couldn't throw them away because we needed our ice axes to cross the glaciers. When we got to Fury Gap we picked up our frozen tarp and all the things that we'd left there—film boxes and that sort of thing, and food and a Primus stove, and we stuffed them into our packs. Then we went down the slope onto some shelves of rock—wet, of course, and cold as the dickens—put a tarp on these rocks, and we three sat on them and then just pulled the tarps over our heads, like a lean-to, and we stayed there for the rest of the storm, until it was light enough to come down the glacier."[26]

That was just about it for Betty. She had had enough and, much to Phyl and Don's dismay, insisted on being taken back to the steamer. The Mundays escorted her to the cannery at the mouth of Knight Inlet, where she caught the steamer and returned home. Phyl and Don painfully retraced their route back up to Franklin Glacier and spent the remaining time in further explorations. It was unfortunate that the weather had turned just as they had been so near the base of the tower. Back in the area on their own, they reassessed the route, planning always for the next season.

On their way out, as they neared Knight Inlet, they fortuitously met up with a provincial surveying party, led by J.T. Underhill, returning from the Klinaklini Glacier. Spurred on by Don's correspondence and his hand-drawn maps, the surveyor general had authorized Underhill to authenticate Don's amateur mapmaking. The party had just completed a triangulation of the mountains, verifying Don's own measurements of Mystery Mountain as accurate to within less than 50 metres. Now officially charted, its elevation was documented at 4,019 metres. It confirmed that

Mystery Mountain was the highest mountain wholly in British Columbia—higher than Mount Robson, which until this survey had been thought to be the highest peak.

That winter, the Canadian Geographic Names Board (after a waffle or two) named the mountain Waddington in recognition of one of the first white men to penetrate Bute Inlet. He led an ill-fated survey for an intended wagon road in 1862. This name was not a choice favoured by the public, who had been caught up in the Mundays' annual trips, following newspaper accounts and Don's published articles in various journals. They much preferred the name Mystery Mountain.

During winter both Don and Phyl presented public lectures promoting the Waddington area and educating the public about this new, hitherto unused recreational area. But their talks were tempered with realism and with a respect for the terrain, weather conditions and technical climbing abilities required to climb in its world. Don wrote. "All probable routes to the summit of Mystery Mountain are guarded by hanging glaciers, icefalls or rock towers ranging from gendarmes to individual mountains in size. The rock is a hard schistose formation breaking into smooth slabs and overhanging faces. The danger from falling rocks was extreme; one rock-fall, amounting to thousands of tons, was seen after the party had decided further advance in that direction was too dangerous." He also went on to say that the route from Fury Gap and over three of the peaks in the formidable west ridge "is the only practicable route, is somewhat intricate, never obvious ... It involves passing under impending ice cliffs of the summit ridge. Frequent losses of elevation cost valuable time ... Armed now with a thorough knowledge of the difficult approaches to the mountain, we feel our 1928 attempt will be successful." [27]

Bert Munday accompanied his brother and sister-in-law on this 1928 expedition. As Don predicted, it was successful, at least in part; they attained the northwest peak, although the main summit tower eluded them. Their push to the top was risky, but a risk they took knowingly. The weather had been extremely poor, with persistent rain and almost incessant wind. All three were frustrated and the enforced idleness challenged their patience. On the morning of July 8, just past 1:00 a.m., wind raged in Fury Gap, but they set out anyway, following their route of the previous year. This day would prove to be the only good climbing day of the entire expedition. Twice they stopped for nourishment and rest; it was to be a long push under a clear sky full of stars.

Top: Part of the 25-kilometre-long Scimitar Glacier from Fury Gap, 1928. Bottom: Don and Bert Munday in camp, Saffron Creek, 1928.

They made their way past the twin Men-at-Arms Peaks, cutting steps up Bodyguard Peak, then on to the high shoulder of Councillor Peak, then along the edge of Angel Glacier. At nearly 6:00 p.m., after traversing four subsidiary peaks, they approached the base of the final peak. "Coarsely granular snow was fairly hard yet lacked cohesion," Don wrote. "I had to strip off the snow and cut steps in blue ice, and also cut clearance for the legs to above the knee. It was a place where no member of the party must slip. A steeper stretch of about 12 feet nearly proved insurmountable. I had to support myself with one hand while cutting with the other." The last 130 metres took over an hour. And then, suddenly, they were at the top: "a short knife-edge between two horn-like, icy cornices flaring up and out. The three of them could barely "straddle the ridge." [28]

But the excitement was short-lived. Phyl's comment summed it up. "It was such satisfaction [getting to the top] but we were absolutely aghast." They were not on the summit of Waddington as they had thought, but on an adjacent peak toward the northwest. The highest spire—mere metres from their reach—towered upwards another 60 metres. They were so close to the summit that they could differentiate the striation on it. "The rocks were not all just plain grey; they were different colours. Most people don't really notice the colours but our eyes were always open for any changes of any sort. We could see the main tower was a difficult climb." [29] They were exhausted. After a brief 15 minutes "on that glorious crest," they turned down. It was a long all-night trek back to Fury Gap. They arrived about 2:00 a.m.

It would be another two years before they next returned. The unexpected death of Phyl's mother in early 1929 may have put a damper on any inclination to climb. Both Phyl and Don's outdoor activities were unusually restrained for the entire year. When they did return, in 1930, they brought skis with them and Don's special concoction of wax (a pine tar mixture). They also had a new objective. Waddington had been their focus previously but this would be their year to branch out to the surrounding mountains and bag peaks. Don and Phyl had honed their skiing abilities over the previous two winters. Combining skiing and mountaineering showed that the Mundays were leaders, for ski-mountaineering was in its infancy. Don and Phyl felt they had something to prove, for many mountain climbers felt "that skiing is fun, but really not a very practical way of getting up or down mountains." [30] But for Don and Phyl skiing increased their mobility, affording them the opportunity to go greater distances. They were very interested in expanding what was possible in terms of winter mountaineering. On

View from the summit of the northwest peak of Waddington, 1928.

the coast the frequency and extent of mountain activities in winter was very modest in comparison to that of the regular climbing season (late spring through autumn), but ski-mountaineering changed all that.

In the Coast Mountains, including those on the North Shore of Vancouver, snow often lies on the ground from the beginning of November to the middle of June, some areas reaching maximum depths of five to eight metres. Snowshoes make for slow going, and crampons perform well on slick glacier ice but not in snow. For climbers on a long trek the most beneficial equipment might very well be skis, which allow greater distances to be covered in less time, and with much less physical effort. Skis would allow even swifter downhill progress than the time-honoured glissading techniques practised by mountaineers on foot.

On the west coast in 1930, skiing's popularity was in its infancy, but in 1931 the Vancouver Section of the Alpine Club of Canada officially opened a ski hut—constructed entirely by members' volunteer labour and donated lumber and other building materials—on Mount Seymour. The club focused on offering ski instruction for mountaineers. It was a training ground to develop the skill that could later be applied in the ascent of truly alpine peaks. The Mundays knew the potential.

"Three seasons in the Mt. Waddington section of the Coast Range fully convinced us that skis were logical equipment to overcome the obstacles imposed by the immense snowfields. Faster traveling meant extending one's effective climbing range, thereby making it possible to take advantage of brief spells of favorable weather where unsettled weather naturally resulted from seawinds sweeping up ... across the glacial mantle of the range."[31]

In early July, after the assistance of their trapper friend Stanton who ferried them and their supplies in his boat to the head of Knight Inlet, Don and Phyl reached Last Valley Camp. A couple of days later they were at their base camp at Icefall Point on the edge of Whitetip Glacier. Here they had carefully cached unused tins of food two years ago. Now they uncovered their stash. Having adequate food on these trips was always a balancing act. All supplies had to be relayed such a great distance over such tough geography. Bringing too much could present logistical problems, and bringing too little of course could make the difference between a successful expedition and a life and death situation. So having extra food without the effort and packing was a nice bit of security.

The mixed weather was not encouraging but on July 17 they ventured out late in the afternoon to try out their skis. They got to the top of Mount Redbreast (2,049 metres) behind camp, the lowest mountain in the district. It was a nice warm-up for the remainder of the week. The following day, they ventured along the Franklin and Whitetip glaciers and skied and climbed Shelf Mountain (2,529 metres). Next they carried their skis across the Franklin Glacier to Dauntless Glacier, until they found enough snow for continuous skiing.

They climbed over loose, lichen-covered rock slabs to reach the arête of the eastern peak of Mount Dauntless. "Phyl grasped the lip of the final yellow slab and hauled herself up high enough to peer over. 'The west peak is about 8 feet higher,' she announced."[32] Down they went, then worked their way up again, this time on the west arête, summiting just after

6:00 p.m.[33] From this vantage Don's aneroid barometer recorded the elevation. They could see that several peaks in the Whitemantle Range were higher so they were not satisfied. Clearly they were on a quest. "There will always be mountains to climb, but not always mountains for original exploration, and these two challenging tasks must command close views into the western section of the Whitemantle Range," wrote Don in *The Unknown Mountain*, his account of the years spent in the Waddington area.

They were on and off skis every day, depending upon the conditions. The icy crevasses and lumpy, pitted, wind-frozen sections of the glaciers forced them off the skis and onto their feet; but skis gave them a huge advantage by allowing rapid travel over the softer snowy patches. "Thanks to our skis, the deep, soft snow troubled us not at all (except for turning)."[34]

First Ascent of Mount Munday

The first ascent of Mount Munday (named in their honour by the Geographic Names Board in 1927) was a highlight of their 1930 expedition, principally because poor weather conditions had prevented them from making an attempt in 1928. "Naturally we wanted to make the first ascent," wrote Don. Mount Munday (3,356 metres) is composed of several peaks, all within 20 metres or so in elevation. It was estimated to be three days on foot from their base camp near Icefall Point. The logistics of carrying food, fuel and equipment had undoubtedly been discussed during the previous winter, but skiing made this expedition doable. Of course, their plans did not unfold smoothly; they had troubles with the ski wax and lost time in stopping to apply more wax. It was all a lesson in experimentation and Don resolved to fix that problem for the next time.

Don described the ascent and descent of Mount Munday:

On wind-compacted snow, without our skis, we mounted the north face of the middle peak, crossed an icy bergschrund, and gained the short summit ridge of snow and rock. The north peak, which is so splendid from Spearmen Col, was definitely below us, the east peak a little higher; the highest of the westerly peaks was the true summit.

Edith Munday (third from right) and her father
(far right) with friends on Mount Seymour, ca. 1930.

We hurried down and across to it ... The dividing notch offered no difficulty other than the thinnest possible fin of new snow between two savage couloirs ... At 5:25 p.m. we swung up on to the narrow summit ... a cold wind whined, sharp as icicles, amid the rocks, and as soon as we reached the snow we raced back to our skis. We gripped them and, still half-numbed, felt like kites about to take to the air as we fought our way down against the blast roaring upward out of the cirque at the head of Waddington Glacier. Spread-eagled, we slid across remnants of the snow bridge at the bergschrund, then on skis enjoyed a run down the still sunny but freezing cirque. Two thousand feet of execrable skiing brought us well down into Ice Valley. Despite skis we sank half-way to the knees in wet, loose snow, with or without a cutting crust." [35]

Close to Icefall Point, they took off their skis and plodded on, arriving at camp after 3 o'clock in the morning, precisely 24 hours from their departure. The trip was a success; both Mundays were enthusiastic about the distances covered and the relative ease of switching from skis to foot when required.

In 1931 they returned to Waddington territory, again with skis. This time they ventured north from Vancouver in a five-metre rowboat fitted with an outboard motor. On board was Edith, whom they left with friends on Read Island before continuing northward. By the third week in July they reached the base camp at Saffron Creek, an hour or two down-glacier from Icefall Point, at the furthest limit of trees. There they set about building a little log cabin, using only a handful of nails, their small axe and a blade from a bucksaw. Their expectations were not grand, the main point being to simplify their routine each year by establishing a permanent shelter and a place to cache supplies that could be used from expedition to expedition. Again, the weather was uncooperative, so they bided their time.

The first workout was a ski ascent of Mount Sockeye (2,737 metres), north of Ice Valley, about mid-distance to Mount Munday. It was a prominent peak that had intrigued them previously. Although they intended to ski, the glacier east of the mountain proved too steep for skis. They had to leave the skis behind and cut steps with their ice axes for most of the 500 metres. The last part leading up to the summit was snow, and would have been excellent for skiing. The note they left to record their ascent states that the visibility en route was "perfect." [36]

The next day of good weather was several days later on August 1 and they set out due west for Mount Jubilee (2,748 metres), which lies between

184

the Klinaklini and Franklin valleys. They travelled down to Confederation Glacier and then—on and off skis—closed in on the mountain. The most important result of their ascent of Jubilee was the information they gleaned from the topography spread out before them from the summit. "Directly across Klinaklini Valley handsome mountains rose to about our height or higher ... The snout of Klinaklini Glacier sprawled ... below in the river's west fork; half in shadow, half a-shimmer, this huge glacier's tributaries mounted to miles of horizon snowfields south of Mt. Silverthrone." [37] Silverthrone had been glimpsed in 1928 from the northwest summit of Waddington, and in 1930 from Mount Munday, and it would be the objective of another expedition, another year. Back to camp, the weather closed in once again, preventing further excursions.

In 1932 they again began their long ocean voyage in their motorized rowboat. This time it was rigged with a removable canvas cover, which kept both the human occupants and the temperamental engine dry. Once again Edith was with them; this time she was to stay with the Stantons while her parents ventured into the mountains to again patiently wait for breaks in the weather.

At their base camp, Phyl had thought to prepare for the possibility of inactive days forced upon them by weather conditions. She had brought embroidery for herself, but she also soon found a task to keep Don occupied. There was a pile of empty tin cans from previous expeditions, and as Don related: "She arranged a collection of old tins for my inspection, suggesting I make stove and stove-pipe for the still-vacant hut built the previous year. I reminded her that kingdoms had been won for the favour of women, but she still preferred the stove—perhaps she felt we already had a mountain kingdom around us. Armed with a can-opener, I went to work, and next day we moved into the hut, where a temperature of 64° F. felt almost tropical." [38]

After 11 days of frustrating rain and inclement climbing conditions, they resolved to make an attempt on Mount Agur, despite the weather. Crossing the Franklin Glacier to the base of Mount Repose, they put on skis in the rain and headed up the Agur Glacier toward the mountain. In the dense fog they lost their way several times and had to retrace their ski tracks and then their steps. Conditions were ripe for avalanches and they exercised great caution, eventually making their way to within 70 metres of the summit. Time was running out and, defeated by the conditions they headed back to camp. Several days later they met up with Edith at the Stantons.

It must have been a frightening experience to be left with strangers in the midst of the wilds, for Edith had not met the Stantons prior to being dropped off. But her stay was not dull, as Don and Phyl found out when they picked her up that August.

> Any adventuring of ours now took second place to the experiences of our eleven-year-old daughter and Mrs. Stanton when they heard a pig attacked by a grizzly bear within a few hundred yards of the house. Armed only with four-gallon kerosene cans and sticks to beat the cans with, Edith and Mrs. Stanton rushed to the edge of the dense thicket in which the gallant boar battled for its life. There for an hour woman and child created the utmost din of which they were capable, hoping to discourage the bear and encourage the boar. It sounded like a hopelessly one-sided battle, but the boar must have been able to slip back and forth through the stout barricades of willows faster than the bear. The pig escaped at last ...[39]

This was by far the most unsuccessful of all their trips, and as such was the subject of much discussion over the winter months. Many weeks were spent in travelling up the coast and relaying supplies from sea level to the glaciers, severely limiting their actual time in the mountains. A chance meeting the following spring led to new opportunities and a change in focus.

Collaboration: The Hall Partnership

A chance meeting on a Vancouver street changed the direction of Don and Phyl's exploration in the Waddington area in important ways. The onerous yearly task of travelling by sea to get as close as possible to the mountains and then laboriously relaying their supplies to the alpine was the price they paid to access the area. It required a lot of time, planning and physical stamina. They had considered alternate routes overland, particularly as surveyor R.P. Bishop in 1922 had been the first to spot their "Mystery Mountain" and had done so inland from near Chilko Lake. Perhaps it was possible that a practical overland route could be found.

But Don and Phyl had learned to be independent. On the last few expeditions it had been just the two of them, and they had worked out a routine. They knew the way in and they knew the way out. Venturing from this pattern and trying an overland route would necessitate a larger party and more complicated logistics, and there were no guarantees. With their very limited resources—and budget—their annual pilgrimages worked.

On Saturday, June 24, 1933, Don bumped into American climber Henry S. Hall Jr. on a downtown street. Both had been at several ACC camps together, and both wrote and published accounts of their various expeditions—Hall in the American Alpine Club's publication, and Don for the Canadian Alpine Club. Both were active members, participating on committees within their respective national clubs. Hall had a great deal of climbing experience in the Rockies and, as the Mundays would soon find out, also in the Coast Range. Hall had been exploring the area for the previous three years, but he had entered from the interior rather than by the ocean.

Hall recorded: "I encountered Mr. W.A.D. Munday on the street entirely by chance. We talked Coast Range, with the quite unforeseen but happy result that he and Mrs. Munday, who were arranging to leave in a few days for Knight Inlet, decided at my suggestion to accompany us instead, and were ready to do so less than forty-eight hours later when we met on the dock for the Squamish boat ..."[40] Don's version reads: "Henry's exciting invitation on a Saturday afternoon—with banks closed—posed some problems for Phyl and me to solve in order to sail from Vancouver at 9 a.m. Monday for Squamish at the head of Howe Sound."[41] But sail they did, by steamer up to Squamish, where they boarded the Pacific Grand Eastern (PGE) railway. It carried them through the Coast Mountains, through the Pemberton Valley to Lillooet and then on to Williams Lake, arriving the next morning on June 27.

Hall was a different breed of climber—affluent and influential. He was a man of generous nature and wide interests (and skills) in climbing ventures. He had been a substantial financial backer for the 1925 joint Alpine Club of Canada and American Alpine Club expedition to Mount Logan, second-highest mountain on the North American continent; and he had little in the way of financial or time restrictions when it came to organizing his own climbing. The opportunity to be part of Hall's fully funded expedition was something the Mundays could not pass up.

Hall's expedition members included not only the last-minute additions of Don and Phyl, but the legendary Swiss climbing guide Hans Fuhrer, who was hired by Hall; New York businessman Alfred E. Roovers; and publisher Donald W. Brown, "enticed by stories of new worlds to conquer."

The Hall party, 1933. Rear (left to right): Pete McCormack, Alfred Roovers, Don, Phyl, Henry Hall, Valleau the cook. Front: Unknown, Don Brown, Hans Fuhrer.

From Williams Lake these six rode in the back of a truck: "Cushioned seats placed on top of the load allowed us an all-round view." They travelled some 240 kilometres across the great grassland of the Chilcotin Plateau and then descended to Tatla Lake. Several miles later, near where the Homathko River leaves the plain and enters the mountains, they linked up with three packers hired by Hall, along with 17 pack horses. This was to be a very different sort of expedition for the Mundays.[42]

"Not being a real rider," Phyl wrote:

> I asked our packer, Pete McCormick, timidly, to be sure I had a good quiet horse. I did not fancy any antics whereby I might be dumped in a swamp, or worse ... We rode down river channels, crashed through flooded thickets, floundered through swamps, until we camped on a dun-like ridge in willow thickets. In chill weather next morning we continued through swamps to old sand dunes, and plunged into deep water where our horses swam to a submerged sandbar which we crossed to the west side of the valley. It was a queer sensation sitting on my horse with the waves splashing over my saddle. After 20 minutes of this, we were mighty glad to get off and walk a while, to warm up. Then came still more deep channels, swamps, down timber, and

coarse rock slides. Pack horses fell, and had to be rescued. There were tense moments ... Next morning we came to the most critical ford of all, the now swollen Homathko River.[43]

After encounters with bears, frightened horses and many more "tense moments," the party emerged from the river in the rain, to camp in a mountain meadow opposite Scimitar Valley. Far to the west, up the valley, lay their objective, Mount Combatant (3,756 metres). The next camp they established—in a cottonwood grove—would be their base camp, less than a kilometre from the ice front of the Scimitar Glacier, at about 1,700 metres in elevation. Phyl's account of the next leg of their journey provides a nice insight into not only how different this trip was for her and Don, but the ingenuity required to handle some very unusual moments.

> We spent a short time exploring for a suitable route up the glacier for the horses, as Pete was determined to be the first to take his horse to the head of the glacier. Personally, I had no objection to having a horse carry my pack. I was getting thoroughly spoiled on this trip. Pete did all the cooking, and the horses all the packing; both of which I always did on our other trips to the mountains.
>
> We had trouble forcing the horses across Scimitar Creek to a favourable place to start up the steep ice tongue. Though not sharp shod, they did well on the ice. But there was one really difficult place, a narrow shelf beside a crevasse. Mountaineering text books tell nothing of the technique of cutting out steps for horses. On the lower side, the ice fell sharply, about 60 feet to a wide water-filled crevasse.
>
> We cut big steps for the horses up the steep ice, which Nigger, a fine young horse, refused to use. Poor thing, he was frightened by their whiteness. The next thing we knew, he slipped, and landed upside-down on a shelf inside the large crevasse. While Pete and Hans took off Nigger's pack, and got him right end up, I cut steps down another crevasse to recover Hans' ice axe, which had fallen in the struggle.
>
> With my husband's hat for a bucket, I gathered material from the moraine, to gravel the nice white steps which Don enlarged, and the poor shivering horse, with bleeding knees, came up quite easily, and was re-loaded. We led each horse up the steps and on up the glacier and very quickly they learned to follow precisely up the 10 miles of this curving corridor.[44]

On July 14 the try for Combatant began, as most climbs do, early in the morning. "We got away in the bright moonlight at 2:45 a.m., mounting the snow and moraine ... Shortly after the start, one of our party had to return to camp, being unwell after Valleau's concoction of mountain goat stew of doubtful quality. We roped up, never dreaming of the number of hours we'd be tied together."

Almost 16 hours later they gained Combatant's narrow summit. It was 7:30 p.m.; the last 800 metres had taken 10 hours to climb. It was far too late to consider a descent until the morning. They bivouacked on a shelf three metres below the peak. It was narrow, and only two of them were able to lie down; the other three, Don, Phyl and Henry Hall, sat with their backs against Hans' legs, feet dangling over the edge. Phyl was lucky. She had "a nick of rock below me, in which to hook the heel of my boot. The coiled rope acted as insulation from the cold rocks. To prevent us from being shoved off, one end was tied around the three of us. There we sat all night on the mountain top, dozing at intervals, and shivering continuously." But still, she continued: "I shall never forget it, and would not swap it for any night in a comfortable bed." Hours later; "stiff and cold, we welcomed daylight, intending to start our descent as soon as it was light enough to travel. Hans brewed some more of his awful unsweetened chocolate, and we did jerks to limber up. Sunrise from this high place was magnificent. It brought warmth and life. The pale colouring faded, and brilliance returned to the sparkling world ... For the next three hours Hans cut steps down the long couloir so steep we had to face inward most of the time, belaying each other carefully to guard against mishap." [45] Arriving at the base of the peak, they rested and slept for a while, activities that proved to be a mistake, as the warm sun softened the snow, making travelling heavy and slow. By the time they reached camp, they had been gone 37 hours.

The following year they reconnected with Henry Hall and Hans Fuhrer. Don had convinced Hall that accessing Waddington from the south side of the mountain presented the best possibilities for success, so they returned to the tried and true route of access from Knight Inlet. They had with them two young men, Philip (Pip) Brock and Ron Munro, to help pack supplies. They made an attempt on Waddington's main tower on August 10, via Dais Glacier, but turned back at about 3,800 metres because of doubtful weather. On August 14 at 3:20 a.m. they set out again, this time for the northwest peak. Above the Dais Glacier they "found a snow couloir leading up to the main ridge and thus joined the Mundays' 1927–28 route from Fury Gap." [46]

190

On the way to high camp. Pack horses crossing the Scimitar and Radiant glaciers, 1933.

The snow was powdery and knee-deep, the slope incredibly steep. Finally, at 2 p.m., they made their final approach. "Hans went up first, saw the rock tower, and burst into a series of exclamations." Then Hall ascended.

> I went up, had a look, and steadied myself on my ice-axe, so unreal and extraordinary is its appearance. The photographs are all disappointing, partly due to foreshortening. This is surely one of the most remarkable culminating points of any mountain range in the world. Our first impression, little altered by an hour's stay on the snow peak, was that the rock tower is next to unclimbable. It is less than one hundred feet higher than the snow peak. The rock itself is not only excessively steep but the most likely routes are protected by overhangs, and by snow formations of uncertain origin … The Mundays said that in six seasons they had not seen these rocks any freer of snow and ice.[47]

A few days later, Don and Phyl ascended a mountain just southwest of Waddington and gazed back at it across the glacier between. Perhaps they made a resolution there, for they named the mountain Finality

The Hall party on Waddington, 1934.

(2,828 metres). Waddington had become their nemesis in some respects. They were the first to document their discovery and to provide detailed and accurate geographic data, including mapping the icefields and surrounding territory. The photographs Don and Phyl took, along with the articles Don wrote for newspapers and mountaineering journals, tantalized other climbers who had now, like Hall and Fuhrer, turned their eyes to this part of the coast. But this attempt in 1934 would be the Mundays' last. Although it must have been extremely frustrating to have spent eight years on the quest, the mountain would not be conquered by them. Despite the uncertainties of weather and the mix of climbing companions, they had reached the northwest peak twice but the technical difficulties presented by Waddington itself may have been beyond them. They prided themselves on not relying on climber's aids such as pitons and that may have put the summit beyond their grasp.[48] The summit of Waddington would elude the Mundays; others would make that final ascent.

Years later a climber asked Phyl why they kept going back to the Waddington territory. She replied: "Why, there isn't any one mountain worth throwing your life away on. Our lives were more important than any mountain. If the day wasn't good, we'd go off and do something else. There is a whole new world out there, hundreds of peaks, hundreds of glaciers, and all of it uncharted. It is all so marvellously exciting. Even though we started out on a quest for our Mystery Mountain, we ended up with a lifetime of options, and a lifetime of adventures. Every time—it doesn't matter whether it's storm or sunshine—it's always worth it."[49]

But by now, their attentions were drawn again—as they had been in 1927—to the unexplored Klinaklini Icefield to the west, with its snowy peaks beyond Mount Bell and Mt. Chris Spencer. Again, exploration by skis proved profitable in decreasing the time required to cover the distances.

Looking south from camp at about 5,000 feet on the east side of the Silverthrone branch of the Klinaklini Glacier, just southwest of Fang Peak, 1936.

The view from Mount Finality presented them with the information they needed to gauge the best options for access. They determined that access to this area would have to be via the Klinaklini River. Expeditions over the next two years all focused on this area.

In 1936 (the year following a frustratingly fruitless trip up the Klinaklini River to find a route in to the glacier), Don and Phyl arranged to rendezvous with Henry Hall on the river at the beginning of August. Hall arranged for two 17-year-olds—William Hinton and Sherret (Sherry) Chase—to pack in with the Mundays and find a way to cross Tumult Creek, the turbulent glacial tributary to the Klinaklini River that had thwarted Don and Phyl the previous year. The Klinaklini Glacier and the great icefield lay beyond this obstacle.

Tumult Creek spread wide and was extremely swift. It was considered "absolutely uncrossable by ordinary means." [50] Tenacity was certainly one of the Mundays' characteristics, and so was ingenuity. This year Don came prepared with a solution to the problem. He brought more than 30 metres of centimetre-wide steel cable and a pulley. The idea was to somehow anchor the wire on opposite shores of the river and then use poles to suspend the wire above the torrent in such a way that they could ferry themselves and their supplies across.

MYSTERY MOUNTAIN YEARS | 193

Don and I left next day with our camp, to climb to the head of Tumult Valley, cross over the glacier which fed this wild creek, and come down on the other side ... We built smoke signals, and next morning the boys came to throw across the light line which we had attached to the cable. They made several tries before I finally caught it by leaping into the edge of the water. The creek was so noisy we could not hear, so all our conversation was done by semaphore. Bill was a scout, and I a Guide, so he read all my messages while Sherry wrote them down in the sand on their higher upper bank.

Finally the cable bridge was anchored on our side to poles we had already brought from high on the moraine above. But there was nothing suitable for a prop, so Don stood on a huge rock just off our shore, holding up the cable on his shoulder while I pulled myself across. It was a tough struggle, especially as the cable was so much higher on one side; I had to jam my arm in the wheel after each pull, to avoid sliding back. The resulting bruise lasted a long time.

Before Don could come over we had to send a good stout pole across, for him to jam in the convenient crack in the big rock. It was always an anxious business crossing, as any mishap would mean being dragged down by the powerful stream. Eventually all personnel, food, and equipment were safely across, and the usual backpacking continued up the long glacier for some 12 miles to our cozy base camp on a heather slope at an elevation of 2,300 feet high on a cliff above the ice ... Next day we left the boys to bring up the cache, while Don and I ... [and] Henry Hall explored further on for a route to Silverthrone, and a possible climbing camp. From high on the slopes above camp, we saw at close range the real magnitude of the Klinaklini Glacier's main ice stream, stretching before us for perhaps 32 miles. The two main branches curved away out of sight westward to splendid peaks on the horizon.[51]

A few days later:

In bright starlight, about 3:30 a.m. ... we set out with skis, for Mount Silverthrone which we had finally located about 8 miles up a branch glacier. The surface was horribly pitted, making either ski-ing or walking tiring. We eventually settled for walking to the pass at the base of the peak, where snow improved enough for skis. These we

On the summit of Silverthrone, 1936.

> wore happily to the base of the last steep pitch immediately below the summit. This last bit was exceedingly steep, so we climbed cautiously one at a time until we forced our way through the slightly overhanging snow wall at the top. Instead of a ponderous snow dome the summit surprised and thrilled us by being a long acute crest of snow, the north face plunging down for 4,000 or 5,000 feet to a branch of an unknown glacier draining westward. We followed cautiously along this narrow crest to a few snowy rocks ... here we built a cairn for the climbing record ... Big billowy clouds had rolled in from the Coast, obscuring the summits of many distant peaks, making mapping difficult. We waited as long as we dared, hoping the clouds would lift from the peaks, that we might see the tremendous sweep of unknown country. Luck was not with us, so reluctantly we left, resolving to return.[52]

A few days later they climbed Silverthrone again in the identical time of 16 hours and found the view much improved. Silverthrone (2,864 metres) was the highest peak for miles around, yet was secondary within the range. What was most impressive was the extent of glaciation revealed to the north, clearly one of the largest ice masses south of Alaska,[53] and the wealth of unexplored mountains. Don and Phyl turned their attentions north to these mountains for the following three seasons.

On the summit ridge, first ascent of Mount Queen Bess, 1942.

Chapter Seven ICEFIELDS AND MOUNTAINS

O NCE THEY TASTED THE FREEDOM and versatility that skis provided in covering distances in the mountains, Don and Phyl were hooked. Many of their mountaineering endeavours for the next decade involved skis and Don regularly wrote up their adventures in the *Canadian Alpine Journal (CAJ)* to promote the sport.

The first article in the *CAJ* on ski-mountaineering appeared in 1930,[1] and several other articles by a variety of climbers were published yearly after then. In 1932 Don wrote in the *Canadian Geographical Journal* of their July 1930 trip over the Whitemantle snowfields, stating that this was "the first time skis had been used to ascend virgin Canadian peaks of truly alpine character."[2] Over the decade, many climbers learned how to ski, but not all were convinced of the merits of combining skiing with climbing. "There are still those who imagine ski-mountaineering to be an inferior form of mountaineering, but an increasing number of climbers are discovering that with requisite skill, good snow and weather, it may be the grandest form of mountaineering," wrote Don in 1937.[3]

But the tide was turning, and the first of what would become annual ski camps was held that same year at Lake O'Hara. Little by little, skiing— not just as an adjunct activity, but as a part of winter climbing—gained ascendancy.

Skiing Garibaldi

In January 1937, Pip Brock, Gilbert Hooley, Don and Phyl spent a wonderful few days in Garibaldi Park on skis. They left the railway at Green Lake and then tramped along the partially frozen Wedge Creek. Skiing was not practical until they neared the end of the first day and camped below Wedge Pass. The following morning they headed for the Spearhead Range. Here the skiing improved, and as Don metaphorically described in a newspaper article: "Life has few thrills to equal ski-ing on a glacier. The

Don, Gilbert Hooley and Pip Brock on skis, Garibaldi, 1937.

quite moderate gradient surprised us with its immoderate speed for an uninterrupted half mile—if champagne has feelings when uncorked, they would match ours during those moments."[4] They succeeded in climbing Wedge Mountain using a new route up one of the rock ribs. It was a satisfying trip, as Brock remarked while on the summit. "Higher than anybody has stood in Garibaldi Park before."[5] It was quite true, for the winter snow gave them a little extra elevation.

Filled with enthusiasm, they resolved to try again. In late April 1937 Don, Phyl and Pip Brock disembarked from the PGE railway at "Mile 34" on the edge of Garibaldi Park. Their departure was later in the year than the Mundays would have wished, but Brock, a university student, had been tied up with examinations and unable to leave a month earlier. They carried two weeks' food, supplies and skis as they followed the 16-kilometre trail through the forest to Cheakamus Lake. They found the lake was only partly frozen and not strong enough to travel across as they had planned. Avalanches fell directly into the lake on one side while the other was rough and rocky. Their goal was to follow the headwaters of the Cheakamus River to reach "snowfields never tracked by skis and glacial peaks never ascended by mountaineers"[6] and to be the first to climb Mount Sir Richard (2,681 metres).

A partially frozen lake was not what they expected, but luckily the ice was thawed along the north shore, allowing a more or less continuous channel. Conveniently, an old raft lay abandoned on the shore. But the next several hours almost stymied their entire trip. "A good raft is a poor craft, and the one we found was a poor raft, barely big enough for two of us and our freight, but too big to push readily through ice which, sometimes eight inches thick (rotted a bit), barred our course in places. Ice blocks impeded paddling, sticky glacial mud or very deep water hindered poling."[7] The first 100 metres took them three hours.

Dogged persistence is perhaps the best characterization of their efforts as the threesome slowly made their way along the length of the lake, towing where possible for the two days it took to reach the mouth of the river feeding into the lake. Here began "obstructed, trail-less mountainside; the valley floor first that was snow-less swamp, then snow-tangled willows."[8] Route-finding while laden with supplies proved to be challenging, requiring a further two days to advance to a camping site at about 3,500 feet. With the "absent-minded flutter of snowflakes" the following day they explored on skis through the canyon which lead abruptly to the lip of the hanging valley of the Sir Richard glacier. Encouraged, they returned to camp, only to be met with slushy snowfalls and rain, increasing the chances of avalanches, making travel dangerous. After waiting it out in camp, the first day of May arrived with blue skies. They advanced up a snow pass only to be met with

gorges draining to the Lillooet River instead of towards Mount Sir Richard. An avalanche started on the north wall and within seconds "the whole face broke loose, a quarter of a mile in width ... when snow-dust settled, warily we set our skis swishing campward."[9] It was a very clear reminder that late spring can be a precarious time to be in the backcountry.

The following day they followed the main river again, descending into the glacier valley. They had not yet seen Sir Richard, but knew that by following the glacier, the view would eventually be theirs. They made their way toward the cirque when they were suddenly overtaken by a gale.

> An odd crosscurrent of wind beat gustily against us so that we struggled toward the cirque's head. Two blue frozen waterfalls hung below a hanging glacier. A glimpse of whitened granite high above the neve rim might be the mountain top.
>
> A practicable ski route led up through broken ice for 2,000 feet. But could so steep a face stand this second day of brilliant sun and warm wind without avalanching? It still gave a margin of safety.
>
> Shining heights of Garibaldi Park, and beyond, came into view. Then, the gale, which had spared us for a time, burst over the north ridge. Unable to progress on skis, we left them flapping wildly though driven mid-length in the snow ... struggling up almost on all fours, I rested every forty steps. Big flakes of blown ice-glaze spiralled brightly over the broad summit. We did not arrive there till 4 p.m. ...[10]

After orienting themselves to the mountains spread beneath them, it was time to return to camp.

> Perhaps if we had our skis on the summit we would have yielded to the alluring unwisdom of descending McBride Glacier, a longer route probably certain to leave us benighted in unknown gorges with snow floors being washed away by sudden river-flood.
>
> Wet snow made descent to the cirque of Sir Richard Glacier less than ideal. We marvelled the sunny slope still refrained from avalanching as we swung back and forth in long tacks. But we rejoiced greatly in skis to make the long return to camp so comparatively

Poling and pulling Pip Brock on raft, Cheakamus Lake, en route to Mount Sir Richard, 1937.

effortless, and, of course, only skis had made the ascent possible under such snow conditions."[11]

It was a long struggle back to camp, for once in the main valley, with night coming on, they found the Cheakamus River in unexpected flood "bursting through the bridging snow and ice by which we had crossed and re-crossed at will." They reached camp at 9:30 p.m. The weather no longer allowed additional climbing. They soon retraced their route to the lake, this time negotiating a heavy thaw. The valley was in a tangle. "Crusty snow, often too patchy for skiing, commonly dropped us through as much as thigh-deep among brush, rocks and logs. Slender logs 50 to 100 feet long across the river were not always walked with complete nonchalance ..." The lake was now ice-free. In a typical Don understatement: "final day to the railway was a bit more exhausting than the first."[12]

Mount Grenville

In the years after their decision on Mount Finality, Don and Phyl continued to explore Waddington territory, focusing on the surrounding mountains and on their mapping. In late July 1941 they wired an invitation to their friend Polly Prescott, with whom they had climbed at several ACC camps. Prescott was in the Rockies for the season, and in fact, was still at the ACC camp (Don and Phyl did not attend that year). Prescott (1903–2004)[13] was a spirited American climber from Cleveland who joined the ACC in 1926; she had a broad base of mountaineering experience and attended the camps for many years. Like Phyl, she was a minority within a male-oriented club, but unlike Phyl (who because of some internal politics in the club had to wait until 1948), Prescott was the first female to be awarded the club's prestigious Silver Rope that certified she could lead climbs.[14] She had experience in the Alps and, of course, in the Rockies. She and Phyl shared an enthusiasm for climbing and appreciated each other's company and support while climbing alongside their (largely) male climbing companions.

Polly Prescott was quick to respond to the Mundays' invitation. "Believing that good fortune knocks but once with such a longed-for opportunity, I joined them in Vancouver on July 31."[15] The destination for this threesome was Mount Grenville (3,079/3,109 metres), northeast of the head of Bute Inlet. Don and Phyl had first sighted the mountain in September 1925 from

Don with Polly Prescott on approach to Mount Grenville, 1941.

Mount Rodney. Its height and dramatic profile had been noted then, but it lay to the east of the anticipated route to their Mystery Mountain, so had not yet been explored.

They left Vancouver in the *Edidonphyl* for the long trip to Bute Inlet. The voyage was less than perfect; despite a recent overhaul of the boat, they lost four days to engine problems. Heading up the inlet, they anchored the boat not far from the mouth of the Southgate River and then relayed supplies in their dinghy to establish a beach camp on the north side of the river, above the high-tide mark. They had food for 20 days. On August 10 they left camp, following the remnants of an old trail up the river to Elliot Creek. They turned north up the creek and entered a deep valley. They "hacked a course" over, through and around logs, bush and rocks. It was a challenge for Prescott, who had never before encountered such a difficult approach. Ten days later they emerged. "Gleaming through the dark forest came ... the inspiriting sight of a glacier cascading 2,000 feet or more over the bare head-wall of the valley to a comparatively low elevation." Two days later they established their base camp just below the snout of the West Grenville

Glacier and enjoyed what would soon be one of the last clear days. "Buoyant-hearted as slaves set free, we set out somewhat leisurely next morning to prospect a route to by-pass the formidable ice-fall. We tramped to the glacier through young alders draped disgustingly with tent caterpillars." The icefall completely blocked any view of the mountain, so they eventually determined to ford Elliot Creek and work their way up to a high camp they established just below the ice tongue of the South Grenville Glacier.[16]

At 6 a.m. on August 24 after making up "triple lunches" they left camp and moved up and along the glacier, which ascended at an easy gradient. Four hours later they were on the moraine at the foot of Grenville itself, "the start of the real climb." It was a long traverse on steep ice until they "discovered a narrow gully cutting the cliff ... wet walls were rotten and shelving. But it led to the steep edge of the ice-cap above the cliffs."[17] They were 100 metres below the summit.

Polly described the panoramic views. "From the ridge the climb was a scramble up easy rocks to an eerie summit composed of two towers. The first one proved to be a few feet higher than the second and we were content to sit there and gaze upon the magnificent and vast panorama, which stretched below us. The great Homathko Icefield, covering about 200 square miles, lay at our feet and on the northern horizon Mt. Waddington remained hidden in soft clouds. As our eyes completed the circle, we picked out Bute Mt., Mt. Rodney and Mt. Gilbert from the endless sea of unnamed peaks."[18]

Grenville was easily the highest mountain in the vicinity and the view was impressive. For Don and Phyl, the observations and photos taken from this summit added more pieces to their mapping puzzle. Here they had another angle to observe the Homathko Icefield and record the topography. But there was no time to linger—it was 7:00 p.m. and the sun beginning to set. "Still simmering with delight, we started down in half an hour. Almost at once a long streamer of cloud raced across the sky and hid the peak." As the wind came up, Don cut steps down the steep and crevassed ice. "By lamplight we got off the glacier about 10 p.m., and at first did fairly well on the glaciated rocks. Then we missed a guiding cairn and clawed around for a long time where we might have shied at going in daylight. Polly's lantern succumbed to bitter wind, but the two women did amazing things with such flashes of light as I could give them from my acetylene lamp. About 1:30 a.m. we rested in a heathery hollow partly sheltered from the wind. I was relieved when my companions proved ready to leave the last cliff till daylight."[19]

On the summit of Mount Grenville, Polly Prescott and Don (with movie camera in hand), 1941.

The following year Don and Phyl chased down another piece of the puzzle by climbing Mount Queen Bess (3,313 metres), on the northern end of the Homathko Icefield. Now they could be comfortable in their assertions about this icefield, having viewed it from all directions and from the peaks of the highest mountains in the immediate area. Documenting such a vast icefield as the Homathko, as well as the Silverthrone and Monarch icefields, gave the Coast Mountains a scientific and geological significance that had hitherto been unrecognized. The Mundays' mapping and photography was opening a previously underrated world.

Mount Queen Bess

"My wife and I had long feared that some enterprising climbing party might reach Mt. Queen Bess ahead of us. Twice we planned trips and were forced to postpone our plans. We found that Henry S. Hall, secretary of the American Alpine Club, had similar hopes ... so we hurriedly unified our plans." [20] After the tremendously difficult approach to Grenville in 1941, the Mundays opted the following year for entering the mountains from the interior of the province, through the Chilcotin, as they had done with Henry Hall earlier in 1933. Again they travelled from Williams Lake to the north end of Tatlayoko Lake, a journey of a day and a half, this time on a mail stage. At the lake lay the ranch of Ken Moore, with whom they arranged pack horses and transportation down the lake. The climbers and horses

made their way along the East Homathko river and then the Nostetuko and Stonsayako river valleys, taking several days to move ever closer to the mountains. Less than a kilometre below the glacier they found the evidence of long-receded ice and the slope steepened. Ancient rockfalls mixed with ice, and cutting steps "became more nightmarish each time." [21]

A succession of rainy days contributed to huge rockfalls; one slid right across the valley leaving in its wake a tremendous dust cloud that hung in the air for almost half an hour. When the weather improved they moved on, continually frustrated by inadequate and inaccurate maps, which led them astray on more than one occasion and, in fact, contributed to their "losing the mountain," as the map showed it on the wrong side of the river! Eventually they mounted the Mantle Glacier. "Crusted snow slowed us and as the slope steepened, ice appeared underneath, with wet, loose snow between— bad alike for cutting steps or trying to use crampons ... we continued our steep diagonal till the ice forced us into the longest gully." [22]

And then:

> rather suddenly the summit ridge took form above us. We emerged from the gully's confinement to the gleaming white rooftree of the world ... We mounted the snow ridge. Loose, incohesive snow—typical at this height in the Coast Range—defied adequate probing with the ice axe to discover possible crevasses into which we might wallow. This superb snow crown must exceed 300 feet in thickness ... We reached the top about 4 p.m. Few of our memorable hours in the Coast Range equaled this. Most of the outstanding summits of the range within a radius of 75 miles stood revealed ... Most of the secrets of the mysterious, immense Homathko Snowfield between Southgate and Homathko rivers opened before us; possibly 300 miles in area, it is probably double that of the famous Columbia Icefield in the Rockies... Descent is often the true test of climbing skill. There is always temptation to relax vigilance. The gully now streamed with water. Somehow the snow failed to quite reach the avalanching stage. We backed down for what seemed an interminable distance, sometimes scraping off the snow to chop steps in the ice. [23]

Several days later they were back at Tatlayoko Lake, vowing to return.

Mount Queen Bess, 1942.

Don's Final First Ascent

In 1946 Don and Phyl "beguiled Henry S. Hall, Jr." to join them in an exploration to find a practical route from Tatlayoko Lake up the east branch of the Homathko River to the base of Mount Reliance, their next first ascent. Departing Williams Lake, they "crowded into the nearly springless rear seat of an auto which smote our spines at every bump, the rebound sucking a swirl of Chilcotin dust through a big hole below the cushion."[24]

Thus began a journey westward toward the Homathko Icefield, which would complete the explorations of this great ice mass they had initiated in 1925. Now they would view it from its eastern aspect. They left on horseback with Harry and Muriel Haynes from their ranch near Tatlayoko Lake, following a course high above the river. They searched for a suitable ford, cutting trail through the alder and kinnikinnick as they neared the river. The spot they selected was swift running, but taken on the diagonal it proved manageable, although as Don recorded: "A horse forced to swim might fail to land above log jams, and no horse could swim back against the current." Phyl's horse "missed its footing when maddened by wasps" as they neared the river. She got clear of the falling mare but hurt her back in the process. She continued on despite her discomfort; it would be several weeks until she recovered fully. Muriel Haynes stayed near the ford with the horses; her husband Harry accompanied the three climbers to a higher elevation. They travelled light. "Our grub did not include an ounce of bacon, though Mackenzie's store in Williams Lake had helped us out with some tinned meat. We had only three pounds of cheese, and of course were short of sugar, butter and most dried fruits."[25]

The weather was brilliant, clear and hot—a rarity, as they knew from all their previous years in mountains. As yet they had met with no snow. Up a canyon, they climbed above a waterfall, and soon they were up high enough to see the outer ridges of Mount Reliance less than a kilometre distant. Finally, at about 6,500 feet, they encountered "Gangplank Glacier," which they followed for some while, climbing ever higher and closer to Reliance. "Quite soon the western view through clouds revealed Tiedemann Glacier's long lane of ice leading past the icy face of Mt. Munday to giant Mt. Waddington." The views were breathtaking. Don wrote:

Don and Phyl looking out toward
Mount Queen Bess from the summit of Reliance, 1946.

It was very grand up here above the ice cliffs, and dwindling cloud soon began to allow the long corniced summit ridge and its two rock towers to outline themselves against a sky of exultant blue. We hoped the eastern peak of Mt. Reliance would prove highest because the other looked hard to get at ... Before we reached the bergschrund we crossed a big curious ridge of snow—probably built by wind—it crossed the snowfield nearly parallel to the summit ridge ... Elsewhere in remnants of recent snow we noted wolf tracks. Here the wanderer had climbed to the rim, looked down the wild southern face and found the descent seemingly not to his liking ...[26]

Henry Hall recorded:

> At 2 p.m. we stepped up onto a sloping, lichen-covered slab, 25 by 15 ft.—the summit. The view was truly magnificent. Nothing like it is ever seen in the Rockies. From 10,500 ft. we could look down to the waves in the rapids of the Homathko, 9,400 ft. below, and, beyond and just to the right, up to 13,260 ft. (or higher) Mount Waddington ... The air was warm and still. We lay out on the rock, when we were not busy with photography or observation, and even talked of spending a night on top, as we had done on Mount Combatant in 1933. To the south and west ... here in one sweep, were more examples of the varied phenomena of glaciation than one could find in seasons of climbing in other ranges. Regretfully we started down at 3:45 ...[27]

Don, too, left reluctantly. This would be his last first ascent.

Don on Queen Bess expedition, 1942.

The *Edidonphyl*

In the winter of 1934–35 Don began an ambitious construction project. He was building a 16-foot launch to replace the small open boat they had been using to take them from Vancouver to Knight Inlet, a distance by water of 240 kilometres. Don's skills as a carpenter, despite his bad arm, still came in handy. The boat—later christened by Edith as Edidonphyl, an amalgam of their three names—was sturdy and a perfect design for their needs.

He started the boat in his basement, but as construction progressed, the entire lower back wall of the house had to be removed. Surely this was not a case of mis-measurement, but an idea that literally grew as he went along. The load-bearing beams of the house wall just barely allowed the boat to be carefully eased out of the basement on rollers through the opening in the wall. Then there was the whole process of getting it from their backyard in North Vancouver down to the ocean without a trailer—a testament to Don's ingenuity and imagination. Edidonphyl was removed from the back-yard to the lane below using skids and then, using the same skids raised into the back of a truck. From the truck it was hoisted into the ocean at the foot of Lonsdale Drive.

Edidonphyl had a cabin and wheelhouse, an inboard motor and sleeping accommodation. It gave the Mundays portability, shelter from the weather and enough space to take others along with them. For several years running the Munday family set out for Waddington country, dropped Edith off with friends on Cortes or Read island and then headed up for the summer's climbs.

The completed *Edidonphyl* in the Mundays' backyard; transporting *Edidonphyl* from North Vancouver down to Burrard Inlet; launching *Edidonphyl* in the ocean, 1935.

Don and Phyl beside their tent, Alpine Club of Canada camp, ca. 1948.

Chapter Eight LATER YEARS

Don's health never completely returned after his military duty during the First World War, though he worked at maintaining his fitness. He built trails and cabins. He never owned an automobile so he walked everywhere. He was strong in many ways: his legs could carry him for miles, his back could support great weights and his arms wielded chopping axes. But he never regained complete use of the fingers on his left hand or his grip strength. The shrapnel-shattered ulna had healed but he had to constantly work his fingers to stimulate the muscles in his left forearm. This he did by carrying in his pocket a small wad of paper that he squeezed and rolled throughout the day. When the climb required reliance on left-handed holds, Phyl would often lead. As she explained, "If we had to do anything, in rock climbing and where it needed a very touchy left hand hold or feeling, then that was when I took over because of his wounded arm. He was strong enough but there were some things he couldn't do as well as he could with his right."[1]

But there was another weakness inherited from his war years. His respiratory system never recovered from the assault of gas at the Somme and he was susceptible to bronchitis and other inflammations of the respiratory system. Winters were the hardest time for Don, with coughs and, at times, episodes of breathlessness. One such incident, in the winter of 1935 while climbing Mount Baker with friends, put the entire climbing party at risk. Don could not proceed, yet the weather was worsening. It might have been this event that cautioned Don against further big winter climbs; his body could not be relied upon. Don stuck to skiing, which in the end served the greater good. As his skills became well refined, ski-mountaineering became incorporated into their high-altitude summer climbing, stretching the distances and easing the fatigue.

Photos of Don from the late 1930s through the 1940s show a man whose face is aged, skin drawn tight over cheekbones, with a look of fragility. Never a large man, his slight frame carried no extra weight, and it didn't

Don and Phyl (second and third from left) with friends at camp, ca. 1948.

take much for him to look drawn and tired. But he was a stubborn man, refusing to take things easy, always exerting himself and pushing his limits.

With the advent of the Second World War, Don was frustrated. He was too old to enlist, even though his mountaineering skills would be useful in combat. The young men were soon away fighting and many jobs became available. Don needed to diversify his source of income, as while the world was at war there was little demand for the type of magazine articles he wrote. In 1942, as a war veteran, he was given priority for hiring and was taken on by the Burrard Shipyards, which turned out one-third of the cargo ships produced in Canada during the war. At first he worked in the stores warehouse and after a year became a sheet-metal specialist, earning a basic rate of 85 cents an hour. At the end of 1945, with the war over, staff reductions eliminated his position.[2]

Don contributed to the war effort in another important way also. In July and August 1943 he and 21 other senior ACC male climbers donated their services to the Department of National Defence and conducted a military training camp for soldiers to teach them manoeuvres on mountain terrain, in both rock and ice conditions. Don's particular duties were to provide practical instruction to the soldiers in snowcraft and bivouacking, and to conduct lectures and demonstrations on these subjects as well. The instructors were expected to impart "methods and tricks of the trade found useful to overcome obstacles, deficiencies of equipment, weather hazards, etc. All instructors should be able to draw on their experiences to make this a worthwhile discussion."[3] Two courses, each of three weeks duration, took place in the Little Yoho Valley in Yoho National Park. Approximately 150 men received training on each course. Don later wrote about his experiences with some soldiers who seemed to have no appreciation for climbing, and who could not see why anyone would bother going to all the trouble and effort to reach the top of a peak.[4]

Don's climbing activities slowed down dramatically during the 1940s with his job, but also because of the war and his own health. The records for the ACC camps show that Phyl alone attended in 1940 and 1943 (while Don was snowcraft instructor in Yoho). But in 1945 they were both present at the Eremite Valley camp and along with another famed climbing couple, Dorothy Pilley and her husband Dr. I.A. Richards, shared guiding assignments for several climbs. Henry Hall led the Mundays and others up Memorial Peak on July 18. In his report following the climb, he captured a little of the competitive edge brought to the climb by the presence of these two couples. "The Richards and Mundays went up the rock arête running straight up from the snowfield to the summit. This has two 'windows' in it and if followed throughout gives interesting easy sound rock climbing."[5]

That year, Don and Phyl also guided members up Angle Mountain, which qualified as a graduating climb. Don summarized the climb: "Left 8 a.m. Summit 3:50 p.m. Descent 3½ hour. Cool day, snow good, but becoming thin on N. face. Considerable time lost due to misunderstanding of visual routes. Inexperience of several of party slowed ascent, but they came down quite well. Miss MacGowan keen, quick to learn, endurance good, should be given a chance at something a little harder. Goldsmith well above average beginner and could tackle something a little harder. Miss M. Lewis merely lacks experience and personal instruction, a little slow at upper elevations, should not try anything harder at present."[6]

In 1948, at the Peyto Lake camp, Don and Phyl led six others on an ice climb to the north face of Mount Thompson. Don provided a thorough report to the club upon their return. The route followed the Peyto glacier "to about the 8000-foot contour line on the Alberta–B.C. Boundary survey sheet. The map does not show the steep narrow glacier in the angle of the NW and NE ridges. The wide moraine-buried tongue changes to steep bare ice which provided continuous step cutting for about 2½ hours, much of it being of a very exposed nature." The route they took "up the icefall had been reconnoitered only from the highway and was chosen only with a view to making a good ice climb. The presence of a movie camera prolonged the ascent considerable. Times were not recorded. Ascent probably took an elapsed time of about nine hours."[7]

At the Freshfield Camp in 1949, Phyl led a "manless" group of six women up Mount David. Don concentrated on photographic opportunities on day hikes, and with Phyl and others took pack horses to the High Camp overnight. The intenseness of their earlier climbing days was gone, but in its place, contentment in being with friends and in the outdoors. Phyl could see Don's gradual weakening—his fatigue and loss of fitness. On August 4, Don and Rex Gibson led six climbers up Mount Freshfield from the High Camp, but this would be Don's last club climb.

On their return to Vancouver, Don participated in the mountain rescue of a climber who had fallen and broken his leg during a descent from one of the mountains in the Tantalus Group, north of Squamish. Not long after, on November 21, Don himself was admitted to Vancouver General Hospital and then, on November 30, transferred to the Vancouver Military Hospital, Shaughnessy. He was weak and ill. Six months later, on June 12, 1950, while still in hospital, he succumbed to lobar pneumonia, with bronchial asthma a significant contributing factor. Don's life of high-altitude climbing, of enduring cold winds, of chills and wet camping had finally taken its toll. Phyl was devastated. She had lost not only her husband, but also her climbing partner. Don's death "marked the end of one of the greatest climbing teams in alpine history," stated the *Province* newspaper.[8] The accolades and tributes poured in.

> The passing of Don Munday closes an epoch in the annals of Canadian mountaineering but leaves a tradition. It also severs one of the most closely knit husband-and-wife teams of admirers, conquerors and exponents of the loftier realms of Nature. Perhaps in likeness to the university dons of his ancestral England, Don has been referred to as the "dean of mountaineering"—a wide term when recalling the early pioneers and writers of exploration in the Alps, Caucasus, Himalayas and Rockies—but certainly befitting his exploits in the BC–Alberta Rockies, the Coast and other ranges in BC, accompanied by his understanding expositions of the history, lore and science of these mountains and of the mountaineering craft ... Don was a true

lover of the mountains in all their phases—not alone in conquest of the peaks, but also in their surrounding beauties, as expressed by his prose, poetry and photography.[9]

Don Munday was dressed as he had requested, in his red mountain shirt and grey pants. On the coffin draped with the Union Jack lay his ice axe and an old hat with a moss garden of wildflowers. The funeral service was well attended by Don's extended family of mountaineers.

The following month, Phyl, accompanied by their long-time climbing companion and friend Neal Carter, boarded a small airplane; the flight—as Phyl recorded—was "financed by the thoughtfulness and generosity of our Mountain friends." The plane flew high over Waddington territory, and when it got above Mount Munday, Phyl released her parcel to the winds. A "tight-top" tin contained some of Don's ashes. Around the tin was tied one of Don's old mountain hats and a small cross of flowers made by Phyl's sister, Betty. The remainder of his ashes was later scattered among the alpine flowers of Garibaldi Park, where Don had "enjoyed his first truly alpine climbs."[10]

Phyllis continued on, stoically attending the ACC camps, leading "Snow School" training sessions for the campers who signed up for instruction as well as mountain first aid. Without Don, she lost her inclination for high climbing, but still loved the camping life and being around mountaineers. In latter years, when her arthritis was bad, she came to camp on horseback or was flown in—she was very much the respected Grande Dame of Mountaineering. Her first-aid work as the "foot-lady in the blister-tent" had become legendary. In July 1972, Phyl attended her 33rd camp set in the Selkirks or Rockies.

Phyl's volunteerism kept her going. In her capacity as the Provincial Wood Lore Commissioner for Girl Guides, she attended Guide camps in B.C. and abroad, and set up badge testing, training and nature hikes. Concurrently, she undertook broader and broader responsibilities with St. John Ambulance, working her way from divisional superintendent to provincial superintendent.

As a pioneering climber who had opened up the mountain world of the Pacific coast, Phyl was somewhat of a legend. She was sought after as a public speaker and as an interviewee. Her message over the decades did not

Phyl Munday at Mount Robson, August 1974, the 50th anniversary of her Robson ascent.

change a great deal. She wanted people to experience nature in its infinite variety and complexity. She wanted people to notice the little things on the side of the trail, the ant nests, and the slug on the branch, the mosses, the dewdrop on a salmonberry. These modest and easily observed aspects were in their own way as magical and important as the snowy peaks on the end of the trail. For Phyl, the end was not nearly as important as the getting there. For a generation of Girl Guides and for newly minted mountaineers and the general public who attended her lectures and lantern-slide shows, this was the message they received and remembered. Phyl made a difference in countless lives by teaching the value of looking at the exquisiteness of the ordinary and the little details on the well-travelled pathways that exemplified the majesty of nature.

For years Phyl had suffered from rheumatoid arthritis in her knees, an affliction she disguised from all her fellow climbers. Climbing could be extremely painful, at times it was all she could do to erect the tent and then crawl into its privacy. There she could rest, and wrap cool compresses around her knees and bind them with a rubberized bandage. In her later years she also suffered with leg ulcers. Between the two afflictions, mobility (such an important part of her lifestyle) became increasingly difficult. But still she kept on over the decades. Don had his weakness, and so did she, but together they had kept the secrets, covering for each other when one was fatigued, or in pain, or the pitch required a strong left hold.

For many years Phyl continued on in the small house on Tempe Crescent in North Vancouver, where the family had moved after descending from their cabin on Grouse Mountain. She surrounded herself with photos of mountains, most of them taken by her and developed by Don in the tiny darkroom he made in the basement. The house was packed with memories and filled with mountain gear, souvenirs and sunshine. Her last years were spent in Nanaimo, first living with her nephew and his family, and then after that in a nursing home. Phyl had lived a long life as a widow without her climbing partner. On April 11, 1990, at the age of 95, she died, almost 40 years after Don's death. A large community of friends that included generations of climbers, Girl Guides, volunteer and church groups, mourned her. Her request was that her ashes be scattered alongside Don's in the alpine meadows of Garibaldi. At the funeral service, the following poem (presumably her own composition) was read.

I Think What Will Happen To Me

When my old body is finished and dies, I'm sure my spirit will come to a place like this: A lovely woodsy trail, a beautiful lake, an alpine meadow, a ridge and a peak.

For all this had been heaven to me while on earth. They are all God's great gifts to man.

I will roam, at will, about the alpine meadows, along the happy rippling streams, the placid ponds and lakes that mirror the grand peaks and passing clouds. They will catch the early sunrise, with promise of the day, and later the glorious sunset, the last of light, then the night sky with bright stars and brilliant moon.

My spirit will wander about in the fields of flowers, reveling in their unspeakable beauty—it will pause to wonder at a rare treasure on some secluded spot. My spirit will also be tuned to all bird songs, and calls of little animals who make their homes in the mountains.

I will ramble high on the ridges where grotesque trees give way to heather and the highest flowers. Then I will join the fresh breezes, gain in strength, and rejoice in the rocks and snows of high places.

I will travel all over the glaciers—which I love so well—and the sparkling snow fields, the deep blue crevasses and shining seracs and the steep snow ridges and rock faces. And finally, with all the world at my feet, I will sit exulted on the summit, and just look, and look, and look, and love it, and thank my Maker for the supreme privilege my old body has enjoyed through the years.

My spirit belongs to all of the mountains—for this to me is heaven. Thank God who has made me like this. How privileged I have been, as Don and Edith shared these joys with me.

If I have been able to pass on, to even one other soul, the great joy and beauty God gave me in life, then I have been rewarded beyond measure.

The Legacy

The Mundays' photographs and written accounts, public speaking and their recorded advocacy for mountain spaces ensure their lasting legacy.

Don carried on a voluminous correspondence with officials in the provincial Lands Department; with the surveyor general and various survey staff; with the federal government and the Geographic Names Board. He maintained an ongoing correspondence with the provincial archivist of British Columbia, consulted historians, read nineteenth-century accounts of overland and maritime exploration and scoured annual reports from the Canadian Pacific Railway survey operations; in short, he did all he could to unearth historical information that might assist in directing their mountaineering expeditions. Don's quest for accuracy in his own reporting and mapping led him to search for corroboration or direction from the records left by explorers, surveyors, pioneers, trappers and miners who might have entered the areas in earlier times. He engaged in lively discourses with individual surveyors and other climbers whose comments could trigger him into passionate diatribes. Don's perspectives were at times broadened through healthy debate of differing interpretations of the historical documentation or alternate observations of the landscape due to taking different routes. Don could be counted on to have an opinion—one backed up by historical data or his own minute observations, mapping or photographs.

Don's research also helped him in his writing, for many of the articles published in the *Canadian Alpine Journal* and other periodicals include the historical context of exploration within the accounts of his and Phyl's climbing activities.

When Don and Phyl began exploring the Waddington territory, they committed themselves not only to exploration but also to recording and documenting the environment. The Mundays applied names to rivers, creeks, glaciers and mountains that had no official names beyond the oral record of First Nations peoples. Don and Phyl's year was broken into two halves—the climbing season and the preparation-for-climbing season. Each was busy in its own way. Winter and spring were the planning and plotting time of the year. Determining the routes, working out the logistics of transportation, timing their entry and exit of the backcountry kept the Mundays focused in their anticipation of the upcoming exploration and climbing times. Don also took this opportunity to transmit the maps, notes, photographs and observations taken on their climbing trips to the British Columbia and Canadian Geographic Boards. Almost without exception the names applied by the Mundays were accepted, and their careful mapping meant this undocumented section of the province became delineated on official maps based upon their information.

Their willingness to share their information and knowledge was also appreciated by their climbing contemporaries. In a coterie of often close-mouthed and competitive mountaineers, this was not always the case.

"We didn't only go into the Waddington country just to climb one mountain and run out and leave it. We went into the Waddington country to find out all we possibly could about glaciers and mountains and animals and nature and everything about that particular area—completely unknown before we went into it—so that we could bring out the information for the interest of other people as well as ourselves."[11]

For the last few years of Don's life his health affected his stamina and endurance. He had to take care not to overexert himself and channelled his need to stay connected to climbing by pulling together his account of their quest for Mount Waddington. He relied on his and Phyl's small climbing diaries, of notes made each winter regarding their routes and application of place-names, and the articles he wrote after their annual explorations. Don spent many laborious hours piecing together panoramic photographs taken from various routes into the area or from mountaintop viewpoints. Using his small manual typewriter, he revised, rewrote and polished his account. In May 1948, after much anticipation and a bit of delay, the end result was *The Unknown Mountain*, published in London, England, by Hodder and Stoughton. It was to become a classic.

Don and Phyl at summit cairn, Mount Victoria, 1925.

LATER YEARS | 223

List of Ascents

Mountain	Height	Year	Ascent
Agur	3,086 m	1932	attempt only
Albert Edward	2,093 m	1938	first winter ascent (skis)
Alouette	1,361 m	1919	
Angle Peak	2,910 m	1945	
Arrowsmith	1,819 m	1925	
Athabaska	3,491 m	1940 Phyl, 1948 Don	
Atwell Peak(Diamond Head)	2,655 m	1911 Don	
Bastille	2,286 m	1938	first ascent
Bastion	2,213 m	1926	
Becher	1,385 m	1938	spring ski
Ben Lomond	1,654 m	1912 Don	2nd & 3rd ascents this trip
Bevel	1,739 m	1932	first ascent
Bishop	1,508 m	1916 Phyl	
Bivouac Peak	3,020 m	1928	first ascent
Black Mountain	1,217 m	1918 Phyl	
Black Tusk	2,315 m	1912 Don, 1921 Phyl	
Blackcomb	2,440 m	1923	first ascent
Blade	2,470 m	1925	first ascent
Blanshard Peak	1,706 m	1918	first ascent
Bookworms	2,331 m	1922?	
Brazeau	3,470 m	1930 Don	
Brunswick	1,785 m	1911 Don, 1916 Phyl	
Burwell (formerly White)	1,530 m	1911 Don, 1916 Phyl	
Calumet	2,977 m	1924	
Camel and Camel Ridge	1,495 m	ca. 1918 Phyl	
Carr (formerly Copper Peak)	2,490 m	1911 Don	1930s first winter ascent
Castle Towers	2,675 m	1911 Don, 1916 Phyl	
Castor	2,779 m	1921 Don	
Cathedral	1,730 m	1915 Don, 1916 Phyl	
Cautley	2,870 m	1952 Phyl	
Charlton	3,217 m	1930	
Charybdis	2,848 m	1930	
Cheam	2,104 m	1925	
Columnar Peak	1,830 m	1911 Don	
Combatant	3,756 m	1933	first ascent
Coquitlam	1,583 m	1918	first ascent
Crown	1,503 m	1911 Don, 1917 Phyl	
Daly	2,166 m	1925	

Mountain	Height	Year	Ascent
Dam	1,340 m	1917 Phyl	
Dauntless	2,853 m	1930	first ascent
David	2,780 m	1949 Phyl	
Davidson	2,516 m	1925	
Deception Peak	2,233 m	1922?	
Defiance	2,666 m	1937	attempt
Dome (Fromme)	1,177 m	ca. 1911 Don, ca. 1916 Phyl	
Elsay	1,422 m	1934 Don	
Ennis	3,122 m	1939 Phyl	
Eremite	2,910 m	1945	
Eureka	1,949 m	1923	
Fang Peak	2,347 m	1936	first ascent
Finality	2,828 m	1934	first ascent
Fireworks Peak	2,968 m	1928	first ascent
Fitzsimmons	2,650 m	ca. 1923 or 1924	
Foley Peak	2,307 m	1924	first ascent
Forbes	3,617 m	1940 Phyl	
Freshfield	3,336 m	1949	
Gardner	7,67 m	1912 Phyl	
Garibaldi	2,678 m	1911 Don, 1921 Phyl	
Garnet Peak	2,876 m	1939 Phyl	
Geddes	3,353 m	1933	attempt
Geikie	3,298 m	1926	
Gendarme	2,927 m	1924	
Glacier Pikes	2,130 m	1911 Don	
Goat	1,319 m	1917 Phyl	
Golden Ears	1,716 m	1911 Don, 1918 Phyl	1911 first ascent
Goodsir	3,567 m	1939 Phyl	
Grenville	3,079 m	1941	first ascent
Grizzly	2,754 m	Don 1921	
Grouse	1,211 m	1911? Don, 1912 Phyl	
Habrich	1,700 m	1912 Don,	
Hanover	1,747 m	1913 Don, 1916 Phyl	1913 first ascent
Hans Peak	3,110 m	1950 Phyl	
Helmet Peak (Helm Pk)	2,146 m	1916 Phyl	
Henry McLeod	3,288 m	1930 Don, 1950 Phyl	
Hollyburn	1,324 m	ca. 1918 Phyl	
Homathko	3,017 m	1947	attempt
Huber	3,368 m	1925	
Hungabee	3,492 m	1925	
Isosceles	2,530 m	1922	first ascent

LIST OF ASCENTS | 225

Mountain	Height	Year	Ascent
Jubilee	2,748 m	1931	first ascent and with skis
Lady Peak	2,178 m	1923 or 1924?	
Lava Mountain (the Gargoyles)	1,830 m	1913 Don	
Ledge	1,920 m	1912 Don, 1919 Phyl	
Lion, East	1,599 m	1911 Don, 1916 Phyl	
Lion, West	1,646 m	1912? Don, 1916 Phyl	
Lyell #1 (Rudolph Peak)	3,507 m	1940 Phyl	
Lyell #2 (Edward Peak)	3,514 m	1940 Phyl	
Lyell #3 (Ernest Peak)	3,511 m	1940 Phyl	
Lynn Peaks	1,015 m	1918	
Lynx	3,170 m	1920	
MacKenzie	2,143 m	1938	
Mamquam	2,595 m	1911 Don	
Martins Peak	3,053 m	1939 Phyl	
Marvel	2,690 m	1927	
Men-at-Arms Peaks	3,190 m	1928	
Meslilloet (Ida, Indian Chief)	2,001 m	1914 Don, 1919 Phyl	1914 second ascent
Moffat	3,090 m	1930 Don	second ascent
Mons Peak	3,087 m	1940 Phyl	
Mumm	2,962 m	1920	
Munday	3,356 m	1930	first ascent and with skis
Myrtle	2,361 m	1928	first ascent
Odaray	3,159 m	1925	
Outpost Pk (Eremite)	2,880 m	1945	
Overlord	2,634 m	1923	first ascent
Parapet	2,470 m	1922	first ascent
Pivot Dome	1,905 m		first ascent
Potato Peak	2,206 m	1956 Phyl	
President	3,123 m	1925	
Price (Red Mt.)	2,052 m	1912 Don, 1930s	1930s first winter ascent
Queen Bess	3,313 m	1942	first ascent
Redbreast	2,049 m	1930	first ascent and with skis
Refuse Pinnacle	2,500 m	1923	
Reliance	3,134 m	1946	first ascent
Resplendent	3,426 m	1920	Via NW arête, new route
Rice Peak	unknown	ca. 1918 Phyl	
Robson	3,954 m	1924	first female ascent
Rodney	2,399 m	1925	
Rogers	3,208 m	1921 Don	
Round Mt.	1,675 m	1913 Don	
Rust (Cinder Cone)	1,901 m	1911 Don	first ascent
Saugstad	2,908 m	1938	attempts

Mountain	Height	Year	Ascent
Schaffer	2,691 m	1943 Phyl	
Seymour	1,450 m	1917 Phyl	
Sheer	1,680 m	1912 Don	
Shelf	2,529 m	1928, 1930	first ascent and with skis
Silverthrone	2,864 m	1936	first and second ascents
Sir Donald	3,284 m	1921 Don	
Sir John Thompson	3,349 m	1925	first ascent
Sir Richard	2,710 m	1937	first ascent and with skis
Sir Wilfred Laurier (Titan)	3,520 m	1925	second ascent
Sky Pilot	2,031 m	1912 Don, 1919 Phyl	1912 second ascent
Sockeye	2,737 m	1931	first ascent and with skis
The Spearhead	2,457 m	1923	
Sphinx	2,410 m	1911 Don	
Spire Peak	2,040 m	1913	first ascent
Stewart Peak	2,230 m	1923	first ascent
Strachan	1,454 m	1911 Don, 1918? Phyl	
Stupendous	2,682 m	1937	first ascent
Surprise Point	2,400 m	1945	
Survey Peak	2,652 m	1954 Phyl	
Swanzy	2,891 m	1921 Don	
Thompson, N. Face	3,089 m	1948	
Tonquin	2,465 m	1926	
Unwin	3,268 m	1930	
Valad Peak	3,250 m	1930 Don	
Vaux	3,310 m	1939 Phyl	
Vice President	3,077 m	1925	
Victoria	3,464 m	1925	
Vigilant	2,841 m	1930	first ascent
Waddington, NW Summit	4,011 m	1928, 1934	first and second ascents
Warren	3,300 m		
Wedge	2,904 m	1936	new route and first winter ascent (with skis)
Welch Peak	2,440 m	1924	attempt
Whistler (London Mt.)	2,210 m	1924	attempts
Whitetip	2,444 m	1928	first ascent
Wiwaxy Peaks	2,706 m	1943 Phyl	
Wonder Peak	2,850 m	1952 Phyl	
Yukness	2,851 m	1943 Phyl	

NOTE: This listing is not definitive; it is derived from references to ascents in the Munday records, ACC accounts and mountaineering publications.

Endnotes

Note: BC Archives has been abbreviated to BCA; Whyte Museum of the Canadian Rockies is listed as Whyte Museum.

Introduction

1 For information on Phyl's achievements and Guiding career, see Bridge, *Phyllis Munday, Mountaineer.*
2 Information on Don's affiliations is found in Neal Carter, "In Memoriam, Walter Alfred Don Munday," *Canadian Alpine Journal,* 1950.
3 Phyllis Munday interview with Susan Leslie, 1978. BCA Tape 160.
4 Siri Louie, "Peak Potentials and Performance Anxieties: Gender, Mountaineering and Leadership in the Canadian West, 1906–1940." Paper presented at Unsettled Pasts: Reconceiving the West Through Women's History conference, Calgary, AB, June 2002.
5 Quoted in Williams, *Women on the Rope,* p. 102.
6 See Helen Lenskyj, *Out of Bounds: Women, Sport and Sexuality* (Toronto: Women's Press, 1986), and Susan K. Cahn, *Coming on Strong: Gender and Sexuality in Twentieth-Century Women's Sport* (New York: Free Press, 1994).
7 See Reichwein, "Beyond Visionary Mountains" and Routledge, "Shifting Seas of Ice."
8 For example, "New Mountain Horizons in Canada: A Record of Pioneer Exploration of Peaks and Glaciers of the Coast and Mountains of Canada, 1925–28," Whyte Museum, AC368 (now at BCA).
9 Determining accurate mountain heights has been aided in recent years by the development of more sophisticated measuring devices. Unfortunately, there is no single authoritative listing of up-to-date heights. The heights given here are based upon several sources.

Chapter One: Early Years and the B.C. Mountaineering Club

1 The year 1888 is confirmed by his birth certificate and his army papers. Don's death certificate gives 1890 as his birth date, which is the date stated in the newspapers at the time of his death and used on most library catalogues, but is incorrect.
2 Munday's parents are mentioned briefly in "Adventure Trails of British Columbia," unpublished manuscript, Don and Phyllis Munday fonds, BCA, MS-2379.
3 Information from Alberta and Manitoba online vital statistics indexes. Half-sister Alice Gertrude Burnell, born in 1872 (by Jessie Munday's first marriage), lived with the family until her marriage ca. 1902. Information from Canada Census, 1901, Manitoba Census 1906.
4 Details about the Munday family's arrival in Vancouver are elusive. Pansy's death certificate suggests she was in B.C. by 1911. Don became a BCMC member in October 1910. Angus Gunn, in his introduction to the expanded edition of *The Unknown Mountain,* p. 4, states 1909 but this statement is not documented. Neal Carter also gives 1909 in his "In Memoriam" article in the *Canadian Alpine Journal,* 1951, p. 146. Don apparently had a second sister who was still alive at the time of his death. I have yet to find documentation about her.
5 Don Munday, "Soul-Standards of Archibald Lampman," *Westminster Hall Magazine,* n.d.
6 Don's poems were published principally in 1913–14. Copies of his poems with notations about their publication appearance are in BCA, MS-2379.
7 The archives of the BCMC hold rich documentation including minute books, correspondence, membership lists, newsletters, photographs and publications. Most of the information about Don and Phyl's affiliation with the club comes from the BCMC archives.
8 Early BCMC history is included in the first publication of the club, *The Northern Cordilleran* (Vancouver, 1913).
9 G.B. Warren, "Bring on the Peaks," Vancouver *Province,* April 16, 1910.
10 "The Cathedral Group," 1913, revised March 26, 1914, BCA, MS-2379.
11 "Mountain Club", Vancouver *Province,* May 27, 1911.
12 "Climbers Conquer Mount Brunswick," Vancouver *Province,* June 30, 1911, p. 13, and Don Munday, "The Lions Group," unpublished manuscript, revised March 24, 1914, BCA, MS-2379.

13 Don Munday, unpublished manuscript, ca. 1938, BCA, MS-2379.

14 Ibid.

15 Ibid.

16 Don Munday, "The Lions Group," unpublished manuscript, revised March 24, 1914, BCA, MS-2379.

17 Don Munday, unpublished manuscript, ca. 1938, BCA, MS-2379.

18 Don Munday, "The Sleeping Beauty," manuscript, ca. 1913, revised 1914, BCA, MS-2379.

19 Don Munday, *Garibaldi Park*, p. 5.

20 "Summer Camp", *B.C. Saturday Sunset*, September 16, 1911.

21 Frank H. Smith, "Cabins, Camps and Climbs," *The B.C. Mountaineer*, 1957.

22 Don Munday, *Garibaldi Park*, p. 2.

23 Dick Culbert, *A Climber's Guide*, p. 32.

24 Fred Smith, "The Sawtooth Group," manuscript, ca. 1914, BCA, MS-2379.

25 Fred Smith, "The Pipes of Pan, Number 2," BCA, MS-2379.

26 At the time of writing, Don speculated on how long this feature would last before erosion crumbled it further. Six years later he noted that the hard traverse across the western face was no longer required; it was an "easy" walk to the top. From Don Munday, untitled draft manuscript [Mt. Ida], BCA, MS-2379.

27 Fred Smith, "The Pipes of Pan, Number 2," BCA, MS-2379.

28 Fred Smith, "The Sawtooth Group," p. 9, BCA, MS-2379.

29 Ibid., p. 14.

30 Ibid., p. 15.

31 Ibid., p. 16.

32 Ibid., p. 17.

33 Ibid., p. 19.

34 Frank H. Smith, "Cabins, Camps and Climbs," *The B.C. Mountaineer*, 1957.

35 Don Munday, unpublished manuscript, "Mount Hanover," BCA, MS-2379.

36 Ibid.

37 Ibid.

38 Ibid.

39 Ibid.

40 Pansy Munday died unexpectedly at the age of 23. Loretto Hanafin was a great friend to Munday. She married Fred Smith in 1916 and continued climbing. Many of her photographs were included in Don's *Garibaldi Park*.

41 Don Munday, scrapbook of poetry, BCA, MS-2379.

42 Don Munday, diary entry June 28, 1917, Museum of the Royal Westminster Regiment, New Westminster, B.C. Some of Don's military memorabilia, including his diaries, housed at this institution. His official military record is in Library and Archives Canada.

43 Phyllis Munday interview with Dan Bowers, March 11, 1973. BCA Tape 160.

44 Ibid.

45 Ibid.

46 Ibid.

47 Phyllis Munday interview with Mary Alice H. Stewart, May 23, 1972, S1/65 Whyte Museum.

48 *Nelson Daily News*, May 12, 1903.

49 Daniel Francis, ed., *Encyclopedia of British Columbia* (Madeira Park, B.C.: Harbour Publishing, 2000), p. 734.

50 Phyllis Munday interview with Susan Leslie, 1978, BCA, Tape 160.

51 BCMC fonds. Membership book includes Miss M. Carr, Elsie Carr, J.P. Carr, F. Carr, all from the same address.

52 BCMC fonds. Membership book, Minute book, December 20, 1915.

Chapter Two: Wartime

1 Phyllis Munday interview with Susan Leslie, BCA Tape 160.

2 Don's official military record is dryer than his own written accounts; see "Adventure Trails of B.C.," BCA, MS-2379.

3 For Don's complete account of the battlefields, see "The Fighting 47th," manuscript, BCA, MS-2379.

4 Don Munday, war diary, 1915–1917, Museum of the Royal Westminster Regiment.

5 Don Munday, "The Fighting 47th," pp. 307–10, BCA, MS-2379.

6 Information on Don's wound, hospitalization, health and military activities are found in his official military record, Library and Archives Canada.

7 According to Don's military record, he was awarded the Military Medal on June 21, 1917, received the letter stating so on July 27 and was presented with the medal on November 15. Museum of the Royal Westminster Regiment.

8 Medical records while at Bearwood, a Canadian Convalescent Hospital.

9 "Vancouver Had First Women's Volunteer Army Corps in 1915," newspaper clipping, n.d.

10 Phyllis Munday interview with Susan Leslie, 1978, BCA, Tape 160. Phyl's mother went to England to visit family just prior to the war. At war's outset she undertook nursing training in England and worked in this capacity until war's end. Information from her obituary and photo documentation in private collection.

11 Information documenting these climbs is found within photos assembled by BCMC member Tom Fyles, private collection.

12 Phyllis Munday interview with Dan Bowers March 11, 1973, BCA, Tape 160.

13 Phyllis Munday interview with Susan Leslie, 1978, BCA, Tape 160.

14 Tom Fyles and Phyllis Munday interview with Dan Bowers, March 23, 1973, BCA, Tape 177.

Chapter Three: Recovery and Discovery

1 Executive minute book, BCMC fonds.

2 Club Cabin guestbook, August 10–11, 1918, BCMC fonds.

3 Don Munday, untitled manuscript fragment, BCA, MS-2379.

4 "Veteran Editor and His Bride," Vancouver *Province*, February 4, 1920, p. 8.

5 Don Munday, untitled draft manuscript [Mt. Ida], BCA, MS-2379. This manuscript also specifies: "The most prominent summit on the ridge east of Mt. Meslilloet was climbed in 1919 from the S.E. from Ann Creek" by Phyl, Don and Tom Ingram.

6 Don Munday, untitled draft manuscript [Mt. Meslilloet], BCA, MS-2379.

7 Ibid.

8 Executive minute book 1919 shows September 30–31, 1919, but the climb actually took place on August 30, 31 and September 1, 1919. BCMC fonds.

9 Don Munday, "Adventure Trails of B.C.," unpublished manuscript, BCA, MS-2379.

10 Don Munday, *The Unknown Mountain*, pp. 1–2.

11 Ibid.

12 Don Munday, "Adventure Trails of B.C.," BCA, MS-2379.

13 Don Munday, file of poems, BCA, MS-2379.

14 Don Munday, diary entry, June 4,

1916. Diary covering 1915–1917, New Westminster Regimental Archives.

15 Ibid. June 18, 1917. Don's first wife was named Flora. The marriage ended by mid-1917 when Don was given leave to return to England, during which time presumably the paperwork was attended to. Don's military papers list his wife as the recipient of his paycheques for a period from late 1915 through the end of 1916.

16 Club Cabin guestbook, February 26 and 27, 1919, membership books, BCMC fonds.

17 "Veteran Editor and His Bride," Vancouver *Province*, February 4, 1920, p. 8.

18 Ibid.

19 Membership Register, Alpine Club of Canada fonds, AC 385/2, Whyte Museum. At a London meeting of the Alpine Club on June 1, 1920, the organization agreed to formal affiliation with the Alpine Club of Canada. *Canadian Alpine Journal*, 1920.

20 Vancouver *Province* newspaper, July 2, 1921, p. 36.

21 Phyllis Munday, "My Memories of North Vancouver," unpublished manuscript, BCA, MS-2379.

22 Phyllis Munday interview with Dan Bowers, 1973, BCA, Tape 177.

23 Don Munday, "Adventure Trails of B.C.," p. 34, BCA, MS-2379.

24 Ibid.

25 Phyllis Munday, "Memories of North Vancouver," BCA, MS-2379.

26 Don Munday, "Adventure Trails of B.C.", pp. 38–40, BCA, MS-2379.

27 Ibid., p. 40.

28 Phyllis Munday interview with Dan Bowers, 1973, BCA, Tape 177.

29 Report of the Vancouver Section of the Alpine Club of Canada indicates two club members (Don and Phyl) attended this BCMC camp. *Canadian Alpine Journal*, 1921.

30 Don Munday, "Summer Camp of B.C. Mountaineering Club" [1921], unpublished manuscript, BCA, MS-2379.

31 Ibid.

32 Ibid.

33 Phyllis Munday interview with Dan Bowers, 1973, BCA, Tape 160.

Chapter Four: Climbing on the Coast

1 Don Munday, "Peaks at the Head of

Pitt River," unpublished manuscript, BCA, MS-2379, and published version in *Canadian Alpine Journal*, 1923.

[2] Ibid.

[3] Ibid.

[4] The camp was cancelled in 1923, but the following year the camp was held at this location.

[5] Neal M. Carter, "Some Reminiscences of 1920–1926 with the B.C.M.C.," *The B.C. Mountaineer*, BCMC, 1957.

[6] Don Munday, "Fitzsimmons," unpublished manuscript, BCA, MS-2379.

[7] In 1911, W.J. McGuighan, G.G. McGeer and the Grouse Mountain Scenic Incline Railway Company received provincial legislation granting them authority to construct a railway winding up the mountain. Information in Registrar of Companies files, BCA.

[8] This company was formally incorporated under the Companies' Act as the Grouse Mountain Highway and Scenic Resort Limited on November 22, 1924, with five principals each holding shares. Registrar of Companies files, BCA.

[9] Don Munday, *The B.C. Mountaineer*, July 1923.

[10] "Grouse Mountain Trail Completed soon; Surveyors Busy," Vancouver *Province*, August 10, 1923.

[11] Phyllis Munday, "Memories of North Vancouver," BCA, MS-2379.

[12] Daniel Francis, ed., *Encyclopedia of British Columbia* (Madeira Park, B.C.: Harbour Publishing, 2000), p. 256.

[13] In response to newspaper coverage of the ascent, Penticton resident Mr. E. Knight responded that he and companion D. Walker had made a previous ascent in 1885. It is probable that the mountains he climbed were up the west fork of Jones Creek, rather than the east fork, hence a different set of peaks. See Knight's attestation in the *B.C. Monthly*, and Don's rebuttal of it in *The B.C. Mountaineer*, September 1924.

[14] Phyllis Munday, "Most Difficult Peak in Cheam Range Conquered by Trio of Vancouver Mountaineers," Vancouver *Province*, October 6, 1923, p. 23.

[15] The Geographic Names Board of Canada officially adopted Williamson's appellations of "Lucky Four" and "Baby Munday" in 1946. Information from B.C. place names website, Government of British Columbia.

[16] Don Munday, *The B.C. Mountaineer*, May 1924.

[17] Don Munday, *The B.C. Mountaineer*, October 1924.

[18] Don Munday, *The B.C. Mountaineer*, June 1925.

[19] Phyllis Munday, "A Pioneer homemaker Mid Mountaintop Snows," Vancouver *Province*, December 29, 1927.

[20] Phyllis Munday, "Memories of North Vancouver," BCA, MS-2379.

[21] Phyllis Munday, "A Pioneer homemaker Mid Mountaintop Snows," Vancouver *Province*, December 29, 1927.

[22] Don Munday, "No Apologies," *The B.C. Mountaineer*, January 1924.

[23] Phyllis Munday, "Memories of North Vancouver," BCA, MS-2379.

[24] Advertisement appearing in successive issues of *The B.C. Mountaineer*, beginning December 1923.

[25] Information taken from photo in private collection.

[26] Phyllis Munday, "Memories of North Vancouver," BCA, MS-2379.

[27] Phyllis Munday, "The Birth of the First Vancouver Company Girl Guides," unpublished manuscript, BCA, MS-2379.

[28] A.A. Brookhouse, *A 'Hike' Up Grouse Mountain. The experiences of an unwilling tenderfoot on his birthday jaunt*, May 16, 1926, Vancouver.

[29] Don Munday, *The B.C. Mountaineer*, December 1924.

[30] "Intrepid Mountaineers Locate Ore for Miners," Vancouver *Province*, July 26, 1924, and "Open Vein Located at Eureka Mine by Mountain Climber," Vancouver *Province*, August 7, 1924.

[31] "Mountaineering as an Aid to Mining," *The B.C. Mountaineer*, July 1924.

Chapter Five: The Alpine Club of Canada

[1] *Canadian Alpine Journal*, October 1924, p. 151.

[2] Alpine Club of Canada, *Gazette*, 1924. p. 13.

[3] Did George Kinney make the first ascent? For an account of the controversy see Chic Scott, *Pushing the Limits*, pp.70–81.

[4] This is the wording on the sign-up sheets for the 1924 camp. Inderbinen Pass as a place name does not exist today. The

name may refer to Alice Pass leading to the Mural Glacier.

5 Siri Louie, "Peak Potentials and Performance Anxieties."

6 Phyllis Munday, "B.C. woman First on Mt. Robson," unpublished manuscript, BCA, MS-2379.

7 Don Munday, "Canadian Climbing Adventures," unpublished manuscript, BCA, MS-2379.

8 Don Munday, "Ascent of Mount Robson," *The B.C. Mountaineer*, August 1924.

9 Phyllis Munday, "B.C. woman First on Mt. Robson," BCA, MS-2379.

10 Don Munday, "Ascent of Mount Robson," *The B.C. Mountaineer*, August 1924.

11 Don Munday, "Canadian Climbing Adventures," BCA, MS-2379.

12 Don Munday, "A Correction," *The B.C. Mountaineer*, September 1924.

13 Alpine Club of Canada, *Gazette*, 1924, pp. 33–4.

14 Allen Carpe, "Climbs in the Cariboo Mountains and the Northern Gold Range, Interior Ranges of the B.C.," *Alpine Club Journal*, 1925, vol. 3, p. 63.

15 Don Munday, "In the Cariboo Range," *The B.C. Mountaineer*, September 1925.

16 Ibid.

17 Don Munday, "The Cariboo Range, Canadian Pacific Railway Surveyors and Modern Climbers," *Canadian Alpine Journal*, 1940, pp. 196–7.

18 Don Munday, "In the Cariboo Range," *The B.C. Mountaineer*, September 1925.

19 Ibid.

20 Ibid.

21 Don Munday, "In the Cariboo Range —Mt. David Thompson," *Canadian Alpine Journal*, 1925, pp. 129–32.

22 Don Munday, "The Cariboo Range," *Canadian Alpine Journal*, 1940, p. 201.

23 Don Munday, "Cariboo," unpublished manuscript, BCA, MS-2379.

24 Although some of the climbing diaries survive, the notes also recorded at the time are not extant, with the exception of a single page of Phyllis Munday's diary July 14–18, 1925, found within Munday Lantern Slides, M 414 box 5, Whyte Museum (now at BCA).

25 Alan Carpe, article in *Appalachia*, June 1928, pp. 5–11.

26 Don Munday, "The Cariboo Range," *Canadian Alpine Journal*, 1940, pp.

194–204. R.T. Zillmerto, editor, *Canadian Alpine Journal*, ACC records, Whyte Museum.

27 According to the geographical place names index on the British Columbia government website, these mountain names were officially adopted in September 1927.

28 Report on Annual Camp, *Canadian Alpine Journal*, 1925.

29 Climbing Sheets, 1925 camp, AC/OM/100A, Alpine Club of Canada fonds, Whyte Museum.

30 Don Munday, "Crossing Emerald Pass in a Blizzard," unpublished manuscript, p. 2, BCA, MS-2379, p.2.

31 Don Munday, "Peaks and Passes in the Rockies," *The B.C. Mountaineer*, 1925.

32 Ibid.

33 Ibid.

34 Don Munday, "Crossing Emerald Pass in a Blizzard," pp. 3–5, BCA, MS-2379.

35 Ibid., pp. 5–6.

36 J. Monroe Thorington, *The Glittering Mountains of Canada* (Philadelphia: John W. Lea, 1925).

37 Dougherty, *Selected Alpine Climbs*, p. 260.

38 Don Munday, "Geikie," unpublished manuscript, BCA MS-2379.

39 "Tonquin Valley Camp," *Canadian Alpine Journal*, 1926, pp. 246–47.

40 Don Munday, "Geikie," BCA, MS-2379.

41 Vancouver *Province*, August 9, 1926.

Chapter Six: Mystery Mountain Years

1 Don Munday, *The Unknown Mountain*, p. 4.

2 Don Munday, "Mt. Arrowsmith," *The B.C. Mountaineer*, 1925.

3 V. Dolmage, "Chilco Lake and Vicinity, British Columbia," *Canada Geological Survey Summary Report*, 1924. Cited in Don Munday, "Explorations in the Coast Range of British Columbia," *Geographical Review*, April 1925, p. 196.

4 Don Munday, *The Unknown Mountain*, p. 3.

5 Don Munday, "Explorations in the Coast Range of British Columbia," *Geographical Review*, April 1925, p. 197.

6 Don Munday, "Mountains of Bute Inlet," Alpine Club of Canada *Gazette*, December 1925, p. 15.

7 Ibid., p. 16.

8 Dick Culbert, in *A Climber's Guide to the Coastal Ranges of B.C.*, (p. 196), credits R. Bishop and J. McPhee with the first ascent, although no date or source is given.

9 Don Munday, *The Unknown Mountain*, p. 9.

10 Ibid., p. 47.

11 Ibid., p. 56.

12 Ibid., p. 58.

13 Ibid., p. 61.

14 Ibid., p. 62.

15 Ibid., p. 84.

16 Ibid., p. 90.

17 Ibid., p. 92.

18 Ibid., p. 94.

19 Don Munday, "Mystery Mountain," *The B.C. Mountaineer*, December 1927.

20 Don Munday, *The Unknown Mountain*, p. 99.

21 Ibid., p. 103.

22 Ibid., p. 104.

23 Phyllis Munday interview with Susan Leslie, 1978, BCA, Tape 160.

24 Don Munday, *The Unknown Mountain*, p. 107.

25 Ibid., pp. 110, 111.

26 Phyllis Munday interview with Susan Leslie, 1978, BCA, Tape 160.

27 Don Munday, "Mystery Mountain," *The B.C. Mountaineer*, December 1927.

28 Don Munday, *The Unknown Mountain*, p. 141.

29 Phyllis Munday interview with Dan Bowers, 1973, BCA, Tape 160.

30 Don Munday to A.A. McCoubrey, January 6, 1937, M200/AC0/29, Alpine Club of Canada fonds, Whyte Museum.

31 Don Munday, "Ski-Climbs in the Coast Range," *Canadian Alpine Journal*, 1932, p. 101.

32 Don Munday, *The Unknown Mountain*, p. 151.

33 Don Munday, "Canada's Newest Mountains," *Canadian Geographical Journal*, December 1932, p. 235.

34 Don Munday, *The Unknown Mountain*, p. 151.

35 Ibid., pp. 154–55.

36 Summit note from Sockeye Peak, July 27, 1931, M200, accession 6465, Whyte Museum.

37 Don Munday, *The Unknown Mountain*, p. 167.

38 Ibid., p. 174.

39 Ibid., p. 180.

40 Henry S. Hall Jr., "Further Exploration and Ascents in the Coast Range of British Columbia," *American Alpine Journal*, 1934, p. 154.

41 Don Munday, *The Unknown Mountain*, p. 191.

42 Ibid., p. 194.

43 Phyllis Munday, "Mountain Memories, Mount Combatant," unpublished manuscript, BCA, MS-2379.

44 Ibid.

45 All quotes above from "Mountain Memories, Mount Combatant," BCA, MS-2379.

46 Henry S. Hall Jr., "The 1934 Attempts on Mt. Waddington," *American Alpine Journal*, 1935, p. 304.

47 Ibid.

48 See Chic Scott, *Pushing the Limits*, p. 113.

49 Phyllis Munday interview with Susan Leslie, 1978, BCA, Tape 160.

50 Henry S. Hall Jr., "Mts. Monarch, Silverthrone and the Klinaklini Glacier," *American Alpine Journal*, 1937, p. 37.

51 Phyllis Munday, "Mountain Memories, Mt. Silverthorne," unpublished manuscript, BCA MS-2379.

52 Ibid.

53 Henry S. Hall Jr., "Mts. Monarch, Silverthrone and the Klinaklini Glacier," *American Alpine Journal*, 1937, p. 39.

Sidebar: What to do about Edith?

1 Don Munday, *The Unknown Mountain*, p. 76.

2 Phyllis Munday, climbing diaries, 1927, 1928, 1930, BCA, MS-2379.

3 Conversation between Edith Wickham and the author, 1986.

4 Queen Margaret School Registers, BCA, MS-1377.

Chapter Seven: Icefields and Mountains

1 Don Munday, "Ski-Climbs in the Coast Range," *Canadian Alpine Journal*, 1930, pp. 101–11.

2 Don Munday, "Canada's Newest Mountains," *Canadian Geographical Journal*, December 1932.

3 Don Munday, book review, *Canadian Alpine Journal*, 1937, p. 148.

4 Don Munday, "Through Garibaldi Park On Skis," Vancouver *Province*, January 30, 1937.

5 Ibid.

6 Don Munday, "First Ascent of Mt. Sir Richard," unpublished manuscript, BCA, MS-2379.

7 Ibid.

8 Don Munday, "To Mt. Sir Richard on Skis," *Canadian Alpine Journal*, 1936, p. 71.

9 Ibid., p. 72.

10 Ibid., p. 73.

11 Don Munday, "First Ascent of Mt. Sir Richard," unpublished manuscript, BCA, MS-2379.

12 Ibid.

13 In her 40s, Prescott joined the Red Cross and served in Casablanca, Naples and Rome during the Second World War. In the 1960s, she joined the Peace Corps and went to Nepal.

14 Siri Louie, "Peak Potentials and Performance Anxieties."

15 Polly Prescott, "The Ascent of Mt. Grenville," *American Alpine Journal*, 1941, p. 424.

16 Don Munday, "Beyond Bute Inlet," *Canadian Alpine Journal*, 1941, p. 25.

17 Ibid. p. 30.

18 Polly Prescott, "The Ascent of Mt. Grenville," *American Alpine Journal*, 1941, p. 428.

19 Don Munday, "Beyond Bute Inlet," *Canadian Alpine Journal*, 1941, p. 31.

20 Don Munday, "The First Ascent of Mt. Queen Bess," *Vancouver Sun*, August 22, 1942.

21 Don Munday, "Mt. Queen Bess," *Canadian Alpine Journal*, 1942, p. 163.

22 Ibid.

23 Don Munday, "The First Ascent of Mt. Queen Bess," *Vancouver Sun*, August 22, 1942.

24 Don Munday, "Mt. Reliance," *Canadian Alpine Journal*, 1946, p. 1.

25 Ibid., pp. 4–5.

26 Ibid., pp. 9–10.

27 Henry S. Hall Jr., "Mount Reliance: Coast Range," *American Alpine Journal*, 1947, vol. 6.

Chapter Eight: Later Years

1 Phyllis Munday interview with Susan Leslie, 1978, BCA, Tape 160.

2 I am grateful to archivist Francis Mansbridge at the North Vancouver Museum and Archives for providing me with Don's employment record at the Burrard Shipyards.

3 Alpine Club of Canada memo to all instructors from President Eric C. Brooks, April 1943, Whyte Museum.

4 Don Munday, "Mountain Troops," *Canadian Alpine Journal*, 1947, pp. 83–90.

5 Alpine Club of Canada climbing sheets and reports, 1945. Whyte Museum.

6 Ibid.

7 Alpine Club of Canada climbing sheets and reports, 1948, Whyte Museum.

8 Medical information contained in Vital Statistics Death Registration. Vancouver *Province*, editorial, June 14, 1950.

9 Neal M. Carter, "In Memorium," *Canadian Alpine Journal*, 1950.

10 Notes made by Phyllis Munday in file she kept regarding Don's death, private collection.

11 Phyllis Munday interview with Dan Bowers, 1973, BCA, Tape 160.

Selected References

Alpine Club of Canada. *Canadian Alpine Journal* and *Gazette*

Bridge, Kathryn. *Phyllis Munday, Mountaineer*. Montreal: XYZ Publishers, 2002.

Culbert, Dick. *A Climber's Guide to the Coastal Ranges of B.C.* Vancouver: Alpine Club of Canada, 1965.

Dougherty, Sean. *Selected Alpine Climbs in the Canadian Rockies.* Calgary: Rocky Mountain Books, 1991.

Dowling, Phil. *The Mountaineers: Famous Climbers in Canada.* Edmonton: Hurtig Publishers, 1979.

Fairley, Bruce. *A Guide to Climbing & Hikes in Southwestern British Columbia.* West Vancouver: Gordon Soules Book Publishers, 1986.

Munday, Don. *Mount Garibaldi Park: Vancouver's Alpine Playground*. Vancouver: Cowan and Brookhouse, 1922.

Munday, Don. *The Unknown Mountain*. Expanded edition including essay "Behind the Unknown Mountain" by Angus M. Gunn. Lake Louise: Coyote Books, 1993.

Reichwein, PearlAnn. "Beyond Visionary Mountains: the Alpine Club of Canada and the Canadian National Park Idea, 1906 to 1969," Ph.D. dissertation, Carleton University, 1995.

Routledge, Karen. "Being a Girl without Being a Girl: Gender and Mountaineering on Mount Waddington, 1926–36." *BC Studies* 2004 (141): pp. 31–58.

Routledge, Karen. "Shifting Seas of Ice: The Mundays and Mount Waddington, 1926–1934." M.A. thesis, Simon Fraser University, 2002.

Scott, Chic. *Pushing the Limits: The Story of Canadian Mountaineering.* Calgary: Rocky Mountain Books, 2000.

Smith, Cyndi. *Off the Beaten Track: Women Adventurers and Mountaineers in Western Canada.* Jasper: Coyote Books, 1989.

Williams, Cecily. *Women on the Rope: The Feminine Share in Mountain Adventure.* London: George Allen and Unwin, 1973.

Archival Repositories

British Columbia Archives
British Columbia Council of Girl Guides, Archives
Museum of the Royal Westminster Regiment
North Vancouver Museum and Archives
Provincial Archives of Alberta
Vancouver City Archives
Whyte Museum of the Canadian Rockies

Acknowledgments

Many people have provided information and guidance. In particular, I would like to thank climber-authors Don Serl and Chic Scott for reading, correcting and providing advice on portions of the manuscript and photos and climber-historian Don Lyon, who assisted with Kootenay and Nelson details. I have endeavoured to be accurate and factual. Any errors are my own, not theirs. Thank you also to Leslee Smith for generously allowing me extended access to her Munday family records; Ches Munday for sharing his memories of Don and Phyl; and Dr. James T. Fyles for allowing me access to his father's photograph albums and lending negatives. Thank you also to Michael Feller of the B.C. Mountaineering Club; Don Bourdan at the Whyte Museum of the Canadian Rockies; Francis Mansbridge at the North Vancouver Museum and Archives; Beth Henson from Girl Guides; and photographer Lance W. Camp. The Access Services staff at the BC Archives have been unhesitatingly helpful.

Photo Credits

BC Archives: Front cover (I-61647), 45 (I-61757, left), 54 (I-61767), 61 (I-61764), 63 (I-61763, top; I-61765, bottom), 64 (detail, I-61698), 65 (I-61721), 74 (I-61716), 77 (I-61758), 78 (I-61772), 89 (I-61736, left; I-61735, right), 93 (I-61720, top; I-61723, bottom), 96 (F-7505), 105 (I-61978), 111 (I-61697, top left; I-61701, bottom left; I-61691, bottom right), 112-13 (I-61699, inset; I-61700), 115 (I-61693), 122–23 (I-68120), 128 (I-61760), 137 (I-68050), 138 (I-68053), 142 (I-68049), 143 (I-68057), 151 (I-68124), 157 (I-68125), 158–59 (E-04949), 161 (I-61988), 162 (I-61707), 168 (I-51589), 169 (I-51587), 170 (E-04995), 171 (E-04998), 173 (H-03440), 179, bottom (I-68086), 181 (E-04954), 188 (I-51586), 191 (I-51582), 193 (I-68096), 195 (I-68108), 199 (I-68140), 203 (I-61645, I-68103, I-68102), 205 (I-68109), 206 (I-68108), 208 (I-68146), 211 (I-68145)
British Columbia Mountaineering Club collection: 87 (bottom left)
Fyles collection: 2–3, 14–15, 23, 29-30, 33, 48–49, 57, 87 (top)
Girl Guides collection: 45 (right)
Lance W. Camp: 219
North Vancouver Museum and Archives: 20 (5660), 46 (5655), 67 (5682), 116 (5677, top)
Provincial Archives of Alberta: 126–27 (P-5004)
Smith collection: back cover, 17, 35, 39, 40, 43, 50, 58–59, 81-82, 85, 86, 87 (bottom right), 90–91, 117, 125, 134, 146-47, 165, 166, 179 (top), 182, 192, 196–97, 200, 210, 212–213, 215, 223
Whyte Museum of the Canadian Rockies: 19 (ACOP 0383), 133 (AC192P/1)

Index

Abbot Pass, 143–44
Agur, Athol, 162, 164, 172
Agur, Mount, 170, 185
Alouette Lake, 61
Alpine Club of Canada (ACC), 8, 10, 76–77, 124, 181
    summer camps, 124–36, 143–44, 149–57, 216–17
Alpine Lodge, 104, 109–17, 121
Alpine Scenic Highway Company, 102
Alta Lake, 96, 101–102
American Alpine Club, 8
American Alpine Journal, 141
Angle Mountain, 216
Appalachian Mountain Club, 8, 124
Arabesque Peaks, 171
Arrowsmith, Mount, 160–61
Asperity, Mount, 171
Asulkan Pass, 87
Avalanche Pass, 96, 98

B.C. Mountaineer, The, 79, 103, 107, 114, 120, 134, 137, 144
Baby Munday, Mount, 106
Bain, A.H., 124
Baker, Mount, 70–71, 214
Bank of Vancouver Mine, 84
Barbican, Mount, 150–51, 156
Bastion, Mount, 149
Bell, Mount, 192
Bella Coola, 167
Berg Lake, 75, 134
Bert Glacier, 170–71
Bishop, Mount, 54, 80, 83
Bishop, R.P., 161–62, 186
Blackcomb, Mount, 97, 101
Black Mountain, 54
Black Tusk, 14, 29
Blade, Mount, 163
Blanshard, Mount, 61–63
Bodyguard Peak, 180
boots, 75–76
Boy Scouts of Canada, 44
Bridal Falls, 105
Britannia, 25, 26
British Columbia Mountaineering Club (BCMC), 8, 18, 47, 73, 76
    summer camps 24, 29, 54, 92–97
Brock, Philip H.G. ("Pip"), 190, 198–99
Brown, Donald W., 187
Brunswick Mountain, 21–22, 32–33, 54
Buchan, John, Baron Tweedsmuir, 167
Buck, Annette E., 129, 135
Burwell, Mountain. *See* White Mountain
bushwhacking, 21

Bute Mountain, 204

Calumet, Mount, 128, 135
Cameron Lake, 160
Camsell, Dr., 97
Canadian Alpine Journal, 8, 12, 75, 79, 94, 129, 140–41, 149, 198, 222
Canadian Geographical Journal, 198
Canadian Geographical Society, 8
Canadian Geographic Names Board, 142, 178, 183, 222–23
Canadian National Railway, 75, 105
Canadian Pacific Railway, 39, 143
    survey, 141, 168, 222
Canyon View Hotel, 19
Capilano Hotel, 19–20
Capilano River, 18, 21, 31, 34
Cariboo Mountains, 136, 142
Carpe, Allen, 136, 138, 140–42
Carr, Elsie, 47
Carr, Frank, 38
Carter, Neal, 92, 97, 101, 218
Cascade Mountains, 71
Castle Towers, Mount, 25, 54, 96, 98
Cathedral Mountain, 34, 38, 54, 83
Cavalier, Mount, 175
Cayley, Bev, 106, 109, 124, 128
Challenger, Mount (renamed Mount Stanley Baldwin), 143
Chamberlin, R.T., 136, 140, 142
Chase, Sherret ("Sherry"), 193–94
Cheakamus Glacier, 98
Cheakamus Lake, 98, 199
Cheam, Mount, 105, 109
Chilcotin Plateau, 188
Chilko Lake, 163, 186
Chris Spencer, Mount, 176, 192
clothing, women's, 55
Coast Mountains, 94, 205
Columbia Icefield, 207
Columbia Mountains, 136
Columnar Peak, 24–25
Combatant, Mount, 171, 189–90, 210
Cooper, A., 109
Copper Peak (renamed Mount Carr), 25, 94
Coquitlam Mountain, 64
Councillor Peak, 180
Crosscut Ridge, 94, 96
Crown Crater 22–24, 121
Crown Mountain, 34, 54, 80

Daly, Mount, 144
Dam Mountain, 54, 64, 80, 73
Darling, Basil S., 31
David Thompson, Mount (renamed Mount Sir John Thompson), 138–42
David, Mount, 217
Davis, Mr., 66
Dawson Range, 86–87
DeBeck, L.A., 19

INDEX | 237

Denny, Norah, 166
Dixon, Andrew, 119
Dome Mountain (renamed Mount Fromme), 55, 103
Drinnan, Andy, 129, 153–54

Eagle Head (renamed Mount Habrich), 27
Edidonphyl, 167, 203, 211
Ellett, Mrs. B., 165
Emerald Pass, 144–49
Enchantment Peak, 32
Eureka Mountain, (renamed Silver Peak), 119–21
Eureka-Victoria Mine, 119–21
Evenglow Cabin, 64, 73, 80, 92, 102

Feuz, Edward and Ernest, 144
Field, 143–44, 149
Field, C., 26–27
Finality, Mount, 191–93
First World War, 38
Fitzsimmons Glacier, 98, 100
Foley, Mount, 105–7
food planning, 68
forest fires, 25, 36, 87
Foster, Dudley, 106
Foster, William, 128
Fowler, E., 19
Franklin Glacier, 173–74, 177, 182, 185
Fraser River, 61
Fraser, Mount, 150, 155
Freshfield, Mount, 217
Fuhrer, Hans, 153–57, 187, 190–92
Fuller, Eric, 106, 109
Fury Gap, 176–78, 180, 190
Fyles, John, 56
Fyles, Tom, 54, 61, 85, 88
Fynn, Val, 153

Gallon, R., 167
Gambs, Gustave, 88, 144
Gardner, Mount, 46
Gargoyles, The, 36
Garibaldi Park, 24, 29, 35–37, 97–102, 198–99, 201, 218, 220
Garibaldi, Mount, 25, 34, 36, 70, 79
Geddes, Malcolm, J., 129–30, 153
Geikie, Mount, 149, 150–57
Gendarme, Mount, 128–29
gender issues, 10
General Stewart, Mount (renamed Stewart Peak), 104–6
Geological Survey of Canada, 164
Gibson, Rex, 217
Gilbert, Mount, 204
Girl Guide movement, 8, 45–47, 117–18, 218, 220
Lone Guiding movement 45, 117, 167
Glacier House, 86, 88–89
Glacier Pikes, 25
Glacier Station, 85, 88

Gladstone, Margaret, 88
Goat Mountain, 54
Golden Ears, 22, 61
Goldsmith, 216
Granite Mountain, 42
Grassi, Lawrence, 153–54
Graves, H.J., 150, 152–53, 156
Gray, William ("Billy"), 19, 21–22, 24, 29
Gray Pass, 94, 95
Grenville, Mount, 202–4, 206
Grouse Mountain, 18, 19, 43–45, 55, 61, 102–4, 109–18

Hall, Henry, 167, 187, 190–94, 206, 208, 210, 216
Hanafin, Ben, 25, 31, 35
Hanafin, Loretto, 36, 79
Hanover, Mount, 22, 31–34, 54
Harling, Sid, 118
Harman, Elizabeth B., 77–79
Harvey, Mount, 22
Haynes, Harry and Muriel, 208
Helmet Peak, 54
Henley, Edith M., 79, 124
Henshaw, Julie, 174
Hermit Mountain, 86
Hinton, William, 193–94
Hollyburn Mountain, 80
Holway Peak, 137
Holy Cross Mountain, 119, 121
Homathko Icefield, 204–5, 207–8
Homathko River, 163, 168–69, 188–89, 208
Hooley, Gilbert, 198
Hope, 104, 106, 119
Horie, Mr., 106
Hostility, Mount (renamed Mount Mackenzie King), 143
Huber, Mount, 144
Hungabee, Mount, 144
hunting, 25, 28, 75

Icefall Point, 175, 182–84
Ida, Mount (renamed Indian Chief, then Meslilloet), 66, 68–70
Ingram, Tom, 66, 71, 77, 79, 160, 162, 164, 170, 171
Isosceles, Mount, 95

James, Arthur Frank, 38, 40, 43–44, 72
James, Beatrice (née Swann), 38, 40, 43
James, Esmée Mary ("Betty") (married name McCallum), 39, 41, 44, 72–73, 173, 175, 177
James, Frank Richard Ingram ("Dick"), 39, 44, 47
Jasper National Park, 149
Johnson, R.C. ("Johnny"), 77, 104, 164, 171–72
Jubilee, Mount, 184–85

Kain, Conrad, 128–32, 134–35
Kinney, Lake, 130–31
Klinaklini Glacier, 177, 185, 194

238

Klinaklini Icefield, 192–93
Kokanee Landing, 40–42
Korten, H., 19

Ladies' Alpine Club, 8
Lake O'Hara, 143, 198
Lambart, Fred, 129, 135
Lava Mountain, 36
Ledge, 25–27
Lefroy, Mount, 144
Leigh, Amy, 167
LePage, Edward, 25, 31
Lewis, Margaret, 53
Lewis, Miss M., 216
Lions, The, 19, 21–23, 54, 80
Loch Lomond, 84. *See also* Summit Lake
Logan, Mount, 187
Lookout Mountain, 87
Louise, Lake, 144
Lucky Four Glacier, 107
Lucky Four Group, 105
Lucky Four Mine, 105–7
Lynn Peaks, 54
Lynx, Mountain, 75, 77, 79, 128

MacGowan, Miss, 216
Mamquam Mountain (formerly Santa Rosa), 24, 34, 70, 79, 100
Mamquam Range, 95
Mantle Glacier, 207
Marpole, Mount, 148
McCallum, Betty. *See* James, Esmée Mary
McCarthy, Albert, 128
McCoubrey, A.A., 174
McLennan Range, 136
McPhee, Jack, 163, 164
McPhee's Landing, 165
Memorial Peak, 216
Men-at-Arms Peaks, 180
Meslilloet Mountain. *See* Ida, Mount
Miller, Ivan R., 124
Mills, R.M., 28
Moffatt, T.B., 129–30
Molly Gibson mine, 41–42
Monarch Icefield, 205
Moore, Ken, 206
Moritz Peak, 128
Mountain Memories, 12
Mumm, Mount, 75, 77, 128, 129
Munday, Albert Rupert ("Bert"), 16, 73, 164, 170, 172, 178
Munday, Caroline Pansy, 16, 35–36, 79
Munday, Edith Phyllis, 11–12, 80–86, 88–89, 92, 109, 114–16, 124, 164, 165–67, 184–86, 211
Munday, Jessie (née Arkell), 16
Munday, Mount, 183, 184, 208, 218
Munday, Phyllis ("Phyl") Beatrice (née James)
    awards and honours, 8, 118, 202
    early years, 38–47

as editor, 12
Girl Guides, 8, 45–47, 117–18, 218, 220
later years, 214–20
marriage, 73–74
memberships, 8, 47, 77–78
rescues, 8, 118
St. John's Ambulance, 8, 46, 53, 218
Munday, Walter Alfred Don
    awards and honours, 8, 53
    early years 16–18
    as editor, 8, 79, 114, 120
    injury to arm, 51–53, 104, 214
    later years, 214–20
    marriage, 73–74
    memberships, 8, 77–78
    obituary, 217–18
    poetry, 18, 36–37
    rescues, 8, 118, 217
    WWI experience, 50–53
Munday, William Thomas, 16
Munro, Ron, 190
Mystery Mountain, 163–64, 170–77, 186, 192.
    See also Waddington, Mount

Nanaimo, 160, 220
Nelson, 39–40
Nelson, Mr., 106
Newport, 28. *See also* Squamish
North Thompson River, 141
North Vancouver, 18, 102, 117, 220
Northern Cordilleran, 29, 94
Norton Lake, 67

O'Connor, Harold, 92, 106
O'Hara, Lake, 136, 144–45
Odaray, Mount, 144–45
Ostheimer, A.J., 129, 130
Overlord Mountain, 97–100

pack horses, 188–89
packs, 99
Paradise Valley, 143
Parapet Peak, 95
Park, J., 19
Park, T., 19
photographs, 157
Pilley, Dorothy, 216
Pitt Pass, 94–95
Pollard, Harry, 129–30
Porter, J.T., 129
Premier Group, The, 142
Prescott, Polly, 202–4
President, The, 148
Ptarmigan, Mount, 128

Queen Bess, Mount, 205–7
Queen Margaret's School, 166

Red Mountain, 98
Redbreast, Mount, 182

INDEX | 239

Refuse Pinnacle, 99
Reliance, Mount, 208
Repose, Mount, 185
rescues, 8, 118, 217
Resplendent, Mountain, 75, 77, 79, 128
Richards, Dr. I.A., 216
Robson Pass, 124, 125, 130, 134
Robson Provincial Park, Mount, 75–76, 85, 124
Robson, Mount, 96, 128–35, 178
Rodney, Mount, 163, 203–4
Rogers Pass, 85
Rogers, Mount, 86
Roosevelt Glacier, 71
Roovers, Alfred, 187
ropes, 141
Round Mountain, 36
Royal Geographical Society, 8, 125, 174
Rust Mountain, 25

Saladana, Joe, 129, 132
Saugstad, Mount, 167
Sawtooth Range, 25, 34
Scar Creek, 168, 169
Second World War, 215
Selkirk Mountains, 39, 85
Sentinel Glacier, 95–96
Serra, Mount, 171
Seymour, Mount, 34, 54, 181
Sharpe, Reverend R., 149–150, 153, 155, 156
Sheer, Mount, 25
Shelf Mountain, 182
Shelley, W.C., 102
Sifton, Mount, 85
Silverthrone Icefield, 205
Silverthrone Mountain, 167, 185, 194–95
Sir Donald, Mount, 86
Sir Richard, Mount, 199–201
Sir Wilfrid Laurier, Mount, 136, 142
Sisters, The, 25–27
ski-mountaineering, 180–85, 192, 194–95, 198–99, 201–2, 214
Sky Pilot, 25, 26
Smith, Fred, 19, 21–23, 25–27, 36, 66, 109
snowblindness, 170
Sockeye, Mount, 184
Spearhead Range, 101, 136, 198–99
Spearmen Peak, 171, 175
Sphinx Mountain, 95
Sphinx, The, 25
Spire Peak, 36–37
Spouse, B., 109
Squamish (formerly Newport), 24–25, 83, 85, 187
Stanton, James and Loretta, 165, 172, 182, 185–86
Stawamus Valley, 25, 27, 83
Stephen, Mount, 145
Stewart Peak. See General Stewart, Mount
Stewart, Miss, 87
Stupendous Mountain, 167
Summit Lake (renamed Loch Lomond), 25
Surprise, Lake, 33

Switzer, J.W., 136

Table, The, 54
Takakkaw Falls, 144
Tantalus Mountain, 70
Tantalus Range, 161, 217
Terra Nova, 45, 56
Tête Jaune, 136
Thompson, Clausen, 92, 95
Thompson, Esther, 150, 152–53, 157
Thompson, H.F., 150, 153
Thompson, Mount, 216
Thorington, J. Monroe, 129–30, 149
Tiedemann, Mount, 171
Titan, Mount (renamed Mount Sir Wilfrid Laurier), 136–39, 142
Tonquin Valley, 149
Townsend, Charles, 108
Trapper Nelson pack, 99
Turret Peak, 157
Tweedsmuir Park, 167

Underhill, J.T., 177
Unknown Mountain, The, 8, 11, 160, 183, 223

Vancouver Mountaineering Club, 18
Vancouver, 16, 42–43
Vernon, 50
Victoria, Mount, 144

Waddington Glacier, 169, 171, 184
Waddington, Alfred, 168
Waddington, Mount, 7, 9, 178–81, 190–92, 204, 208–9, 223
Walker, Tommy, 167
Wates, C.G., 153
Watson, Major General D., 50
Wedge Mountain, 101, 199
Welch Glacier, 106, 108
Welch, Mount, 105, 108
Welcome, Mount (renamed Mount Sir Mackenzie Bowell), 142–43
Wheatley, Bill, 106
Wheeler, Arthur O., 79, 128–29, 144, 174
White Mountain (renamed Burwell), 19, 34, 54
Whitemantle Range, 169, 183
Wigwam Inn, 56, 66
Williamson, Arthur Shewan, 102, 104, 106, 118
Withers, A.L., 136
Women's Volunteer Reserve Corps, 53
Worsley, Marg, 53, 61, 64

Yoho National Park, 144–45, 215

Zillmer, R.T., 141–42